RESPONSE TO DEATH

Response to Death

The Literary Work of Mourning

Edited by CHRISTIAN RIEGEL

The University of Alberta Press

Canadian Review of Comparative Literature/
Revue Canadienne de Littérature Comparée

Published by

The University of Alberta Press
Ring House 2
Edmonton, Alberta
Canada T6G 2E1

and

**Canadian Review of Comparative Literature/
Revue Canadienne de Littérature Comparée**
317 Arts Building, University of Alberta,
Edmonton, Alberta
Canada T6G 2E5

LIBRARY AND ARCHIVES CANADA
CATALOGUING IN PUBLICATION

Response to death : the literary work of
mourning / edited by Christian Riegel.

Co-published by the Canadian review of
comparative literature/ Revue canadienne de
littérature comparéé, as vol. 30, no. 1 (2003).
Includes bibliographical references and index.
ISBN 0–88864–421–3

1. Bereavement in literature. I. Riegel,
Christian II. Title: Canadian review of
comparative literature.

PN56.D4.R48 2005   820.9'3548
C2005–900676–5

NOTICE TO LIBRARIANS: Response to
Death: The Literary Work of Mourning is *co-
published with the Canadian Review of Comparative
Literature/Revue Canadienne de Littérature Comparée
and is also the Canadian Review of Comparative
Literature/Revue Canadienne de Littérature Comparée*
30.1 (2003) (ISSN: 0319–051X)

Printed and bound in Canada by Houghton
Boston Printers, Saskatoon, Saskatchewan.
First edition, first printing, 2005

The University of Alberta Press is committed to
protecting our natural environment. As part of
our efforts, this book is printed on stock
produced by New Leaf Paper: it contains 100%
post-consumer recycled fibres and is acid- and
chlorine-free.

The University of Alberta Press gratefully
acknowledges the support received for its
publishing program from The Canada Council
for the Arts. In addition, we also gratefully
acknowledge the financial support of the
Government of Canada through the Book
Publishing Industry Development Program
(BPDIP) and from the Alberta Foundation for the
Arts (AFA) for our publishing activities.

Contents

Foreword

LAMENT AND MOURNING have long been part of the burial and memory of the dead. The reaction to and interpretation of death became important for poets, philosophers and historians, as it had long been for priests. The progress of body and soul is a concern in Homer, Herodotus, Plato and Plutarch. The matter of mourning and mirth, death and life are also biblical. Since its development as a modern discipline, psychology has made feelings about suicide and death, about mourning and its effects part of its purview. In *Response to Death: The Literary Work of Mourning* editor Christian Riegel has brought together a collection ranging from the Middle Ages to the present. In his Introduction, Riegel places the essays in context and focusses on his interpretation of death and mourning.

Response to Death makes a significant contribution to literary studies and the subject of death and mourning, which touches all our lives and many fields of human endeavour. The importance of this collection lies in its very breadth in examining the work of mourning in literary texts from the first centuries of literature in English to the present. These literary manifestations of death and mourning have implications well beyond this particular kind of cultural representation. As Riegel suggests, the act of writing itself can perform a psychological function and becomes the work that is required to mourn loss. Moreover, according to Riegel, the readers discover in this work instructive models for coping or participate in public memorials or commemoration (sometimes over the death of public figures). Riegel aptly recognizes the social and historical aspects of mourning in addition to this literary element. He finds a context from ancient Greek lament and tragedy to the formal elegies of the nineteenth centuries and the elegy, anti-elegy, elegaic fiction since. In a suggestive phrase, Riegel says that the work of mourning provides "the staging ground for emotion." These literary texts express loss and try to make up for it or at least come to terms with it because the work can never replace that which it represents. Recuperation and revival never quite happen. Still, as Riegel notes, literary history shows that while these words fail, they succeed at supporting the survivors in working through and understanding their loss. This is the perspective that *Response to Death: The Literary Work of Mourning* takes. For so long, writers have been representing loss and mourning even if twentieth-century intellectual efforts have made us concentrate on these matters anew. This volume provides a context for these theoretical approaches and crosses cultures from the Middle Ages onwards.

Riegel reminds us that mourning is an intricate and needed activity that consoles in the face of pain. This collection crosses disciplines, periods and cultures as does the work of our journal over the past thirty years and of the Library of the *Canadian Review of Comparative Literature* of which it is a part. The last two volumes in the CRCL Library have been on the future of literary studies and on the politics of cultural mediation. This publication will help to explore the boundaries of literature, history and culture.

Mourning the dead is something that crosses cultures. Before Freud's thoughts on death and grief, many texts took a cross-cultural and typological view of killing, death and dying. European cultures came to see their own beliefs about and images of death in the contexts of other cultures. Many views of death and mourning in the arts and human sciences have been represented in Western culture and beyond. That is why such a comparative and interdisciplinary volume is important not simply in the important field of mourning but across a range of methods and departments. The sheer richness of this collection should be suggestive to a wide group of students, scholars and general readers.

After reading the essays in this collection, I came to reflect on mourning in terms of my own work and in central texts in our culture. Briefly, I would suggest that Christian Riegel's Introduction and editorial work and the contributors' essays in this collection have the power to make us understand more deeply the nature of loss and mourning. Other readers might apply what they have come to see as a result of this volume to aspects of their own lives and interests, literary and otherwise. Two brief contexts come to mind, one from the Bible and the other from Shakespeare. They are canonical as sources of mourning, but mean something to me personally. The context of mourning shifts in the Bible, the King James or Authorized Version, which became so central to English literature, as it represents mourning in different situations. Job 30:31 proclaims: "My harp also is turned to mourning, and my organ into the voice of them that weep." Psalm 30:11 moves from the metaphor of turning music to mourning to one of the transformation of mourning into dancing: "Thou hast turned for me my mourning into dancing: thou hast put off my sackcloth, and girded me with gladness." Ecclesiastes 7:2 contrasts the solemnity of mourning and death with feasting: "It is better to go to the house of mourning, than to go to the house of feasting: for that is the end of all men; and the living will lay it to his heart." At 7:4, this contrast is made more explicit, and mourning and wisdom become identified in opposition to a kind of joy: "The heart of the wise is in the house of mourning; but the heart of fools is in the house of mirth." Isaiah 60:20 promises an end to mourning: "Thy sun shall no more go down; neither shall thy moon withdraw itself: for the LORD shall be thine everlasting light, and the days of thy mourning shall be ended." Eternity will repair the ruin of death that causes loss and mourning.

Hamlet's distraction is as much a key to loss as Job's suffering. There are many representations or interpretations of mourning in literature, but these help me to read this collection and to take from it new ways of seeing other literary representations of loss and mourning and to look at the experience of them in life in different ways. Christian Riegel mentions loss from Homer to the present and alludes to Shakespeare, and this is perhaps the key moment of mourning in the Shakespearean canon. Claudius provides advice to their son and his nephew: "Tis sweet and commendable/ In your Nature Hamlet,/ To giue these mourning duties to your Father" (Hamlet, First Folio, 1623, lines 268–70). The new king qualifies his commendation: "But you must know, your Father lost a Father,/ That Father lost, lost his, and the Suruiuer bound/ In filiall Obligation, for some terme/ To do obsequious Sorrow" (271–74). Mourning, for Claudius, is natural, is part of the march of generations from birth to death to birth to death and so on. Sorrow, however, has its term. Claudius sees impiety in extending mourning beyond this period. The king, who turns out to be a usurper who murdered his brother for the crown, reiterates the notion that such mourning is against heaven and strings together adjectives that show up Hamlet's weakness, naïvety and lack of education or discipline. Claudius argues for a reality principle (to borrow Freud's phrase): "For, what we know must be, and is as common/ As any the most vulgar thing to sence,/ Why should we in our peeuish Opposition/ Take it to heart?" (280–83). Why oppose the way things are? Claudius returns to the notion of impiety, a sinful faultiness in such a kind of mourning: "Fye, 'tis a fault to Heauen,/ A fault against the Dead, a fault to Nature,/ To Reason most absurd, whose common Theame / Is death of Fathers, and who still hath cried, / From the first Coarse, till he that dyed to day,/ This must be so" (283–88). This sense of commonness and the cycle in the death of fathers is meant to have Hamlet leave mourning after a term and to return to reality, reason and necessity. Yet Hamlet is stubborn in his grief and the work of mourning persists. *Hamlet* is a long mediation on loss and mourning as much as revenge, but lest this turn into something long itself, I think it best to return to the work of mourning that Riegel and his contributors have done so much with.

In *Response to Death*, Riegel has provided a wonderful range of essays that give a literary exploration of loss and mourning, one so rich that it supplements and complicates the fascinating psychological and philosophic examinations of the subject by Freud, Lacan, Derrida and others. Theory reads literature and literature theory in a movement in which the one makes the other richer and more comprehensive. The work of mourning can be found in the making, reading and interpretation of literature and life. A mutual movement between experience and imagination is something that Riegel and the authors of the essays suggest.

––––––

THE ESSAYS that Riegel has brought together in *Response to Death* provide a rich sense of the complexity and diversity of mourning in time, place and kind of writing. Some medieval and early modern literary and dramatic texts are where this pursuit of mourning begins. This collection opens with Leanne Groeneveld's consideration of mourning, heresy and resurrection in the York Corpus Christi Cycle, more specifically of that cycle's representation of the disciples' mourning as excessive and as a cause and a sign of weak or heretical faith and its use of Saint Augustine as a means of representing the disciples' grief. The plays provided a warning to their audience of the dangers of mourning the dead too much. A close connection between resurrection and transubstantiation in late medieval culture permitted the plays to exploit the disciples' grief, for the York playwrights could then identify the disciples as Lollards (Wyclifites) and employ their example to condemn heretical beliefs on the doctrine of transubstantiation in the fifteenth-century.

In the following century Shakespeare explored a more secular course in mourning. Heather Dubrow, echoing Eugene O'Neill, explores the politics of grief in Shakespeare's epyllion or minor epic, *Rape of Lucrece*. Arguing that the rhetoric of mourning in *Lucrece* sheds light on the rhetoric and rhetoricity of other Shakespearean texts, Dubrow maintains that the poem also suggests new approaches to mourning. Dubrow notes that Freud and many neo-Freudians have emphasized the psychological dangers of grief but that Shakespeare's *Lucrece* also stresses the political perils. More particularly, this poem calls attention to the way in both individuals and a society mourning engenders what Dubrow terms "liability and volatility." Shakespeare thereby suggests how mourning generates power and authority while threatening agency.

Lisa Dickson discusses the death of kings and how the nation is mourned in the three parts of Shakespeare's *Henry VI*. Dickson asserts that eulogizing Henry V at the opening of the First Tetralogy is ineffective in the face of the power of death: Henry VI cannot defend his sovereignty or unify his nation. For Dickson, these history plays suggest that the sovereign ideal is not simply lost but is unattainable. The corpse of Henry V at the beginning of 1 *Henry VI* and Henry V's triumph at the end of *Henry V* (its events happened before but written after) have some meaning for the life and death of kings, nations and historical narratives.

Melanie E. Gregg examines the language of lament in the French lyric poem of sixteenth century. She maintains that these women poets were dissatisfied with the limits of rational language to express their experiences and thus turned to their bodies to represent the ineffable. The best examples of this poetry of grief and mourning and of instances of this feminine language of the body (*avant la lettre*) included poems by Philiberte de Fleurs, Madeleine des Roches, Catherine de Bourbon, Gabrielle de Coignard and Marguerite de Navarre. For Gregg, women's love lyric, secular *complaintes*, or devotional compositions, also support this argument. In England and France, then, the subject of mourning had important roles to play in interpreting the classical, biblical and national pasts as well as in making room for women to manoeuvre in poetic and literary space.

In subsequent times, especially in the nineteenth and twentieth centuries, the matter of mourning continued to be a key cultural practice. Stephen Behrendt connects the mourning of two princesses in Britain, one near the beginning of the nineteenth century and the other near the end of the twentieth. He links mourning, myth and merchandising in the death of Princess Charlotte in November 1817 to the public grief over the death of Princess Diana of Wales in 1997 and the subsequent commercial activities of mourning her. According to Behrendt, these events serve as reminders of how public mourning rituals stabilize and restore society. He argues that, in such cases, mourning becomes a public performance that brings together the people and the elite as a common public. Thus, rituals of mourning can be democratic.

Another analysis of mourning in the nineteenth century occurs in Barbara Hudspith's discussion of the relation between Mary Ann Evans's (George Eliot's) grief at the death of her father, Robert Evans, and the creation of *Adam Bede*. Hudspith also looks at the connection between the author's mourning and that of her protagonist. Moreover, she examines the issue of the links between mourning and biography and interprets Adam's situation in terms of healthy grief and pathological grief.

Garry Sherbert analyzes a twentieth century text, Djuna Barnes's *Nightwood*, as an anatomy of melancholy and unfinished work of mourning. Sherbert says that the ongoing critical debate about whether incest happens between the main character, Nora Flood, and her grandmother suggest that this is unfinished mourning because her memory of their relation conceals as much as it reveals. For Sherbert, as readers, we harbour the absence of death. Nora's dreams and the crypt of her grandmother are two productive examples of exterior resistance and interpretive efforts to internalize, to make an anatomy of her melancholy. Thus, Nora's and Barnes's work of mourning is also the reader's.

Poets continued in the twentieth century to take up the ancient laments and elegies. Ernest Smith argues that John Berryman's *The Dream Songs* mythologizes the loss and the figure of the father as do some important poems of

Sylvia Plath. Smith asserts that their poems concerning the father are among the most memorable and involve new directions for the elegy despite a honouring of the conventions of the genre. Both poets challenge previous works of mourning. In Todd F. Davis's and Kenneth Womack's essay on mourning in another central American poet, Donald Hall, they maintain that in *Without* (1998), Hall remembers his life with the poet Jane Kenyon as she wrestles with and dies from leukemia. Hall expresses grief and tells stories at once in an "ethics of mourning." For Davis and Womack, Hall succeeds, by publishing this book and giving poetry readings, in expressing his grief and sharing it with others, so that Hall not only makes a memorial of Kenyon's life, but also renews his own.

Hybrid genres also do the work of mourning. Thomas M.F. Gerry discusses Lola Lemire Tostevin's *Cartouches* (1995), which includes poems and journal entries in French and English that provide a meditation on death and the act of remembrance. In the ritual she creates, Tostevin is the mourner who remembers her father as she remembers her self. Here, Gerry suggests, is a community of mourning.

Discussing maternity, mourning and nation in Janet Frame, Sara Suleri and Arundhati Roy, Katherine G. Sutherland argues that the association between these aspects is a recurring theme in the writing of women in post-colonial nations. Moreover, she says that this "representational matrix" may cast some light on the understanding of nationality. Sutherland's tentative hope is that by coming to terms with the embodied experiences of women, we might avoid brutal, grotesque and abstract myths of nation.

With a particular focus on the works of Paul Monette, Lloyd Edward Kermode argues that the active engagement between the work of the AIDS elegy and the future of a community of sufferers justifies a separation of this kind of elegy from classical pastoral elegy with its tendency to reflect and console the now. Kermode maintains that this new kind of elegy involves a political movement in the world along with the grievous physicality, despair and inscription of AIDS in discourses of the body. The AIDS elegy is social and literary at once.

Mourning becomes us and we become it. In a culture that sometimes hides death and the dead, the work of mourning is a necessary matter of expression and renewal. Christian Riegel and the contributors he has brought together here have provided us with a music and dance to remember. For that, we can look backward with something to look forward to. The collection, like Hamlet's mourning, is itself but gestures beyond itself. This work on mourning is a matter worth exploring.

JONATHAN HART, EDITOR

Canadian Review of Comparative Literature/
Revue Canadienne de Littérature Comparée

Acknowledgements

THIS VOLUME DEVELOPED over several years and ultimately came to fruition with the help of Jonathan Hart, editor of *The Canadian Review of Comparative Literature/Revue Canadienne de Littérature Comparée*, for which I am grateful. He also helped make possible the co-publication with the University of Alberta Press. I wish to acknowledge Irene Sywenky at CRCL, and Alan Brownoff, designer, and Peter Midgley, copyeditor, at the University of Alberta Press, for their excellent work in bringing this volume to press as painlessly as possible, and especially Mary Mahoney-Robson, editor, who has once again allowed me to make use of her talents. The Press would also like to thank Gail Lint and Barb Johnson at the The Alberta Foundation for the Arts for rephotographing the cover image. Thanks to my research assistant, Justin Dittrick, for his invaluable help with manuscript preparation. I would like, finally, to thank Eugene Bertoldi, Eleanor Bertoldi, Jeanette Lynes, Nat Hardy, and Katherine Robinson for their sustaining friendship.

Portions of chapter 2 appear in *Shakespeare and Domestic Loss: Forms of Deprivation, Mourning, and Recuperation* and are reprinted with the permission of Cambridge University Press.

This book has been published with the help of a grant from the Humanities Research Institute, the University of Regina.

Introduction

The Literary Work of Mourning

Yet once more, O ye Laurels, and once more
Ye Myrtles brown, with Ivy never sere,
I come to pluck you Berries harsh and crude,
And with forc'd fingers rude,
Shatter your leaves before the mellowing year.
Bitter constraint, and sad occasion dear,
Compels me to disturb your season due:
For Lycidas is dead, dead ere his prime,
Young Lycidas, and hath not left his peer
Who would not sing for Lycidas? he knew
Himself to sing, and build the lofty rhyme.
He must not float upon his wat'ry bier
Unwept, and welter to the parching wind,
Without the meed of some melodious tear. (lines 1–14)

THE OPENING LINES of John Milton's *Lycidas* reflect many central concerns of the literary work of mourning. The first line indicates the constant and repetitive nature of death in human experience, for Milton's narrator/elegist, the Swain, notes that he is required to mourn "Yet once more." The difficulty and devastation of being required to mourn yet again are noted when his fingers are "forced" to "pluck" the berries of poetic inspiration with "Bitter constraint." Milton's Swain underscores the manner with which serious loss must be responded to despite the fact that it is never wished for when he remarks that he is "Compel[led]...to disturb" the plants before their "season due" (7). The Swain's response, a literary one, is to create a work of mourning to not only grieve for the dead Lycidas but also to help himself to work through his grief. As he states, "Who would not sing for Lycidas?" (10) so that he can "bid fair peace" (22) to his lost friend.

What Milton realizes in this poem, as do so many other writers across history, is that death is the constant of human existence. Where there is life there will also inevitably be death, and because death often has devastating emotional consequences for the living, especially when the loss is a loved one, humans have developed means for coping with severe loss. The ways that humans deal with death are most accurately described as the work that is performed and accomplished by mourning; when mourning is indicated in a literary text of any kind, poetry, fiction or non-fiction, it is known as a literary work of mourning. Psychic processes are engaged through absolute necessity as requirements to meet the devastation of loss. Alongside the psychology of an individual's grief, societies have developed various other means for shaping and aiding the responses to immediate death.

The work of mourning, as artistic construct, falls within both parameters. For the individual creator, the act of writing itself often performs a psychic function and becomes the work that is required to mourn loss, and for the receptors of the text, the work provides instructive models for coping or has the specific function of public memorializing (such as in the case of the many elegies that commemorate the death of public figures). Furthermore, the work of mourning is a multifaceted literary text partaking of the processes of mourning while simultaneously being a product for public reception.

In this guise, the work of mourning is an inherently socio-historical construct. Ancient Greek lament and tragedy provides a particular context to the understanding of mourning as a social and as an individual practice that is obviously very different from the formal elegies of the nineteenth century or the varied texts of mourning—elegy, anti-elegy, elegaic fiction, and so on—of the twentieth and now twenty-first centuries. Likewise, the epic pronouncements upon heroic death of Homer contrast with the perspectives of the anonymous *Song of Roland*. Be it Sophocles or Shakespeare, or Tennyson or Plath, or any of the many other examples from literary history, humans have found the need to express mourning—and see it articulated—in literary terms.

The work of mourning functions as the staging ground for emotion, at times as performance of emotion for the creator and otherwise as focalizer for mourners and their grief which they can see reflected to them in the literary work. Frequently, the work of mourning will fulfill both purposes. At all times, the work of mourning is an attempt to make present that which is irrefutably lost, and within that paradoxical tension lies a central tenet of all writerly endeavour that deals with the representation of death. However much a writer labours to inscribe the lost one, the resulting product can never become that which it seeks to replace. Death is the ultimate void that all signatory practice fails to recuperate. The work of mourning is always a limiting attempt at revival and at representation, though that attempt itself is important and necessary to the mourning subject. What literary history tells us is that while words always fail to replace a lost one, they can succeed at helping the survivors to work through and understand their loss.

Response to Death: The Literary Work of Mourning has as its purpose to present a literary-historical perspective on the work of mourning. While much of contemporary thinking about mourning is informed by twentieth-century intellectual endeavours, literature tells us that writers and thinkers have been contemplating how to deal with death for centuries—probably since the beginning of literary culture. And so, it is useful to place contemporary thinking within a literary-historical context that informs current aesthetic and social practices in regards to the work of mourning. As this volume is not intended as an encyclopedic look at the history of the work of mourning, it begins its cross-cultural examination of the work of mourning in the middle ages and moves chronologically forward from there to the late twentieth century.

Before turning to closer discussion of the individual essays in this volume, it is necessary to further consider the terms mourning and work, which are in common usage in a wide range of discursive situations, but that require specific definition as they pertain to their use in this volume.[1] Mourning is an inherently complex and necessary activity that has the aim of providing consolation in the face of pain. The psychic nature of mourning is complemented by its socio-cultural context, for grief is framed, ordered, and filtered by the historical, social and cultural setting of the mourning subject. As sociologists have noted, it is a condition whereby an individual, in response to a death or serious loss, suffers the "shattering of a sense of ontological security" (Mellor 12). Ontological security, notes Anthony Giddens, refers to an individual's "sense of order and continuity in relation to the events in which they participate, and the experiences they have, in their day-to-day lives" (cited by Mellor 12). A mourning individual will call into question "the meaningfulness and reality of the social frameworks in which they participate" (Mellor 13). This questioning and challenging of social existence is correlative to the psychic processes at work as psychologists have pointed out. Ester R. Shapiro argues that death "forces us to dissolve and re-create the deepest human bonds that form us" (4), and John Bowlby in his book *Loss* underscores the idea that mourning is a condition whereby the emotional investment in the deceased requires psychic response:

> All who have discussed *the nature of the processes engaged in healthy mourning* are agreed that amongst other things they effect, in some degree at least, a withdrawal of emotional investment in the lost person and that they may prepare for making a relationship with a new one. ([italics in original] 25)[2]

Psychological thinking in the twentieth century about the nature of mourning is most heavily influenced by Sigmund Freud's essay "Mourning and Melancholia" that appeared in 1917. Here, Freud explored the conception of mourning as work, which was to spur on later thinking about this notion of the work of mourning. Freud describes mourning as the process of "releasing the tie between an individual and the objects (including other people) in the environment into which the person invests emotional significance, particularly other persons" (Sanders 22); this process involves a great deal of psychic labour and of active labouring, or working, at mourning. As Alessia Ricciardi points out, "[m]ourning is not simply an emotion for Freud, but a performance of a work that...is a psychically transformative activity" (21). A point that is sometimes overlooked in translation, but that is integral to understanding Freud's conception of the work of mourning, is that the German word for mourning *Trauerarbeit*, is more fully encompassing than the English translation. In German the word is literally "mourning-work" and can mean "work of mourning," as in a text of mourning, or "the work that is required to mourn." Freud elaborated the second meaning most fully by using metaphors of work (as in labour) to define mourning, considering it "in terms of the economics of the mind" (126). Grief-work is difficult and time-consuming, as Freud states: "The task [of mourning] is...carried through bit by bit, under great expense of time and cathectic energy" (126).[3] As Robert Kastenbaum points out, it is an involved and complex process: "Griefwork is carried out through a long series of confrontations with the reality of the loss" (322). Kathleen Woodward provides a useful delineation of Freud's definition of mourning:

[Mourning] is psychic work which has a precise purpose and goal: to "free" ourselves from the emotional bonds which have tied us to the person we loved so that we may "invest" that energy elsewhere, to "detach" ourselves so that we may be "uninhibited." Mourning is "necessary." It denotes a process which takes place over a long period of time. It is slow, infinitessimaly so, as we simultaneously psychically cling to what has been lost. (85)

Later thinkers extend Freud's conception of the possibility of the work of mourning, theorizing the role of language in terms of the labour required. For grieving to be effective, the emotions of loss must be translated into words and must be articulated. The work of mourning, notes Robert Stamelman, "penetrates the being of language, filling it with a sorrow so abundant and... so fecund that the worded grief displaces the loved object, its source" (50–51). Jacques Derrida, in his essay "By Force of Mourning," remarks on the relationship of the dual senses of "work" in regards to mourning:

Work: that which makes for a work, for an *oeuvre*, indeed that which works—and works to open: *opus* and *opening*, *oeuvre*, and *ouverture*: the work or labor of the *oeuvre* insofar as it engenders, produces, and brings to light, but also labor or travail as suffering, as the engendering of force, as the pain of one who gives. Of the one who gives birth, who brings to the light of day and gives something to be seen, who enables or empowers, who gives the force to know and to be able to see—and all these are powers of the image, the pain of what is given and of the one who takes pains to help us see, read, and think. (171)[4]

Derrida's emphasis on the notion of opening is significant to understand the concept of the work of mourning as it is employed in this book, for as much as the texts of mourning we encounter are chronicles of an individual's struggle to mourn, they also open readers to the particulars of grief. We are thus aided not only in our understanding of grief-work in our own age and socio-cultural context (as varied as they may be) but we are opened to a history of literary expression that serves to signify other socio-cultural moments. By looking back at the labour of mourning in other contexts we are opened to other works of mourning and that opening in turn reflects upon ourselves and our contextual understanding of the work of mourning. And so, reading the work of mourning, Derrida tells us, is a reflexive process that we are forced to engage in by the very fundamental nature of the subject matter we are reading.

While there is significant variation in the theoretical notion of what grief-work can achieve in twentieth-century thinking, from Freud's structural movement that results in loss being put behind the grieving subject (thus a moving through), to Lacan's idea that loss takes on an "interminable, monotonous tempo...a rhythm that flattens the singularity of the object and renders its historical circumstances irrelevant" (Ricciardi 43), the special focus of *Response to Death: The Literary Work of Mourning* is on the literary response to death and loss. As the discussions in the individual chapters attest—in their collectivity—writers have approached the idea that writing can somehow partake of a labour of mourning for many centuries. Thus, the focus is on Derrida's sense that grief-work is an opening to emotion and to loss, and that this process (or perhaps processes) is a valuable and necessary one.

———

EACH CHAPTER in *Response to Death: The Literary Work of Mourning* interrogates the notion of the work of mourning within a specific historical and literary context, beginning with medieval England and moving forward to the contemporary era and within English, French, American, Canadian and French-Canadian linguistic and cultural settings. Far from invoking a singular template of how mourning is invoked and employed in the texts under examination, the chapters respond to the particular requirements of a text's articulation of mourning and proceed with the concept of the work of mourning broadly defined. Thus, this volume can more readily be read within a comparative understanding of literary history and expression. The notions of comparison, literature, and history—and indeed the work of mourning—should in the context of this collection of essays be taken in the plural, for as Herb Wyile and Jeanette Lynes remark, "literary history is hardly a consensual, communal project to which scholars make their contributions, but rather a site of conflict, debate, and revision" (117).[5]

———

THE INTERSECTIONS of the work of mourning and faith in the York Corpus Christi cycle of late medieval plays are examined by Leanne Groeneveld in "Mourning, Heresy, and Resurrection in the York Corpus Christi Cycle." A central question that is addressed is how the teachings of the church on the nature of grieving are reflected in the plays. These plays fulfill an instructive function on how to mourn the dead, and of how to think of the dead, that is not addressed in other medieval treatises or doctrinal documents. The grief of Christ's disciples upon his death is depicted as paralyzing and excessive in the cycle and over the course of the sequence of plays, they learn the proper ways in which to mourn. Contemporary audiences, Groeneveld notes, were able to learn about correct ways to mourn the dead. The cycle's dramatization of grief serves to warn of the dangers of excessive grief and of the importance of learning the proper ways of carrying out the work of mourning. As guidance to mourning, teachings of the church fathers, and in particular Augustine, are employed. Thus, the work of mourning is linked closely with the proper expression and understanding of faith, and, by the end of the York cycle, it is made clear that those who refuse to accept Christ's body in any form are the only ones who will not ultimately escape eternal grieving.

William Shakespeare's contemplation of the political perils attached to mourning are explored in Heather Dubrow's contribution, "Mourning Becomes Electric: The Politics of Grief in Shakespeare's *Lucrece*." The connections between loss and narrative are examined to show how this well-known poem of Shakespeare's presents a rhetoric of mourning; the poem, in turn, reflects upon other texts by Shakespeare to display new considerations of mourning practices. Shakespeare posits that there are political perils attached to mourning alongside the psychological ones most frequently focused on in Freudian and neo-Freudian contemplations of mourning. The work of mourning in Shakespeare's *The Rape of Lucrece* involves the dynamic of loss and recovery through narrative by the very activities of storytelling and the substitution of an individual's story for a competing one. Also examining work by Shakespeare, Lisa Dickson looks to the three parts of *Henry VI* to explore the complexity of the work of mourning in "The King is Dead: Mourning and Nation in the Three Parts of Shakespeare's *Henry VI*." As with Dubrow, Dickson notes that Shakespeare's conception of the work of mourning reflects an understanding of the personal and political aspects of grieving and that these two frequently overlap and affect each other. Indeed, the work of mourning is coexistent with the crisis of national identity evidenced in the plays. Dickson argues that the tetralogy forms an extended lamentation for a lost ideal of sovereignty. The fractured body politic is reflected in the mutilated and fractured bodies that are subject to the work of mourning of the grieving characters in the plays, and that the work of mourning is thus a metaphor for the loss of the notion of an ideal state.

The interest that Shakespeare displays in his writing with regard to the work of mourning is exemplary of the English fascination with death and grieving during the Renaissance. As Melanie Gregg argues, sixteenth-century France was equally preoccupied with how the work of mourning should be best articulated and understood. In "Women's Poetry of Grief and Mourning: The Language of Lament in Sixteenth-Century French Lyric," Gregg notes that the French feminist theories of *écriture féminine* in recent thinking are anticipated by the constructions of language evident in the work of Renaissance women Philiberte de Fleurs, Madeleine des Roches, Catherine de Bourbon, Gabrielle de Coignard, and Marguerite de Navarre. These women turned to the forces of their bodies to express the ineffable; the language of the body became feminine in their lyric. By working against existing cultural beliefs about grief reflected in many male poems of the mid-sixteenth century—poems where grief was rejected and that reflect a movement of anti-mourning—these female poets were able to assert the emotional and physical aspects of grieving, of the work of mourning, and thus the feminine poetic presents a fundamentally transgressive response to grief.

The public performance of mourning that accompanied the death of the Princess of Wales, Charlotte Augusta, in November 1817 is the focus of Stephen C. Behrendt's essay, "Mourning, Myth, and Merchandising: The Public Death of Princess Charlotte." He explores how the public mourning of Charlotte Augusta became a commodified process of exchange: physical objects and artifacts could be bought by individual members of the public, which then provided forms of gratification for the mourner. These public rituals of mourning are inherently restorative and stabilizing, and, because of their public nature—rather than the private mourning of the elite level of society Charlotte belonged to—are democratizing. The grieving public was able to claim the Princess as their own, an identification as commoners. Behrendt examines the range of aesthetic consumer goods, such as prose and poetic writing, visual art, and other items (such as ceramic pieces, stamps and commemorative coins) that were produced in the period after Charlotte's death to establish the function of the very public work of mourning for individuals, who were able to find corollaries between their own life experiences and that of the mourned subject. Thus, comfort was drawn in recognizing the narrowing of the gap between the mythical world of elite society (and specifically royalty) and the more mortal individuals of the common world. Behrendt notes the striking similarities between the public mourning of Princess Diana and Princess Charlotte and concludes that these similarities reveal a societal impulse to mythologize a popular subject in periods of domestic instability and crisis that supercede the constraints of a specific historical context. Thus, the work of mourning as described by Behrendt is likely to occur at any time when a certain set of cultural and societal conditions occur, as was the case with Charlotte and then Diana.

Focusing primarily on close textual reading through the lens of twentieth-century psychotherapy, Barbara Hudspith in "Adam's Mourning and The Herculean Task in *Adam Bede*" examines the work of mourning carried out by the protagonist, Adam. Hudspith delineates the double-edged nature of Adam's work of mourning, for it functions as a curse and as a blessing, as a wound and as a gift that allows the reparation of not only the immediate loss but also of the conflicts associated with the loss. Eliot prioritizes the work of mourning as process in *Adam Bede*, as Eliot traces Adam's immediate response to loss that is followed by his painful yet ultimately effective working through of deep loss.

Garry Sherbert's examination of Djuna Barnes's novel *Nightwood* marks the shift to twentieth-century texts in this special issue. In "Hieroglyphics of Sleep and Pain: Djuna Barnes's Anatomy of Melancholy," *Nightwood* is theorized as an unfinished work of mourning, following Freud's opposition of mourning and melancholia. Invoking Abraham and Torok's revision of Freud's work on mourning, and employing Jacques Derrida's writing, Sherbert explains Nora Flood's struggles to effectively mourn her grandmother as a resistance to the interiorizing and idealizing powers of language: she is unable to successfully articulate her work of mourning and thus she mourns interminably, staying instead in a melancholic state. Readers of *Nightwood* participate in the work of mourning without closure by the very act of reading itself as this act assembles and ultimately dissembles the loss, never consoling; thus, Nora's work of mourning also becomes the reader's work of mourning.

In "Colossal Departures: Figuring the Lost Father in Berryman's and Plath's Poetry," Ernest Smith examines the changing nature of elegy in mid-century poetry in America. Both Berryman and Plath engage the issue of paternal loss and the subsequent anger at what they sense as abandonment. For Smith, Plath and Berryman are engaged with the work of reconciling the ambivalent emotions of love and hatred for the father that shadows their adult lives. Conventions of elegy are refigured to fulfill the highly personal nature of their loss; elegy becomes the domain of private psychic exploration and thus is a challenge to the earlier much more public expressions of the genre. The work of mourning performed in Plath's and Berryman's elegies is related to the needs of mourners in the twentieth-century; that this work does not in the end result in consolation as the generic requirements of elegy demand is a sign of the changing understanding of mourning and psychic processes in mid-century America.

Where in Barnes the work of mourning is relegated to failure, to an absence of closure and consolation—and indeed in Plath and Berryman as well—the poetry of contemporary American writer Donald Hall is seen as a positive attempt to articulate and to engage in the process of writing grief in Todd F. Davis's and Kenneth Womack's essay, "Reading the Ethics of Mourning in the Poetry of Donald Hall." *Without*, which was written as a response to the death of Hall's wife, poet Jane Kenyon, presents his struggle to transform the reality of his loss into an aesthetic realm. Narrative effectively becomes therapy whereby grief and anger are worked through. Davis and Womack's approach stresses the notion of an ethics of mourning; this ethics recognizes that the desolation of loss can be countered by the balm of language. In *Without*, they argue, the grief and anger over Kenyon's death is recontextualized as well as narrated in the realm of art. The resulting text that readers encounter presents the work of mourning in both senses, as product and process; further, *Without* requires of its readers active participation in the work of mourning that comprises its text.

The expression of the work of mourning within a postcolonial and Canadian context is the focus of the following two essays in the volume. Katherine G. Sutherland, in "Land of Their Graves: Maternity, Mourning and Nation in Janet Frame, Sara Suleri and Arundhati Roy," examines mourning as a social practice that engages in conceptions of nationhood. Invoking nineteenth-century Canadian writer Susanna Moodie, Sutherland argues that the work of mourning involves understanding how the death of her children and the subsequent grief are similar to the separation she suffered at leaving her mother nation (England) and the eventual attachment to the new nation. Mourning is conceived by Sutherland as an expression of cultural value and as a discourse of nationalism. The association between mourning, maternity and nationality are recurring themes in women's postcolonial writing and thus present new perspectives on notions of nationality. The idea of nation in women's postcolonial writing is constructed through intimate, material, and bodily associations by the representation of mothers, sisters, and children. Lola Lemire Tostevin's focus is less on the political than it is on the aesthetic and the personal, writes Thomas M.F. Gerry in "'If Only I Were Isis': Remembrance, Ritual, and Writing in Lola Lemire Tostevin's *Cartouches*." The work of mourning in *Cartouches* is a postmodern contemplation of mourning as an enacted ritual of movement towards renewal and consolation whereby the interplay between the text as product and as simultaneous process of mourning is highlighted. Gerry focuses on the multidimensionality of the readerly and writerly processes involved in partaking of Tostevin's work of mourning. For readers of *Cartouches*, the process of narrative-making is a necessary and active one as we are participants in the charging of language with intention. For Tostevin herself, the collection is a working through of the grief at her father's death and the subsequent process of identity-renewal at the loss.

The final essay in this volume addresses the urgency presented by contemporary disease by asking how the work of mourning can be produced in AIDS elegy. In "Using Up Words in Paul Monette's AIDS Elegy," Lloyd Edward Kermode asserts that AIDS elegy functions successfully on the level of artistry but is also a politically and socially effective means of cultural productivity. Kermode relates Monette's elegiac practice in the collection of poems, *Love Alone: Eighteen Elegies for Rog*, written upon the death of his partner Rog, to conventional elegy and argues that convention is both employed and broken. AIDS elegy shifts from the pastoral influences in conventional elegy and alters the traditional apotheosis to the creation of healing for the future. The focus of *Love Alone* becomes dual, chronicling the poet's own movement towards consolation and speaking more largely by providing what Kermode describes as politically-active documentation that results in readers being drawn into the inscriptions of AIDS within contemporary discourses of the body.

As all the texts examined in the essays in this volume attest, from medieval English drama to Shakespeare's work, to contemporary explorations by writers such as Hall and Tostevin of the form that grief takes, the work of mourning is complexly conceived and thus reflects the social and psychological complexity of specific contextual responses to death. A comparative view of the work of mourning across the centuries, and within varying sociocultural and national contexts, reinforces the interconnectedness of the central tenets of the literary response to death. As much as linguistic and contextual concerns—and indeed the approach to the work of mourning—differ between the texts examined in *Response to Death: The Literary Work of Mourning*, the fundamental nature of death in relation to the human condition is asserted in the collectivity of plays, poems, and novels.

NOTES

1   For further discussion of these concerns, see my discussion in *Writing Grief: Margaret Laurence and the Work of Mourning* (Winnipeg: U of Manitoba P, 2003).

2   While variously constituted in the specific processes involved, the general notion of the gradual breaking of the emotional connection to the dead person in order to move on is a common and accepted one in psychological writing. Formal theorization begins with Freud in his 1917 essay "Mourning and Melancholia" (*A General*

Selection From the Works of Sigmund Freud, ed. John Rickman [Garden City: Doubleday, 1957]), but includes numerous commentators. Amongst these are David A. Crenshaw in *Bereavement: Counseling the Grieving Throughout the Life Cycle* (New York: Continuum, 1990), Peter Marris in *Loss and Change* (New York: Pantheon Books, 1974), Beverly Raphael in *The Anatomy of Bereavement* (New York: Basic Books, 1983), and Elizabeth Kübler-Ross in *On Death and Dying* (New York: Macmillan, 1969).

3   Later on the same page Freud refers to "mental economics," thus reinforcing this image of labour and complexity (126).

4   These words are from a talk Derrida gave at a conference honouring Louis Marin, the visual artist and critic. Derrida's words serve in themselves as a self-conscious work of mourning, while at the same time further define the concept.

5   See also, Christian Riegel, "Recognizing the Multiplicity of the Oeuvre," *Challenging Territory: The Writing of Margaret Laurence*, ed. C. Riegel (Edmonton: U of Alberta P, 1997) for further discussion of plurality and literary history, pp. xi–xxiii.

Mourning, Heresy, and Resurrection in the York Corpus Christi Cycle

FROM SOME TIME around 1376 to some time during the 1570s, a remarkable annual theatre event took place in the northern English city of York. On the Feast of Corpus Christi, manufacturing and trading guilds collaborated to present to an audience of both citizens and tourists as many as fifty plays dramatizing biblical events from the Fall of the Angels to the Last Judgement. Beginning at 4:30 in the morning and ending shortly after midnight, they pushed and pulled their "pageants" or wagon stages through the streets of the city, performing their individual dramas at designated stations at the doors of citizens' houses, at major intersections and before the gates of parish churches.

An official record or register of the plays produced by the individual guilds was compiled sometime between 1463 and 1477. This register records (for the most part) a version of the cycle as it was performed in the latter half of the fifteenth century;[1] marginalia in a mid-sixteenth century hand indicate that many plays underwent substantial revisions between their initial transcriptions and their later (literal, in production) incarnations. One of the plays noted as revised is The Supper at Emmaus (Play 40),[2] the first of a series of plays (extending to Christ's Ascension) that dramatize the disciples' deep despair after Christ's crucifixion and burial.

That the disciples grieve Christ's death in this particular fifteenth-century post-Passion sequence is not especially interesting or unique—in other late medieval biblical plays, they lament the fact and manner of his death, usually at length. What is unique is the York Corpus Christi cycle's careful representation of the disciples' mourning as excessive and, there-fore, as both a cause and a sign of weak, even heretical faith. I will argue that these plays dramatize an interpretation of the disciples in their doubt and despair first put forward by St. Augustine, who, in a number of sermons, reads them as proto-dualists because they initially doubted the resurrection. This use of Augustine allowed the cycle to represent the disciples' grief to double purpose. First of all, the plays illustrated to their audience the dangers of excessively mourning the dead; the disciples move from improper to proper expressions of sorrow, demonstrating the manner in and degree to which mourning should be performed as they shed their heretical beliefs about Christ's particular, and humanity's general, resurrection. The close association of resurrection and transubstantiation in late medieval culture then allowed the plays to exploit the disciples' grief to a second purpose: because Augustine identified the disciples as proto-dualists and used their example to condemn fourth-century Manicheans, York playwrights could identify the disciples as Lollards or Wyclifites and use their example to condemn fifteenth-century heretical beliefs on the doctrine of transubstantiation. The York disciples' disbelief in Christ's resurrection and their unrestrained mourning could be read as both cause and product of an anachronistic Lollard doubt about the true presence in the consecrated host.

Both the disciples' act of mourning and the playwrights' examination of classical and contemporary Christian belief begin in Play 40 of the York Corpus Christi cycle with The Supper at Emmaus. Here the disciples' intense sorrow becomes first and most evident as Cleophas and Luke lament the fact and manner of Christ's death in over sixty lines of heavily alliterative and repetitive verse. That the lines are filled with alliteration suggests the characters' deep-felt emotion:

> That lorde þat [that] me lente [gave] þis liffe [life] for to lede [lead],
> In my wayes þou [you] me wisse [guide] þus will of wone [distraught].
> Qwen [when] othir men halfe [have] moste mirthe to þer mede
>   [reward],
> Þanne [then] als a mornand [mourning] manne make I my mone
>   [complaint]. (Play 40.1–4)

That portions of the last line of each (increasingly alliterative) stanza repeat in the first line of each stanza following suggests, as Alexandra Johnston notes, that Cleophas and Luke "are locked in their despair as they re-tell the story of the crucifixion" (244). Although moving forward in their physical journey to Emmaus, Christ's followers are trapped in a spiritual cycle (or spiral) of grief:

II Perigrinus   In *frasting* [trial] we *fonde* [found] hym full faithfull
                    and free,
                 In his mynde mente he neuere *mysse* [harm] to
                    no man.
                 Itt was a sorowe, *forsoth* [in truth], in sight for
                    to see
                 Whanne þat a *spetyffull* [cruel] spere vnto his
                    harte ranne.
                 In *baill* [torment] *þus* [thus] his body was *beltid*
                    [embraced],
                 Into his harte *thraly* [violently] *þci thraste* [thrust];
                 Whan [when] his piteffull paynes were *paste*
                    [over, finished],
                 þat *swet* [dear] thyng **full swiftely he** *sweltid* [died].

I Perigrinus   **He sweltid full** *swithe* [quickly] in *swonyng*
                    [swooning], **þat swette.**
                 Allas for þat *luffely* [beloved] þat laide is
                    so lowe,
                 With *granyng* [groaning] full *grissely* [grisly] on
                    grounde may we *grette* [weep],
                 For so *comely* [worthy] a *corse* [person] canne I none
                    knowe. (40.49–60)

When Christ appears to the pilgrims and speaks to them, interrupting the stanza form, he attempts to break the cyclic expressions of grief the men have established and are reluctant to abandon. He asks, "What are þes *meru-ailes* [marvels] þat *3e* [you] of mene / And þus *mekill* [greatly] mournyng in mynde þat 3e make, / Walkyng þus *wille* [distraught] by þes wayes?" (40.67–69). Cleophas and Luke immediately resume their mournful alliter-ative and cyclic verse even as they respond to Christ's intentionally disruptive question:

I Perigrinus	Why, *herde* [heard] *þou* [you] no *carpyng* [speaking] nor crying
	Att Jerusalem *þer* [where] *þou* haste *bene* [been],
	Whenne Jesu *þe* Nazarene
	Was *doulfully* [cruelly] **dight to *þe* dying** [put to death]?

| II Perigrinus | **To *þe* dying** *þei* **dight** hym *þat defte* [gentle] was and *dere* [...]. (40.77–81) |

This heavy lament continues for another forty-eight lines before Christ interrupts the men again, condemning their behaviour and reading their grief as evidence of weak faith: "A, fooles *þat* are *fauty* [mistaken] and failes of youre *feithe* [faith], / Þis *bale* [pain] *bud* [it was necessary that] hym *bide* [endure] and *belde* [save] *þame* in blisse— / But 3e be *lele* [faithful] of youre *laye* [law] youre liffe holde I *laith* [in aversion]" (40.130–32). Christ's condemnation and second interruption of the pilgrims' grief brings the two men to their senses at last, disrupting the verse form. Although lines remain alliterative in the play, stanzas are now shared between speakers and repetition is used to different effect.[3]

When the pilgrims realize with whom they have been talking, they resolve to tell their "felawes" (fellows) about their experience (40.187–90). However, Play 41 opens with the disciples in Jerusalem, still unaware of the events that have transpired in Emmaus and lamenting Christ's death and their own persecution at the hands of the Jews:

Petrus	Allas, to *woo* [woe, misery] *þat* we wer *wrought* [made],
	Hadde never no men so *mekill þought* [much worry],
	Sen [since] that oure lorde to *dede* [death] was brought
	With Jewes *fell* [cruel];
	Oute of *þis steede* [place] *ne durste we noght* [we dare not go],
	But here *ay* [always] dwelle.

Johannes	Here *haue* [have] we dwelte with *peynes strang* [strong pains];
	Of oure *liffe vs lothis* [we hate], we *leue to lange* [live too long],
	For *sen* [since] the Jewes *wrought* [did] vs þat wrong
	Oure lorde to *sloo* [slay],
	Durste we neuere [we don't dare] come þame *emang* [among them],
	Ne hense to goo [nor to leave]. (Play 41.1–12)

When Christ miraculously appears to these disciples, they, following the gospel account, wonder if the apparition they see is a ghost or "sperite" (41.35, 37). Christ appears again, condemns them for their lack of faith and for their grief, and reassures them that he is no ghost:

What thynke ȝe, madmen, in youre thought?
What mournyng in youre *hertis* [hearts] is brought?
I ame Criste, *ne drede ȝou noght* [do not fear, doubt];
Her may ȝe se
þe same body þat has you *bought* [saved, redeemed]
Vppon a *tre* [tree]. (41.43–48)

Christ offers to eat roast honeycomb, "To make youre *trouthe* [faith] sted-fast and grete, / And for ȝe schall *wanhope* [despair] forgete / And *trowe* [believe] in me [...]" (41.74–76). He suggests that only true belief will allow the disciples to abandon their despair—faith and grief are, therefore, finally incompatible.

At this point, Thomas enters the scene, approaching the sequestered disciples from a distance. He too is hopelessly sad and expresses his pain using familiar terms and verse form:

Allas for *sight* [grief] and sorowes sadde,
Mornyng makis me *mased* [bewildered] and *madde*;
On grounde nowe may I *gang* [go] vngladde
Boþe *even and morne* [night and day].

þat *hende* [worthy man] *þat I my helpe of hadde* [from whom I received
help, strength]
His liffe has **lorne** [lost].

Lorne I haue þat louely light,
Þat was my maistir moste of myght. (41.97–104)

As Thomas considers the pain suffered by Christ during his Passion, he
is overcome with emotion, crying, "Allas, for sorowe myselffe I *schende* [kill]
/ When I thynke *hartely* [truly, sincerely] on þat *hende* [worthy man] [...]"
(41.115–16). He declares on behalf of all the other disciples, "So wofull
wyghtis [people] was *neuere* [never] none, / Oure joie and comforte is all
gone. / Of mournyng may we make oure *mone* [complaint] [...]" (41.121–23).
Thomas is therefore understandably shocked to discover that his fellows
no longer grieve Christ's death but instead proclaim his resurrection.
Indignant, Thomas declares that he will not believe until presented with
proof of the supposed miracle:

Tille [until] þat I see his body bare
And *sithen* [after that] my fyngir putte in *thare* [there]
Within his hyde,
And fele the wounde þe spere did *schere* [cut]
Riȝt [right] in his syde,

Are [before] schalle I *trowe* [believe] no tales betwene. (41.158–63)

Christ then appears, invites Thomas to probe his wounds, and commands
him to "be no more *mistrowand* [lacking in faith / misbelieving], / But *trowe*
[believe] trewly" (41.179–80), which Thomas of course immediately does.
Unfortunately, the disciples' eventual unanimous acceptance of the resurrection does not put an end to their grief. At the beginning of Play 42, they
even lament Christ's imminent ascension:

Johannes	The missing of my *maistir trewe* [true, faithful,
	good master]
	That *lenghis* [remains] not with vs *lastandly* [always],

Makis me to morne *ilke a day newe* [each day again]
For *tharnyng* [lack] of his company. (Play 42.9–12)

Fortunately, Peter explains, this sorrow, caused by the disciples' separation from their Lord, is mitigated to some degree by the promise of an eventual and eternal reunion:

Bot *ʒitt* [yet] in all my *mysselykyng* [sorrow]
A worde þat Criste saide comfortis me:
Oure *heuynes* [heaviness] and oure mournyng,
He saide, to joie turned *schuld* [should] be. (42.17–20)

The believer's separation from Christ and from all loved ones who die is temporary, for, as Christ himself explains later in the play, all will unite again in future, both spiritually in heaven and physically on earth. On the Day of Judgement, Christ promises, "man by *cours of kynde* [in due course] schall ryse / Allþogh he *be roten ontill noʒt* [has rotted to nothing]" (42.105–06) and "schall [...] be broght / Wher [Christ] schall sitte as trewe *justise* [judge] [...]" (42.108–09).

The disciples' new, more tempered grief seems acceptable to Christ, as he no longer reprimands them. Before he ascends in Play 42, he chooses instead to remind his followers of their past sins, encouraging them not to re-offend by explaining the consequences, both past and potential, of their former doubt and excessive sorrow:

In grete *wanne-trowyng* [weak faith] haue ʒe bene,
And *wondir* [extremely] harde of hartis ar ʒe.
Worthy to be reproued, I *wene* [believe, think]
Ar ʒe forsothe, and ʒe will see
In als *mekill* [much] als ʒe haue *sene* [seen]
My wirkyng proued and my *posté* [power].

Whan I was *dede* [dead] and laide in graue
Of myne *vpryse* [resurrection] ʒe were in *doute* [doubt],
And some *for* [about] myne vprysing *straue* [argued]
When I was laide als vndir *clowte* [shroud]

So depe in erthe. But *sithen* [since] I haue
Ben *walkand* [walking] fourty daies aboute,
Eten [have eaten] with ȝou, youre *trouthe* [faith] to saue,
Comand [have come] emange ȝou inne and oute.

And þerfore beis no more in *were* [be no more in a state of confusion,
    misery]
Of myne vpperysing, day nor nyght. (42.83–98)

Christ warns the disciples that their initial disbelief in his resurrection,
evinced by their grief and mourning and by their petty arguing, has not only
been a sign of, but has also produced, schism within the disciples' ranks:
"Youre misbeleue," he tells them, "leues *ilkone seere* [each one separate]"
(42.99). Fortunately, from this point on in the cycle—with only a couple of
exceptions in the plays of Pentecost (Play 43) and the Assumption of Mary
(Play 45)—the disciples leave their own mourning and lamentations and
instead speak of receiving and giving comfort. After the appearance of two
angels at Christ's Ascension, James proclaims, "Loued be þou lorde *ay* [ever]
moste of myght, / Þat þs, in all oure grete *disease* [discomfort], / Vs comfortist
with thyne aungellis bright" (42.233–35). More encouraging still, James
tells the Virgin Mary that he and the other disciples will in future focus on
lessening her sorrow at the loss of her son: "Oure comforte, youre care to
kele [relieve], / *Whill* [while] we may *leue* [live] we schall not faile" (42.269–70),
he promises her. The disciples, good Christians who now put their faith in
the resurrection, no longer require consolation at separation from their
loved one but instead comfort another believer who mourns.

Christ's repeated condemnation of the disciple's initial immoderate
grief in York can simply be read in light of that ubiquitous medieval adage,
"measure is treasure." In all things, ordinary Christians were advised to
assume the stoic middle-ground—for example, in the fifteenth-century play
Mankind, Mercy counsels the title character not to shun all food, drink, or
fashion but always to indulge in moderation. He advises Mankind,

Mesure ys tresure. Y forbyde *yow* [you] not þe vse.
Mesure *yowrsylf* [yourself] euer; be ware of excesse.

þe superfluouse *gyse* [manner of living] I wyll þat ȝe refuse,
When nature ys *suffysyde* [satisfied], *anon* [immediately] þat ȝe sese.
(ll. 237–40)

This stoic approach to the pleasures of life also applied to those experiences that were painful or sorrowful. Thus Saint Ambrose, in his sermon "On the Belief in the Resurrection," recommends to his fellow Christians "that moderation in adversity which is required in prosperity" (175). "If it be not seemly to rejoice immoderately," he asks, "is it seemly so to mourn?" Of course not, he concludes: "want of moderation in grief or fear of death is no small evil" and so should be avoided.[4]

Ambrose's advice and reading of bereavement is typical of the Latin fathers, who, while discouraging over-indulgence, allow that grief is a natural response to the death of a loved one and is not necessarily sinful in itself. Jerome, in a letter to Heliodorus on the death of his nephew Nepotian, writes that he and his friend, grieving properly, do not sorrow for the young man but for themselves, because they "cannot bear the feeling of his absence" (125). Augustine writes in Sermon 173 that Christians inevitably sorrow when they observe a lifeless body because they are aware that the invisible spirit has departed (in *Patrologia Latina* Vol. 38, 939). Separation from one's family member or loved one is recognized as a natural, sanctioned cause of grief, which perhaps explains why in York the disciples' sorrow at Christ's ascension is never condemned.

Yet, according to Ambrose in his sermon "On the Death of Satyrus," those who die "seem to be not lost but sent before, whom death is not going to swallow up, but eternity receive" (172). The separation of the living and the dead is only temporary, as believers will be reunited in heaven, and so a true Christian's grief should be measured and moderate. If it is not, if his or her grief is instead excessive and inconsolable, it likely arises not from good, natural impulses but from sin and lack of faith. Ambrose writes that "there is a very great difference between longing for what you have lost and lamenting that you have lost it" (162): the former is a natural sorrow by which one does not incur "any grievous sin"; the latter is a "distrustful sadness" that "proceeds from unbelief or weakness" (162). The "difference between the servants of Christ and the worshippers of idols" is that "the latter weep for their friends, whom they suppose to have perished forever" (172). Thus excessive grief signals that the mourner is either a pagan or, amongst those who profess to be Christians, an heretic.

This is not to say that intense mourning was never appropriate and therefore never sanctioned: humankind did not always have the hope and assurance of eternal life. Before the advent of Christ and his crucifixion, if not after, violent sorrow was an appropriate response to death, as Jerome explains in a letter of consolation to Paula. Here he cites a number of Old Testament examples to prove that grief had its place under the old Law. He notes that "lamentation was made for Moses; yet when the funeral of Joshua is described no mention at all is made of weeping" (52). "The reason, of course," he explains, "is that under Moses—that is under the old Law—all men were bound by the sentence passed on Adam's sin, and when they descended into hell were rightly accompanied with tears" (52). He also offers the example of Jacob who, dressed in sackcloth, mourned the death of Joseph and refused to be comforted. Jerome writes: "Jacob, it is true, mourned for Joseph, whom he fancied slain, and thought to meet only in the grave [...], but he only did so because Christ had not yet broken open the door of paradise" (51). Of course, once that door was finally and forever opened, any sorrow stemming from the belief that death is permanent became a "superstition" and a grievous sin. Jerome singles out Jews for condemnation, as they "go on their weeping to this day" (52). And yet, he allows, "they are right to weep, for as they do not believe in the Lord's resurrection they are being made ready for the advent of antichrist."

This last point is of interest, as Jerome seems to identify belief in the resurrection of Christ as the central consolation of Christianity. Christ's bodily resurrection, a sign of his victory over the grave, was a promise of spiritual salvation but was even more a guarantee of the physical salvation to come at the general resurrection. Augustine is more emphatic on this point: in the same sermon in which he identifies the lifeless corpse as a source of legitimate sorrow for those left behind, he identifies that same corpse as a source of tremendous comfort and consolation. The dead body has a dual effect on mourners because it reminds them at once of their separation from their loved one and of their joyful reunion to come, when "'the lord himself, with a cry of command, with the call of the archangels and with the sounding of the last trumpet, will descend from the sky; first the dead in Christ will rise, and then we who are still living will, with them, be caught up into the clouds and will meet with Christ in the air" (1 Thess. 4.16–17, cited in Sermon 171, in *Patrologia Latina* 38.939). "Let sorrow perish when consolation is this great," Augustine exclaims, "let light cleanse sadness from the soul, let faith expel sorrow."[5]

Augustine's assertion that the resurrection of bodies at the end of time is the ultimate source of comfort for the bereaved accords with his repeated insistence that resurrection is Christianity's central tenet. In Sermon 241 he writes:

> The belief in the resurrection of the dead is the distinctive belief of Christians. Christ, our Head, in His own person revealed this to us, that is, the resurrection of the dead, and He furnished us an example of this belief, so that His members might have hope for themselves in regard to that which had already happened to their Head. (*Sermons on the Liturgical Seasons* 255)

"Pagans, wicked people and Jews believed in the Passion of Christ," he explains in Sermon 233, but "Christians alone believe in His Resurrection. The Passion of Christ discloses the miseries of this life; the Resurrection of Christ points to the happiness of the life to come" (217).

Belief in the resurrection, of Christ and of Christians more generally, was also considered central by Augustine because it distinguished orthodox believers from heretics, specifically from the Manichaeans and the Priscillianists, who denied that Christ had a physical body and therefore rejected the doctrine of resurrection. Augustine's discussion of these dualist heretics in his sermons on the Easter season is striking, as he compares them to the disciples in their disbelief after Christ's resurrection. In Sermon 236, he writes:

> If at any time the Resurrection is preached in these days and the account seems to some listener to be nonsense, do not all agree that such a person is greatly afflicted? Do not all denounce, shun, and avoid this person, close their ears and refuse to listen to him? Behold what the disciples were after the death of Christ: they were that which we abhor. Like rams, they had the plague from which lambs shrink. (232)

In Sermon 237, Augustine discusses in particular the disciples' initial belief that Christ had returned as a ghost:

> They saw [...] and because they did not believe that their own eyes were seeing aright, they thought they were deceived. For they 'thought that they saw a spirit,' as you have heard. The wavering Apostles anticipated what the worst heretics later believed about Christ. For there are people today who do not believe that Christ had a body, because they rule out the parturition of a virgin and they refuse to believe that Christ was born of a woman. [...] All that appeared to the eyes of men, as the Manichaeans believe, was spirit, not flesh. (235–36)

In his very next sermon, Augustine reiterates this reading of the disciples' misreading of Christ's appearance, stating, "They [...] were disturbed; they 'thought that they saw a spirit.' That is what is thought by those who do not believe that He had a true body; these are the Manichaeans, the Priscillianists, and other scourges not worthy to be mentioned" (Sermon 238, *Sermons on the Liturgical Seasons* 240–41). Augustine then asks, "What do you think, O Catholic? What do you think, O faithful spouse?" and encourages those who believe truly to "Forgive those who think what the disciples in their confusion previously thought" (241). Again, he explains that the apostles "thought, as the Manichaeans and as the Priscillianists think today, that the Lord was only a spirit without a true body." The only difference between the apostles and these "worst heretics" is that the former "did not remain in their error" but allowed themselves to be instructed and corrected by Christ.

Augustine here represents the disciples as proto-heretics, as dualists. This representation fits with his and other church fathers' more general readings of excessive grief and mourning as evidence of false or lack of faith in Christians, and therefore of heresy. The disciples existed at a crucial moment in time: they witnessed the very events—the crucifixion and resurrection—that eliminated, for true believers, eternal physical death and spiritual damnation, the only legitimate reasons for or causes of immoderate mourning. They should have moved effortlessly from Jewish sorrow to Christian joy, from the old law to the new, from sacrifice to sacrament, but they did not. They remained for a time in a liminal, dangerous state that could have led to, and that Augustine suggests did in fact anticipate, later schisms within the church.

Augustine's reading and representation of the sorrowing disciples as heretics is clearly dramatized in the York Corpus Christi cycle. As discussed in the first section of this paper, repeated reference is made to the disciples' false or "fauty" beliefs in the York resurrection sequence; their grief, their arguments over the truth of Christ's resurrection, and their resultant lack of unity anger Christ and are unequivocally condemned by him. In the Play of Pentecost, the latter shortcoming (the disciples' lack of unity) becomes particularly troubling as they ponder their future roles as teachers and missionaries. Here, in accordance with the biblical account (Acts 1.12–26), Peter suggests that the eleven disciples must nominate someone to fill Judas' place so that they will make an even number; this will facilitate the preaching of the gospel for, Peter states at the very end of the play's first stanza, "Twelue may be *asoundir tone* [parted] / And sett in *parties seere* [separate groups]" (43.11–12). By dividing into smaller groups, the disciples will be able to spread their message further and will win more converts; however—and at this point York deviates from the scriptural account—the disciples must take care that their division in number not result in a division in doctrine. At the very end of the second stanza and thus in obvious juxtaposition with his recommendation that the disciples divide their labour, Peter warns, "*senne* [since] we *on þis wise* [in this manner] / Schall his [Christ's] *counsaile* [message] *discrie* [proclaim], / *Itt nedis* [it is necessary that] we vs *avise* [take care] / Þat we saye no3t *serely* [variously]" (43.21–24). The disciples must be careful not to promote schism within the church and therefore, as in Augustine, must be careful not to sow the seeds of heresy.

That the York Plays dramatize Augustinian readings of biblical events is not an original or particularly contentious point: Alexandra Johnston, in her article "*The Word Made Flesh*: Augustinian Elements in the *York Cycle*," offers convincing external and internal evidence that Augustine's writings were accessible and familiar to both the York playwrights and their subsequent revisers, whoever they were. She discusses a surviving late fourteenth-century catalogue from the Austin friary at York which reveals that the library contained most of Augustine's works, some of the more popular even in multiple copies (226–27). The many references to and interpretations of Augustine in the plays, she suggests, can be explained by the easy accessibility of his texts and therefore the playwrights' intimate knowledge of them. Johnston goes on to argue that the cycle's representation of Christ, the word incarnate, as well as its basic prosodic structure and form very clearly reflect (her term is "exploit") Augustinian theology and theories of language.

However, that the York Corpus Christi cycle echoes Augustine at this particular point in the text is a bit surprising. Augustine's representation in his sermons of the disciples as temporary heretics served a specific purpose at the time when he was writing: it allowed him to address the very real, very pressing problem of dualist heretics in the church of his day. However, this representation seems to serve no purpose in the York Plays: there were no dualist heretics in England in the fifteenth century when the plays (in this form) were being performed.

Why, then, would the York Corpus Christi cycle retain and represent Augustine's reading of the mournful and skeptical disciples as dualist heretics? The answer to this question may lie in popular readings of those heretics who did trouble England at the time: the Lollards or Wyclifites. These heretics were not, strictly speaking, dualist, but could, if creatively read, be compared to their historical and continental counterparts. For example, it seems that Lollards were popularly believed to be immoderately—if disingenuously—mournful and melancholic. In a sermon delivered sometime between 1389 and 1404, an anonymous preacher alludes to (though he unfortunately does not explain) a connection between sorrow and Lollardy:

we se now so miche folk & specialiche þes lollardes, þay go barfot,
þei gon openhed, ȝe, þei wassche soþylike hir cloþes with-owten
with teres of hir eȝen, þat miche oþ þe peple is fowle blynded &
deseyuyd bi hem. For þei wene þat tei haue plente inow with-in hem
oþ þe water of holi leuyng, & truliche it is noþyng so.
(Grisdale 65, ll. 494–99)

[We see today so many folk, and especially these Lollards, go bare-
foot, go bare-headed, even wash (soak) their clothes with the tears of

their eyes, so that many of the people are horribly blinded and deceived by them. For they think that they have plenty of the water of holy living inside them, and truly it is not so.]

More than ten but less than thirty years later, the infamous Margery Kempe became a victim of this popular belief. When in Leicester, she was accused of being "a fals strumpet, a fals loller, & a fals deceyuer of þe pepyl" (*The Book of Margery Kempe* 112, ll. 1–2), at least in part because she felt compelled to "brekyn owte wyth a lowde voys & cryen *meruelowslyche* [marvelously, amazingly] & wepyn & sobbyn ful *hedowslyche* [hideously]" after beholding a crucifix in the local church (111, ll. 12–14).

Thomas Netter, in his weighty condemnation of the evils of Wyclifism, the *Doctrinale Fidei Catholicae*, also suggests that Lollards are particularly sad or melancholic and offers a possible reason why this is so. Whereas Augustine and the other Latin fathers trace heretical sorrow to a disbelief in the resurrection of Christ and of humankind at the end of time, Netter suggests that the Lollards' heretical sorrow stems from a rejection of Catholic practices and rituals. For example, he writes that the Lollards follow the Jews in their rejection of church dedications and other celebrations and so have adopted the joylessness of Jewish worship:

It ought to be noted that when the Jews throughout the world had been captured by the Gentiles, they discontinued the practice of dedicating Churches, which custom of the Church Fathers Christians preserved [...]. Along with renouncing the dedication of their temple[s], the Jews renounced being joyful. When these [practices] were adopted by the Wyclifites, they had no joy in Church festivals, but were somber as were the Jews. (3: 978)[6]

More famously, or infamously, the Lollards denied the devotional, educational, and emotional value of images, which they condemned and periodically smashed and burned. They considered pilgrimages to shrines, often occasions of merriment, to be sinful; the time wasted on such activities could and should be spent ministering to poor men and women who were more perfect images of Christ than any statue of wood or stone could ever be.

Related to this rejection of images (and almost as famous) was the Lollards' rejection of transubstantiation. According to orthodox Catholic doctrine the host really and completely transforms into the body of Christ at the words of consecration; it retains its bread-like appearance after the substance of bread has been annihilated because in it there are *accidens sine subiecto*, accidents or qualities without substance. John Wyclif, founder of the Lollard heresy, was a metaphysical Realist and so rejected, first, the notion that substance or essence could be destroyed and, second, the notion that accidents or appearance could exist independently of essence. He insisted instead that the consecrated host is *panis in natura et corpus Christi in figura*:

> In its substance, the consecrated bread is still what it appears to be: bread. But in figure, it is (and does not merely signify) the body of Christ. On the natural level as bread, one might say the Host is a sign of the *corpus Christi*; but on the higher, figural level, by virtue of the consecration it is *vere et realiter* the body of Christ. (qtd. in Szittya 158)

The actual physical substance of flesh, according to Wyclif, is at no time present in the consecrated host. Instead, the body of Christ appears in the wafer in much the same way as an image appears in a mirror, and is similarly distanced from its object or source (Phillips 253). Thus, Wyclif argues, those who worship the Eucharist as though it is Christ are as guilty of idolatry as those who worship images: they are guilty of actively venerating an object created by human hands that is not in itself divine.

Netter responds to this argument by calling Wyclif and his followers throw-backs and judaizers whose beliefs trouble the line between the old law and its fulfillment. Netter categorically denies Wyclif's assertion that, in substance at least, the host is merely a sign of Christ's body:

> Behold, wretched Wyclif: the blood on the altar is not *type* but *truth*, is not *figure* but *clarity*, is not the *shadow* of Christ's blood, but it in *nature*. The type of his blood was the blood of the paschal lamb; the type of his blood was the blood of the temple; the type of his blood was the sprinkling of the priests. What do you think about this? (2: 180)[7]

Netter then accuses Wyclif of idolatry, reasoning, "just as one is reckoned an idolater who worships with divine reverence that thing which is not God, so is he who denies divine reverence to that which is truly God" (2: 165).[8] By not recognizing Christ's body in the sacrament and not giving the Eucharist the reverence it is due, Wyclif and his followers are acting like idolatrous Jews and Pagans.

This debate's importance to the York Plays and their representation of the disciples is nowhere made explicit, but the Lollards' doubts about transubstantiation seem strikingly similar to the disciples' doubts about the resurrection. In other texts this similarity is perhaps clearer. For example, in the treatise "Seven miracles of Corpus Christi" from the Vernon manuscript (c. 1390), an otherwise righteous man denies that the substance of the host is Christ's flesh. The man is not identified as a late medieval Lollard for good reason—the compiler of the Vernon manuscript borrows the treatise from Robert Mannyng of Brunne's early fourteenth-century text *Handlyng synne*, which is itself an English version of William of Wadington's thirteenth-century *Manuel de pechez* (Rubin 219)—but his heretical views are very similar:

> And, *for* [because] þe *fend* [fiend] wolde him haue *schent* [destroyed]
> He *leeuede not* [did not believe] in þe sacrament,
> And seide, hit was not Ihesu
> Þat Conceyued was *þorwh* [through] gret *vertu* [virtue],
> Ne Ihesu was not þat *Oble* [host, wafer]
> Þat was *reised* [raised] atte *sacre* [the words of consecration]
> And þat þe folk honourede to; *To leeue hit was not to do* [it was not to
>   be believed]. (Horstmann p. 201, ll. 111–18)

The heretic confesses his disbelief to two holy abbots, who try to convince him with examples and arguments that the bread really does convert to flesh; however, he remains sceptical and, like Thomas, declares he will not believe until he sees Christ's body displayed before him: "And *al* [still] he seide hit was lye, / But *ʒif* [unless] he *seʒe* [saw] hit wiþ his eʒe" (ll. 127–28). The very next Sunday, after the words of consecration, the heretic sees the Eucharist transform into a small child; this child is then, before his very eyes, sacrificed and cut to pieces by an angel. The priest offers the heretic a portion of the child's bleeding flesh, which, unlike Thomas, he declines to touch. However, like Thomas, the heretic immediately converts and, the treatise tells us, lives as "a good mon [man] for euer-more" (202, l. 182).

The close association of transubstantiation and resurrection we see here was supported in part by their increasing association in church ritual from the fourteenth to sixteenth century. Medieval Catholics were required to communicate at least once a year (Rubin 148) and generally did so on Easter Sunday. During Holy Week in many churches in England, both Christ's burial and resurrection were re-enacted; a consecrated host was placed in a "sepulchre" on Good Friday and was guarded until Easter Sunday, when it was removed and placed on the church's altar (Rubin 294). By the fifteenth century, the connection between the consecrated host and the resurrected body was further reinforced as, in some English churches, the host was placed inside "an image of Christ with a hollowed chest" before it was "buried" inside the Easter sepulchre (Rubin 294) and raised victorious on Easter Sunday.

Holy Week was not the only time in the liturgical calendar that Catholicism's two central doctrines were paired, however. The Eucharist had its own feast day, the feast of Corpus Christi; celebrated on the first Thursday after Trinity Sunday, it was originally marked in York with an ecclesiastical procession in which both clergy and laity followed the host as it was carried through the city streets. Some time later the cycle, itself processionally staged, developed and eventually became so large and so popular that by the third quarter of the fifteenth century it displaced the ecclesiastical procession to the following day. This left "the cycle of plays as the principal celebration of the feast proper" (Beadle 28)—which again implies a close connection between transubstantiation and Christ's physical resurrection. The cycle must have been considered an appropriate celebration and explication of the miracle of the Eucharist, yet the Eucharist is not its ostensible subject. The cycle represents instead the entire span of Christian history, reaching its climax at Christ's resurrection. As the corpus Christi was consumed by communicants on Easter Sunday, it appears that Easter Sunday was consumed by audience members on the feast of Corpus Christi. Resurrection and transubstantiation are again linked.

In the York Plays, Cleophas and Luke, infirm of faith as they are, leave both their sorrow and their doubts about the resurrection when Christ breaks bread with them at the castle of Emmaus. Some lines are missing from the manuscript, but we know that near the end of Play 40 Christ blesses the bread in some manner and disappears. On the basis of this miracle and other "werkis" that the mysterious pilgrim "wrought," Cleophas and Luke deduce that the man with whom they were travelling and talking was Christ—it was he they "*saugh* [saw] [...] in sight" (40.179). Cleophas then examines the bread Christ blessed and quite enthusiastically proclaims that no greater miracle has ever been witnessed, a declaration Luke immediately seconds:

I Peregrinus We saugh hym in sight, nowe *take* we *entent*
  [pay attention, learn]
  Be [by] *þe brede* [bread] *þat* he brake vs so *baynly*
  [willingly] betwene,
  Such wondirfull *wais* [course of events] as we haue
  wente [known]
  Of *Jesus þe gente* [the gracious Jesus] was *neuere none*
  seene [never before seen].

II Peregrinus *Sene* [seen, witnessed] was *þer neuere* [never before]
  so wondirfull werkes,
  Be [by] see ne be sande, in *þis* worlde so wide.
  Menskfully [in a fitting manner] in mynde *þes* materes
  now *merkis* [let us take note of, remember],
  And preche we it *prestly* [quickly] *on euery ilke side*
  [everywhere]. (40.179–86)

Unfortunately, the two men never reveal what is miraculous about the bread, and therefore we must turn to other dramatic representations for a possible explanation. In the N-Town play, Cleophas and Luke notice that Christ has broken the bread "as *evyn on twast* [in two] / As *ony* [any] sharpe knyff *xuld kytt* [should cut]" (38.285–86); they conclude "therby" that the vanished pilgrim was really Christ. This "brekynge of bred ful evyn *asoundyr* [asunder]" in N-Town (38.291), as lovely a stage effect as it is, does not seem to be the miracle performed in the York play, however; more likely, the miracle represented here is similar to that represented in the Towneley play of the Pilgrims. In Towneley, Cleophas reveals that he and Luke recognized Christ by the manner in which he broke bread:

> I had no knawlege it was he,
> Bot for [except that] he brake this brede in thre,
> And delt [gave] it here to the and me
> With his awne [own] hande. (27.334–37)

Christ breaks the bread into three parts for a purely practical reason—after all, three men are sitting down together for a meal; and yet, he breaks the bread in this manner for a purely symbolic reason as well—at the fraction in the mass, the priest breaks the host into three equal parts. In Towneley, Christ seems to be conducting (a very condensed) mass on stage; the bread he breaks may even be a Eucharist. Given that the host's transformation into flesh at the words of consecration was considered the greatest of miracles, the unparalleled "werkes" Cleophas and Luke in York claim to have witnessed may at least include the host's transformation into the body of Christ, signalled by the bread's (new) wafer-like appearance.

Because Cleophas and Luke "saugh" Christ "in sight," recognized his body, and believed in the resurrection, they are finally able to understand the true nature and profound significance of the bread they hold in their hands. In a single moment, they convert both from Judaism and heretical dualism to Christianity and from heretical Wyclifism to orthodox Catholicism. In the process, they find themselves liberated from their crippling grief, which mutates into a milder natural sorrow at separation from Christ when he ascends to the right hand of God.

Of course, separation from Christ and from all dearly-departed loved ones (and therefore even the slight sorrow this separation generates) is temporary: we see this promise dramatized in York in the play of Last Judgement (Play 47). At the end of time, grief becomes the exclusive property and eternal state of those who, unlike Cleophas, Luke, and the other disciples, never did convert, but who stubbornly refused to recognize Christ's body in any form. After the final trumpet sounds, the first evil soul

(*I Anima Mala*), realizing what is about to happen, exclaims on behalf of all of his fellows, "Allas, allas, þat we were borne, / So may we synfull kaytiffis say" (47.113–14). The wretch then very helpfully identifies for the audience the sin for which he and many others will be eternally condemned: "Allas, we wrecchis [...] are forlorne, / Þat never ȝitt [yet] serued God to paye [to please], / But ofte we haue his flessh *forsworne* [denied]" (47.117–19). In York, it seems that Christ damns souls first and foremost for denying and abjuring his body, in whatever form that body chooses to take. Hell and sorrow are reserved primarily for heretics, for dualists and Lollards who, "for pompe of wikkid pride," "Wepe [...] may with many a teere" (47.158, 159).

This threat of eternal damnation lent an urgency to the lessons offered with such marvellous dramatic economy in the post-Passion sequence of the York Corpus Christi cycle. Audience members, through the example of the disciples, not only learned orthodox Catholic doctrine on the nature of Christ's resurrected and transubstantiated body; they also (eventually) saw modelled before them the proper way to mourn the dead after death's defeat by Christ. This final lesson, although probably less profound to the York playwrights, was likely more valuable to its original audience, as this lesson was seldom offered and encountered elsewhere. Medieval treatises on the true nature of the host abound, but few texts of advice or consolation appear to have been written and circulated for those faced with the hard and yet relatively mundane task of faithfully mourning their dead.

AUTHOR'S NOTE

This article was accepted to the current collection just before Sarah Beckwith's important study of the York Passion sequence became available, and so I have not been able to incorporate or address any aspects of her argument here. Readers interested in this topic are encouraged to see her *Signifying God: Social Relation and Symbolic Act in the York Corpus Christi Plays* (Chicago: U of Chicago P, 2001).

1. One play—Adam and Eve in Eden—was not received and copied into the register until 1559. Other plays—The Marriage at Cana and Jesus in the House of Simon the Leper—were never entered. See Richard Beadle, ed., *The York Plays* (London: Edward Arnold, 1983) 418, 440, 441.

2. See Beadle 456.

3. Whereas repetition at the end and beginning of stanzas previously suggested that each pilgrim was feeding off of or encouraged by the other's grief, repetition now is used to suggest the men's desire that Christ remain with them: "*Bide* [remain] with vs **sir pilgrime, we praye 3ou.** // **We praye 3ou, sir pilgrime**, *3e presse no3t to passe* [do not insist on leaving]" (40.144–45); as well as Christ's graciousness in accepting their invitation: "Sir, I muste nedis do as **3e bid me.** // **3e bidde me** so *baynly* [willingly] *I bide for þe beste* [it's best—or good—that I stay]" (40.152–53).

4. Ambrose here is echoing Seneca, who, in a letter written to Lucilius on the death of Flaccus, does not forbid mourning but insists that it be done in a controlled manner. "We [...] may be forgiven for bursting into tears," he writes, "if only our tears have not flowed to excess, and if we have checked them by our own efforts" (429). "Let not the eyes be dry when we have lost a friend, nor let them overflow," he advises. "We may weep, but we must not wail" (429–31).

5. The translation is my own. The original reads: "'Quia ipse Dominus in jussu et in voce archangeli, et in novissima tuba descendet de coelo, et mortui in Christo resurgent primi: deinde nos viventes, qui reliqui sumus, simul cum illis rapiemur in nubibus obviam Christo in aera'. [...] Pereat contristatio, ubi tanta est consolatio: detergatur luctus ex animo, fides expellat dolorem."

6. The original reads: "Notandum videtur, quod genti per mundam captivae obsolevit usus dedicandi Ecclesias; quem morem Patrum Christiani conservant [...]. Unde Judaei simul cum templo dedicatione ejus, ne jucundentur, renuntiant. Cum his item captivi Wiclevistae, ne iucundentur in Ecclesiae festivitate, judaice contristantur."

7. The original reads: "Ecce, miser Wicleff: ergo sanguis in altari non est *typus*, sed *veritas*; non est *figura*, sed *claritas*; non est *umbra* Christi sanguinis, sed *natura*. Typus ejus fuit sanguis Agni paschalis: typus ejus erat sanguis sanctuarii: typus aspersio sacerdotum. Cujus putas?"

8. The original reads: "sicut est idololatra repuntandus, qui colit divino cultu, quod Deus non est: ita cui cultum divinum denegat ei, qui vere Deus est."

Mourning Becomes Electric

The Politics of Grief in Shakespeare's Lucrece

A POEM ABOUT DIVISION and divisiveness in their many forms, Shakespeare's The Rape of Lucrece has generated a telling debate within the academy about whether its focus is on gender or on the politics of republicanism.[1] Critics have also disputed to what extent anyone or anything besides Tarquin is responsible for Lucrece's suffering: should one blame patriarchy in general? her husband's boast? the victim's own naïveté?[2] One of the most intriguing preoccupations of this poem, however, has received little attention: its conclusion raises broad issues about the workings of loss and of mourning. The relationship between a mourner and the object of his or her grief, Shakespeare's narrative demonstrates, may be as charged and ambivalent as that between Lucrece and her husband—and, indeed, fraught in some of the same ways. A mourner's expressions of grief may also be as implicated in rhetoricity in the many senses of that term as Tarquin's self-justifications.[3]

The Rape of Lucrece recounts the story of a chaste wife, Lucrece, who awaits her husband, Collatine, while he is away on a military expedition. Aroused by Collatine's boasts of Lucrece's beauty, Tarquin, a scion of the ruling family, calls on her. Unable to seduce her, he rapes her and departs, "A captive victor that hath lost in gain" (Line 730).[4] Lucrece, overwhelmed with shame, summons her husband home; after telling her tale to him, her father, and other nobles, she commits suicide. At the end of the poem, her husband and father mourn her; Brutus interrupts and, vowing revenge, leads an insurrection that culminates in deposing Tarquin's family and instituting a republican government.

Whether one maintains that the poem as a whole centres on politics in the common sense or on the politics of gender, its conclusion is indisputably concerned with many types of power. The competition between

Collatine and Lucretius, as well as Brutus's assumption of leadership, render mourning political in two different senses of that adjective (and thus, incidentally, admonish us to deploy the word in question, currently a well-worn and highly valued coin of our realm, with care). First, Shakespeare's text contrasts the apparently apolitical mode of mourning practised by the victim's father and husband with Brutus's response, which is both politic and political. Second, Shakespeare explores how and why Lucretius and Collatine themselves become rival mourners, struggling with each other. In examining such problems, the poem illuminates the imbrication of bereavement and power.

The mourners at the end of the poem manifest significantly different linguistic and syntactical patterns as the repetition and exclamation of Lucrece's relatives is contrasted with Brutus's syntax of rhetorical question and declaration. Collatine and Lucretius repeat the same words ("Woe, woe" [1802]), make the same points over and over, and the very sky resounds with their echoes: "The dispers'd air, who holding Lucrece' life / Answer'd their cries, "My daughter!" and "My wife!" (1805–06). Brutus, in contrast, scornfully demands "is woe the cure for woe?" (1821). In thus rejecting a principle of Paracelsian medicine, he rejects lyric stasis in favour of narrative movement. Brutus's repudiation of similitude and repetition on the linguistic level foreshadows his renunciation of it on the political level when he prevents the Tarquins from adding further episodes to their lengthy history of tyranny. Hence he also effects a fundamental change from the long-standing monarchical succession—not coincidentally itself a form of repetition—to republicanism.

Speech acts also distinguish the two forms of mourning. Within the global speech act of lament, Lucretius throws out a question that is not rhetorical and that neither he nor his listeners can answer: "Where shall I live now Lucrece is unlived?" (1754). He then delivers two commands that, being infelicitous in the technical, linguistic senses of that term, draw attention to his inability to command the forces he addresses. "O Time, cease thou thy course" (1765), he cries, shortly afterwards adding "Then live, sweet Lucrece" (1770)—but of course neither of these demands can be met.

Brutus, in contrast, opens not on a futile command but on one likely to be obeyed: "Thou wronged lord of Rome...arise" (1818). He proceeds to give advice, buttressing his opinions with rhetorical questions like "Do wounds help wounds" (1822), where the answer is assumed and hence controlled. Like a skilled courtroom lawyer, he avoids asking questions whose answers he does not already know. His oration then culminates on another speech act, the vow, which he takes and invites others to imitate as well. Thus his injunctions, requests, and rituals are social, drawing in his listeners. And thus too his commands and questions strengthen his authority by asserting his possession of it, his right to issue commands and have them obeyed— much as assuming the right to protect can assume and thus intensify power. In so doing, he reminds us that speech acts may create social interactions and hierarchies rather than merely reflect pre-existing status systems, as the first generation of speech act theorists had typically assumed.[5]

If Brutus's words and gestures are oriented outwards, towards his listeners and their shared future, the same may be said of his actions. The linguistic contrast between the two responses to Lucrece's death is paral- lelled by the contrast between a mourning that in several senses remains rooted in the domestic and one that in several senses moves outside the home and towards the political arena.[6] In that second, politicized version of mourning, inspired and led by Brutus, the Romans "did conclude to bear dead Lucrece thence, / To show her bleeding body thorough Rome, / And so to publish Tarquin's foul offense" (1850–52). Notice in particular that the use of the verb "publish" in relation to Lucrece's body—the term deployed in an earlier, critical reference to Collatine's boasts of her beauty (33)— signals the movement from the private sphere of home to the public arena of the marketplace, from complaint to epic action, from grief to anger, and in a sense from female to male.

This episode also shifts from female to male in that, as many critics have noted, Lucrece has moved—and been moved—from the role of a subject lamenting her rape to an object deployed in the mourning rituals of others. Incisively analysed by Catherine Belsey and other critics, the emphasis on possession and property earlier in the poem thus extends into its conclu- sion as well.[7] It is telling that Brutus appropriates first Lucrece's knife and then her body, and in so doing contributes another version of chiasmus to the related but significantly different instances analysed by Joel Fineman.[8] If the blade becomes a synecdoche for the body it has injured, so too the body becomes a kind of knife, a weapon in Brutus's struggle against the Tarquins. Lucrece is turned into a stage property, and Shakespeare the actor knows well how props can be deployed to prop up authority.

In so doing, as we have seen, Brutus demonstrates three interrelated strategies for politicizing loss and hence establishing one's own carefully crafted and craftily careful position within that future. First, the linguistic repudiation of repetition represents and helps to establish other forms of change. Second, an assumption—in both senses of that noun—of authority generates power. And finally, controlling the immediate discursive future through such techniques as rhetorical questions both figures and fashions control over the long-term political future.

But how does the text evaluate Brutus's version of mourning against that of Collatine and Lucretius? In my book, *Captive Victors: Shakespeare's Narrative Poems and Sonnets*, I maintained that Brutus's response to Lucrece's death is deeply suspect, an instance of an unscrupulous politician appropriating tragic events to build his own political power. Though I still cannot agree with Annabel Patterson's rival contention that Brutus's behaviour is uncritically celebrated, I want to argue now for a middle position between my original assertion and her interpretation; his behaviour as chief mourner involves some of the ambivalence this and other Shakespearean texts associate with protection.[9] Admittedly, the lamentation of Collatine and Lucretius, arguably rendered farcical by their inappropriate argument, makes Brutus's behaviour look much better than I originally acknowledged. Yet the text does not completely absolve that revenger from culpability: the repetition of "publish" surely hints that the decision to invite the public world to enter your house or, inversely, to carry the iconic representative of that house to the marketplace, can be dangerous and self-serving.

Mourning becomes political in that Brutus cleverly uses it to effectuate a fundamental change in government, reminding us that the skillful deployment of loss can be a weapon as effective as the knife Lucrece and Brutus variously deploy. But mourning is also political in this text in a second, broader sense. That is, it generates, as well as figures in, struggles for power not only between Brutus and the two other men but also between the rival mourners Collatine and Lucretius, who frenetically debate who has the greater right to grieve. In a poem concerned with displacement of several sorts, whether it be Tarquin's usurpation of Collatine's place in bed or the exile of the tyrannous family, Collatine's rivalry with Lucretius is tellingly evoked in such terms: "Collatine...bids Lucretius give his sorrow place" (1772–73).

Not the least reason the poem connects mourning and rivalry this way is narratological. The desire to narrate is often an attempt to gain—or, more to our purposes here, to regain—control over realized or anticipated losses. In Hamlet's insistence that Horatio remain alive to narrate his friend's tale; in Venus's partial (in both senses) account of the would-be lover she was unable to control in life; and in so many other episodes, Shakespeare's poems and plays demonstrate that failures to affect the text of experience frequently generate a drive to effect a literal text. Witness, among many other examples, Desdemona singing Barbary's song shortly before dying.

More specifically, as that instance of Ophelia's funeral suggests, narration often involves an attempt to reassert power by conquering a rival, and this is frequently a rival associated in some way with loss. To begin with, it can be argued that all narration is grounded in rivalry. Peter Brooks has compared storytelling to the competing narratives analyst and analysand produce in psychoanalytic encounters.[10] Might one not go on to assert that narrative itself is virtually always the result of a rivalry, whether overt or suppressed—that is, the competition between the present writer and contemporaries or predecessors, between earlier works in the genre and this one, or more broadly between the different ways the story could be told, such as the lyric interludes often encased in narrative, and the principal version that has been chosen? And if narrative involves, as many theorists have suggested, an agenda of controlling or even subjugating, the rival who is subjugated is often the agent or representative of loss. For example, telling stories about loss can establish a successful rivalry with those masterly narrators of master narratives, God and chance. The impulse to narrate a tale about loss is an impulse to wrest control from such powerful agents of it, rewriting the story with a different author and authority. Similarly, when Brutus publishes the story of Lucrece's fate, he substitutes his version of it for the ones that Tarquin had threatened to tell, and in so doing not coincidentally substitutes himself for Tarquin politically.

Above all, however, narration facilitates the reassertion of control by preventing or overcoming interruption, the linguistic analogue to spatial invasion. Many theories for the driving force behind narrative have been adduced—it is variously described as an impulse to gain knowledge, to conquer a city or a woman's body, and so on. But we should add that the drive to narrate is also a drive to forestall or contain interruptions, whether actual or threatened. In their characteristic emphasis on co-operation between speakers and listeners, the discourse analysts, a varied group of linguists who study conversational interactions, often underestimate the frequency and virulence of struggles between the audience members who attempt to break into a story and the narrators who attempt to hold them at bay.[11] Indeed, such resistance by narrators is one of the principal ways storytelling challenges loss and the competing would-be speakers who may be associated with it. According to common rules of conversation, the storyteller has the floor until he or she establishes closure. Loss by definition interrupts an ongoing story, a relationship, a life. Hence successful storytelling counters both the interruptions effected by a death or other form of loss and the threatened interruptions of a rival narrator by insisting on its own unbroken continuity. Lucretius and Collatine break into each other's lamentations— but neither grabs the mike, as it were, from Brutus when he cuts off the Tarquins' reign and avenges the cutting off of Lucrece's life through his own uninterrupted story.

The imbrication of loss and narrative in *The Rape of Lucrece* recurs throughout its author's canon. The dynamic of loss and recovery, Shakespeare repeatedly demonstrates, involves not only telling a story but also substituting one's own version for a competing alternative one. Deprivation breeds emulation. Much as death is warned not to be proud because Donne can and will recount a more persuasive tale about it, so Shakespeare's romances substitute their narratives for those of tragedy. And so too, the final scene in *Othello* is a struggle between narratives no less driven by competition than Iago himself. Similarly, Henry V's St. Crispian Day speech trumps anticipated and dreaded loss with an alternative narrative, which is itself a tale about people telling the correct tale. The connection between loss and the competing stories about it is not the least reason for Shakespeare's characteristic preoccupation with the workings of rivalry; and that preoccupation is not the least reason for his interest in loss.

But if the rhetoric of mourning in *Lucrece* illuminates the rhetoric and rhetoricity of other Shakespearean texts, it also gestures towards new approaches to mourning itself. The conventional wisdom, as promulgated by Freud and many neo-Freudians, stresses the psychological perils of grief;

Shakespeare's poem draws attention to the political perils as well, cogently demonstrating the liability and volatility mourning engenders in both individuals and society. In so doing it demonstrates as well how mourning, even as it threatens the agency of the bereaved, can at the same time generate power and its cousin authority.

NOTES

1. See, respectively, Coppélia Kahn, *Roman Shakespeare: Warriors, Wounds, and Women* (London: Routledge, 1997) 27–45; Annabel Patterson, *Reading Between the Lines* (Madison, WI: U of Wisconsin P, 1993) 297–312.

2. See, e.g., my study, *Shakespeare and Domestic Loss: Forms of Deprivation, Mourning and Recuperation* (Cambridge, Eng.: Cambridge UP, 1999) 210n.94; Kahn 27; Patricia Parker, *Literary Fat Ladies: Rhetoric, Gender, Property* (London: London, 1987) Chapter 7; Nancy Vickers, "'The blazon of sweet beauty's best': Shakespeare's *Lucrece*," *Shakespeare and the Question of Theory*, ed. Patricia Parker and Geoffrey Hartman (New York: Methuen, 1985).

3. Although the relationship between rhetoric and mourning in the poem has been neglected, many Shakespeareans have incisively discussed the use of language in the poem from other perspectives. See especially Joel Fineman, "Shakespeare's Will: The Temporality of Rape," *The Subjectivity Effect in Western Literary Tradition: Essays Toward the Release of Shakespeare's Will*, (Cambridge, Mass.: MIT Press, 1991); Katherine Maus, "Taking Tropes Seriously: Language and Violence in Shakespeare's *Rape of Lucrece*," *Shakespeare Quarterly* 37 (1986): 66–82.

4. I cite G. Blakemore Evans, *The Riverside Shakespeare* (Boston: Houghton Mifflin, 1974).

5. Among the best challenges to that assumption by earlier speech act theorists is Susanne L. Wofford, "'To You I Give Myself, For I Am Yours': Erotic Performance and Theatrical Performatives in *As You Like It*," *Shakespeare Reread: The Texts in New Contexts*, ed. Russ McDonald (Ithaca: Cornell UP, 1994): 147–69.

6. On the significance of enclosed spaces in this poem and other Shakespearean texts, see esp. Georgianna Ziegler, "My Lady's Chamber: Female Space, Female Chastity in Shakespeare," *Textual Practice* 4 (1990): 73–90.

7. Catherine Belsey, "Tarquin Dispossessed: Expropriation and Consent in *The Rape of Lucrece*," *Shakespeare Quarterly* 52 (2001): 315–35.

8. Fineman, "Shakespeare's Will" esp. 173–75.

9. For those earlier arguments, see Heather Dubrow, *Captive Victors: Shakespeare's Narrative Poems and Sonnets* (Ithaca: Cornell U P, 1987) 125–28; Patterson, *Reading Between the Lines* 301–09.

10. Peter Brooks, *Psychoanalysis and Storytelling* (Oxford: Blackwell, 1994) 46–75.
11. For an overview of the movement, see Malcolm Coulthard, *An Introduction to Discourse Analysis* (London: Longman, 1977).

The King Is Dead

Mourning the Nation in the Three Parts of Shakespeare's Henry VI

THE NATION IS IN CRISIS. Jack Cade and his peasant followers have killed all the lawyers and are advancing through the city while the King, debating the merits of appeasement, is exhorted by his Court to flee London for Warwickshire. Separated from this scene of state deliberation by a few feet of stage space, but nevertheless central for the way it compels our gaze, is a severed head, cradled like a baby in the arms of a Queen distraught with grief. The scene attacks our modern sensibilities with its inappropriateness, with a grotesque incongruity that disturbingly, nervously, verges on the comic. It takes an agonizing twenty-five lines of dialogue for the King to acknowledge this monstrous embrace between his Queen and the remnant of her lover, and even then, his statements oddly reflect none of our horror at this intrusion of the dead into the presence chamber; or at least, his words reflect a horror of quite a different kind:

> KING. How now, madam?
> Still lamenting and mourning for Suffolk's death?
> I fear me, love, if that I had been dead,
> Thou wouldest not have mourned so much for me.
> (2 *Henry VI* 4.4.21–24)[1]

The Queen's strangely equivocal response, "No, my love, I should not mourn, but die for thee" (4.4.25), is followed by the entrance of a Messenger who informs King Henry that the rebel Jack Cade has declared for the throne, "And calls your grace usurper openly / And vows to crown himself in Westminster" (4.4.30–31). This scene, coming in the middle of Shakespeare's first English tetralogy, emblematizes the highly complex work of mourning in these plays, for the Queen's grief is more than personal, and the death that is mourned is not of an individual, but of an ideal.

Moving rapidly from Margaret's lament to challenges to Henry VI's sovereignty, this scene is a picture in little of the extended lamentation that structures Shakespeare's first historical tetralogy. Among the most violent of Shakespeare's plays (*Titus Andronicus*, of course, taking the uncontested lead), the early histories dealing with the reign of Henry VI and the intestine Wars of the Roses have their fair share of strong characters driven by ambition and battle lines drawn between parties—the Lancasters and the Yorks—contending for absolute power. However, unlike the violent tragedies, these plays are characterized by the absence of an ego, a Macbeth or Richard Gloucester, whose megalomaniacal desire drives the plays from death to death in a logical progression toward a definable goal. The *Henry VI* plays do not offer the consoling presence of an evil genius whose violence we can condemn with moral confidence and whose extirpation we can applaud as the triumph of good over evil in a bloody, but ultimately fair fight.[2] However, like Thomas Dekker's *The Wonderfull Yeare*, which is offered as a chronicle and lament for Plague-ridden London in 1603, Shakespeare's first tetralogy attempts to "boldly rip up and Anatomize the vlcerous body of the *Anthropophagized* plague" (Dekker 26), revealing a unifying structure of mourning which codifies apparently meaningless violence and offers a sustained examination of a crisis within the very metaphors of social embodiment from which social identity derives.

In its ideal ceremonial form, the scene of mourning mobilizes these metaphors of social embodiment, seeking to situate the tincture of temporal decay in a discourse transcendence. This transcendence is achieved through an appeal to the *universitas*, that politic body that defines both the mourners and the dead as individual aspects of a functional, unified national self. In the three parts of *Henry VI* and *Richard III*, however, the ceremonies of state are invariably fractured and disrupted by mangled bodies, interrupted eulogies, news of lost territories, rebellions and dire prophesies of lost national identity. At every turn, the appeals made to England as a unified and transcendent entity are undermined by division, limitation and mortality. In these plays, the customary progression from "The king is dead" to "Long live the King" is disrupted by Henry VI's inability to bear—or to bring to bear in his all too limited mortal form—the vast, unifying power of the politic body. It is the impossibility of a mortal embodiment of sovereignty that defines the particular nature of the plays' despair. In an often repeated pattern, the confrontation between the living and the dead staged in these plays is coextensive with the fragmentation of the state, dramatized in a sustained litany of self-loss and bodily mutilation. Beginning with the first scene of 1 *Henry VI*, funeral and mourning go in lock step with a crisis of national identity. The tetralogy's overarching structure of mourning, therefore, is not necessarily to be found in the invariably ironic funerary rituals; the tetralogy itself forms an extended lamentation for a lost ideal of sovereignty that once, through the metaphor of social embodiment, made meaningful the individual's relationship to the transcendent life of the national self.

———

IN ORDER TO UNDERSTAND fully the rivetting tableau of Henry VI's quizzical condemnation of Queen Margaret's grief, and the scene's relationship to sovereignty and national identity, it is necessary to return to the first scene of the preceding play, 1 *Henry VI*, and the funeral of Henry V. As the first of a series of mangled rituals, the 177 lines of this scene occupy the uncomfortably extended pause between the customary declaration, "The king is dead!" and the response, "Long live the King!" Ideally, this juxtaposition of the announcement of death and the declaration of allegiance is designed to permit no interregnum, no gap in the continuity of royal claims to territory and power (Kantorowicz 411–12).[3] Linking in this way funeral to coronation, the ceremony permits the new king seamlessly to take up the space vacated by the old, asserting the unbroken presence of a power that is at once immanent in the individual and an expression of "the eternal continuity and immortality of the great collective called the human race" (Kantorowicz 277), in this case, the English race. The royal funeral then, with its procession of peers and its effigy of the monarch lying in state, enacts the complex conceptual work of mourning that turns the confrontation with mortality into a celebration of *universitas*, the union of the people and the territory of the nation with tradition and posterity. In this sense, the king was by no means a mere figurehead of state apparatus, but was both the ruling head of a body of which the people, past, present and future, comprised the "limbs" and "members" and the nation as a whole personified.[4]

The noble funeral enacted a subtle shift of emphasis from the loss of the individual to his or her participation in a living social body, a body that celebrates in the scene of mourning its unbroken progression through time.[5]

The eulogy for Henry V that opens the tetralogy purports to enact just this turn from the limitations of the corporeal to the ideal embodiment of the nation, but the significant absence of a successor produces, not unity, but fatal fragmentation. Henry V conceptually outlives his own death as well as the play that bears his name to hover like a spectre over the reign of his son in the three parts of *Henry VI*. Part One begins with the funeral procession of peers pacing behind the king's hearse in a dead march. "Hung be the heavens with black, yield day to night!" (1.1.1) Bedford intones, perhaps referring to the funereal cloths draping the stage, a conventional decoration for tragedies,[6] but expressing as well the nature of the world that takes form as the procession of mourners fills the stage. As the funeral speeches progress, Henry V materializes in the language of the peers as the ideal embodiment of power: "England ne'er had a king until his time," Gloucester eulogizes, continuing, "What should I say? His deeds exceed all speech. / He ne'er lift up his hand but conquerèd" (1.1.8, 15–16). Positioned as the model of kingship, with his "sparkling eyes" that drive back his enemies like "midday sun fierce bent against their faces" (1.1.12, 14), Henry V is described in terms of a well-known vocabulary of spectacular power. The eulogy for Henry seeks to fulfil the promise of one of Elizabeth I's mottos as it appears on the most famous of her many portraits, the so-called *Rainbow Portrait*: "*non sine sole iris*: No rainbow without the sun." Here, the Latin, *iris*, refers simultaneously to the rainbow of peace and to the all-seeing eye of the sovereign, while the sun is, of course, the monarch herself, the condition of peace. Appropriating the Elizabethan image of the sun, Henry's spectacular presence, "replete with wrathful fire" (1.1.12), is a violent, penetrating light that conquers where it shines; as the sun, it is aloft, seeing to all horizons, transforming where it touches. Henry is not so much a living being as he is a condition of life, not a creature illuminated by Gloucester's praise, but a source of all illumination.[7] Foregrounding Henry's supernatural presence, envisioning him, with his "arms spread wider than a dragon's wings" (1.1.11), as a colossus, naming him "a king blessed of the King of Kings" (1.1.28), his eulogy begins the process of idealization, enacting the turn from the mortality of the body hidden in the coffin to the unassailable, because invisible, transcendence of his memory. Dead, idealized, incorporeal, Henry is the uncontested icon of sovereign mastery.[8]

This transformative process of mourning does not come to fruition, however, for the declaration that the king is dead does not progress to the salutary invocation of the *universitas* in the second part of the ritual utterance, "Long live the King." Bedford's prophesy, "A far more glorious star thy soul will make / Than Julius Caesar or bright—" (1.1.55–6), is cut off by the rapid entrance of Messengers with the news "Of loss, of slaughter, and discomfiture. / Guyenne, Champagne, Rheims, Orleans, / Paris, Guysors, Poictiers, are all quite lost" (1.1.59–61). Exacerbating the fomenting rivalries amongst the peers, the news also goads them to renewed military action to protect England's dwindling foreign empire. For Bedford's transcending gesture is substituted another, more dire and painfully ironic, prophesy: No rainbow without the sun. Overcome with the sense of England's loss, Bedford declares, "Instead of gold we'll offer up our arms, / Since arms avail not, now that Henry's dead" (1.1.46–7). These arms he proposes to lay upon the altar are both the arms of war and the coats of arms representing the peers' hereditary right and place in the hierarchy of the nation. The image neatly invokes in one gesture of impotence the history of the nation, the martial glory that subtends it and the limbs of the social body which are now paralysed and ineffectual without the royal head. Not soon to be cured, this malaise, Bedford prophesies, will visit future generations' "wretched years" until "Our isle be made a nourish of salt tears, / And none but women left to wail the dead" (1.1.48–51). It seems that once the paragon of kings is dead the nation can cohere for no more than 50 lines before exploding under pressures from within and without.

The special dangers of the eulogizing impulse are made manifest here, for no one left in the world of the living can hope to fulfil the promise of this all-powerful, idealized kingship. While the visible trappings of the royal funeral establish the background for the customary celebration of the continuity of the state, the action of the scene belies this expectation. Between the lamentations over the hearse of the dead monarch and Gloucester's declared intention to "proclaim young Henry king" (1.1.169) there intervene 169 lines concerned with praise for the king that was, news of foreign massacre, and the outbreak of civil broils. Occupying over 25 percent of a scene which covers as much ground as this one—from establishing the animosity between the Bishop and the Protector, to the loss of seven French cities and the chief English hero, to preparations for war and for a coronation—the eulogy for the old king leaves precious little space for praise of the new. Henry V's body, memory, fame and loss dominate the conceptual space of the scene, a careful disproportion of stage time that emphasizes the impossible standards set for the young king whose physical absence is indicative of a political vacuum that enables factionism to flourish where monologic power should reign.[9] The absence of Henry V, signalled by his body inhearsed on stage, represents the physical, political and conceptual absence of his son, who makes no appearance until Act three, who, with only 157 lines out of a possible 2676, speaks a mere 6 percent of the play that bears his name, and whose speech, when we finally hear it, is invariably characterized by wheedling, deference, and disastrous misunderstanding. When he is mentioned at all in this scene, young Henry is an "effeminate prince" (1.1.35) offered up as an object of the peers' ambitious jarring.

This absence and its consequences are rehearsed several times in 2 and 3 Henry VI. In one of his first scenes as an adult king (2 Henry VI, 2.3), in fact, Henry speaks but nine lines of a possible 218: three of them are questions, in one he pleads for peace, and the remaining ones express only his lack of interest in state affairs. His first act of government takes the form of an abstention over the choice of regent of France: "For my part, noble lords, I care not which: / Or Somerset or York, all's one to me" (1.3.99–100). In the opening scene of 3 Henry VI, York sits in the throne while Henry stands to disinherit his son in favour of the house of York, a decision that, as Margaret observes, can only lead to his death: "To entail [York] and his heirs unto the crown, / What is it but to make thy sepulchre / And creep into it far before thy time?" (1.1.235–37). Fulfilling a pattern of displacement and effacement, this act of disinheritance makes Henry a ghost, a king in name only who "shalt reign but by their [the Yorkists'] sufferance" (1.1.234). Having thus divorced the Crown from its power (dramatically signalled by the divorce of the powerful Margaret from the bed of the politically impotent king), Henry is left to steal disguised into his own kingdom from exile in Scotland, "To greet mine own land with my wishful sight" (3 Henry VI 3.1.14), only to utter a eulogy to his absence: "No, Harry, Harry, 'tis no land of thine; / Thy place is filled, thy sceptre wrung from thee, / Thy balm washed off wherewith thou was anointed" (3.1.15–17). His disguise signals metonymically his role as a Player-King, a proxy for his own throne. When the disguise is removed, he is revealed to be neither the holy palmer he aspires to be, nor a king, but, literally, a has-been. Calling himself "Harry," the king marks his demotion from Dignity to mere, unanointed, man. That the king is dead is loudly proclaimed. That a new king has taken his place is barely whispered.

The consequences of this disruption of the work of mourning are manifest, for the death of the monarch entails a radical challenge to the identity of the peers who follow his bier. Breaking into Gloucester's accolades at Henry V's funeral, Exeter's contribution to the eulogy pulls the transcendent images of glorious sovereignty back to temporal loss and an undeniable sense of abandonment:

Henry is dead and never shall revive.
Upon a wooden coffin we attend,
And death's dishonorable victory
We with our stately presence glorify,
Like captives bound to a triumphant car. (1.1.18–22)

Exeter begins with a reassertion of absence and loss and then immediately links the ritual of mourning to that of the triumph, where the vanquished are paraded before the victors as objects of spectacle humiliation. The speech is heavy with contemporary horror of death's levelling decimation of individuality, what Sir Thomas Brown called "the disgrace and ignominy of our natures, that in a moment can so disfigure us that our nearest friends, wife, and children stand afraid and start at us" (qtd. in Neill 9). Writing in the first half of the 1590s, Shakespeare would have experienced as a London dweller the seemingly inescapable, indiscriminate ravages of the Plague, as Death's Triumph, a popular artistic subject, rolled inexorably through the streets, touching rich and poor alike, negating in its final reduction of individuals to base matter, all pretensions to status. Michael Neill describes the typical representation of Death's Triumph this way: "...mounted in splendour, like the monarch of some Renaissance royal entry, King Death rides through the world on a magnificent parade chariot, hauled by a team of jet-black oxen over the heaps of his victims, grinding their corpses into the final anonymity of earth" (89). The juxtaposition of Exeter's image of Death's Triumph with Gloucester's encomium is exemplary of the perversity of the

Triumph itself: "This absurdity," Neill continues, "is most apparent in the mordant contradiction between the ceremonial formality of triumphal pageantry and the grotesque disorder represented by the indiscriminate piles of carrion beneath Death's wheels" (91). As its dramatic *raison d'être* is to exhibit within the framework of formal mourning the collapse of order attendant upon the death of Henry V, the funeral scene itself mimics the representational economy of the Triumph of Death. Immediately following Exeter's references to the peers' humiliation by Death, a dispute breaks out between Winchester and Gloucester over who can praise the dead king with most integrity. As if on cue, the Messengers enter with news of the threats to English interests in France. One gets the sense from the impropriety of this sequence of events that Death's stately pageant has passed over the stage and left behind it what Dekker calls in *The Wonderfull Yeare* the Plague's "main army," a "mingle-mangle" (31).[10]

In the same pamphlet, Dekker refers to the kingdom of Death as the "wild Irish country of worms" (39), associating the suddenness of plague death with what to the contemporary imagination was anarchy beyond the English colonial pale, the untamed, unintelligible, perpetually resistant Celtic Outside. The comparison neatly designates England as a nation of life and order and Ireland as its constitutive Other. Death, like anarchy and rebellion, is nationalized, and those who die become Life's expatriates or exiles, or, in the case of Exeter's contribution to the eulogy, captives in a humiliating triumph. Rather than celebrating the continuity of the state, the funeral in its ironic turn from idealizing eulogy to Death's Triumph drags the living into the "wild Irish" space of war, dismemberment and anarchy, challenging in this way the very foundation of Englishness. The notion of the "wild Irish," for all its importance as a specific colonial Other with specific ideological challenges to the English nation as an incipient imperial power, participates analogically in a more general conceptual structure that encompasses all national Others whose presence defines, even as it threatens, the borders of the English self. Thus, in this sense, the shift in Exeter's speech from admission of humiliation in Death's Triumph to a condemnation of the "subtile-witted French" who, he insists, "By magic verses have contrived [Henry's] end" (1.1.25, 27), marks an attempt to expel Death beyond the borders, to consolidate his forthright Englishness through opposition to a sly and subversive French Other. Henry's death, in other words, is figured as an invasion from without, a perversion even of nature itself by the unnatural practices of witchcraft, and the humiliating fall beneath Death's wheels is a sign of English difference and uniqueness as the privileged domain of life expressed even in the moment of its dissolution.

But Exeter's attempt at consolidation through the designation of a constitutive Other is ineffectual, for the Other he seeks to extirpate has been shown to exist as virulently within the pale, in the form of jarring peers, as it does without. Beginning with the solemn, hierarchically ordered procession of peers onto the stage, the scene exhibits a visual disintegration as the peers exit individually, to prepare for war, or the coronation, or, in the case of Winchester, a self-styled "Jack out of office" (1.1.175), to pursue treason. He tells us of his intention to "steal" the king from his seat in Eltham "And sit at chiefest stern of public weal" (1.1.176–77). The last line of the scene, then, signals the turn from celebration of universitas to individual, atomizing ambition, this gesture of individuality partaking of the language of disorder and disintegration associated with the grinning King on his pageant chariot. Ending with this intimation of usurpation which will be the theme of the following three plays, the scene points to a prior usurpation by King Death, whose levelling presence undermines the transcendent gestures of funeral which enable the salutary appeal to the universitas, as Randall Martin astutely observes: "While like any Elizabethan funeral the implied purpose of this moment is to affirm lineal and political succession as part of an eternal natural order, its symbolic shading and dislocated ritual exposes [sic] such a connection as purely contingent" (259).[11] The great continuity of the social body threatens to reveal itself as the great undifferentiated mass of physical decrepitude, a disintegration of the systems of status and fealty, where, as at the end of a chess game, wrote George Strode in 1632, "the men are tumbled together and put into the bag" (qtd. in Neill 14).

So powerful is this horror of dissolution that it seeps beyond the funeral context to stain the language of the plays that follow, where the social body continues to struggle to cohere in the face of the erosion of England's territory and the crippling absence of a king capable of embodying the abstract power of the universitas. In the opening scene of the 2 Henry VI, where Henry VI meets his new French bride, Margaret of Anjou, the subject is marriage, but the pattern established in the funeral scene is repeated. The scene begins with ceremonial processions, and quickly devolves into the fragmentation and "mingle-mangle" of lost identity. As in the funeral scene, the formal gestures toward the life of the nation implicit in a political union with foreign nobility are undermined by our knowledge that this union is a sham. Suffolk has already declared his intention to marry Margaret to Henry in order to facilitate his sexual and political ambitions: "Margaret shall now be queen, and rule the king; / But I will rule both her, the king, and realm" (1 Henry VI 5.5.106–7). The consequences of Suffolk's and Margaret's adulterous relationship and its grisly outcome will be discussed at length below. At this point it suffices to observe that the marriage, which should be a celebration of continuity and renewal, is coded by our foreknowledge of duplicity and faithlessness as yet another exploitation of Henry's displacement from the centre of power.

Again, this vacuum produces directly a crisis of identity. Reading the terms of an injurious nuptial agreement that divests England of great swaths of French holdings, Gloucester is struck with a "sudden qualm...at the heart" (1.1.53), registering the loss of territory contained in the articles as a bodily infirmity that has, he says, "dimmed mine eyes that I can read no further" (1.1.54). Protector of the realm and the peer most associated with the nation as *universitas*, Gloucester's identification with the land makes it impossible for him to read or speak the terms of its loss. Gloucester's next speech invokes the dead Henry V in a familiar litany: "What? Did my brother Henry spend his youth, / His valor, coin, and people in the wars?/..../ And shall these labors and these honors die?" (2 Henry VI 1.1.76–77, 93), he asks. He then moves to a nomination of the peers in language that turns their martial presence, and their connection to the nation as landed, hereditary lords, into *memento mori*. He asks: "Have you yourselves, Somerset, Buckingham, / Brave York, Salisbury, and victorious Warwick, / Received deep scars in France and Normandy" only to see "Your deeds of war, and all our counsel die?" (1.1.83–85, 95). Positing a social body defined as martial and sacrificial, Gloucester's roll-call appeals to an image of a state written in scars upon the bodies of peers who are united in a common martial and political effort to keep the French in thrall. York's assertion that "France should have torn and rent my very heart / Before I would have yielded to this league" (1.1.123–24) identifies the mutilated body of the noble soldier as the external sign of the *universitas* as it is expressed in a discourse of nationalism, for the heart of the martial hero is the measure of the nation itself. Posed against this model of state embodiment, in much the same way as Henry V's eulogy is balanced by Death's Triumph in the earlier scene, is Warwick's anguished sense that his scars are made meaningless without the territory they represent: "And are the cities that I got with wounds / Delivered up again with peaceful words? / Mort Dieu!" (1.1.119–21). Divested by "peaceful words" of the conquered land that makes their sacrifices meaningful, the peers' bodily signs become unintelligible cyphers. As Martha Hester Fleischer observes, in the iconography of the English history play the onstage representation of the wound (signalled by the scar, the bandage or the crutch) is the physical manifestation of valour "in virtually any context" (19). Here, the perversion of these signs is part of a larger pattern of distorted and desecrated iconography that signals the decay of systems of meaning in the tetralogy.

————

I HAVE ANALYZED these two scenes of state, one funeral and one wedding, in order to establish a framework for our return to the scene of macabre mourning that began this discussion. Gesturing toward the established rituals of mourning, the funeral scene dramatizes the idealizing work of mourning as the commemoration of the dead becomes part of a language of continuity, defining the English nation through the idealized vision of a sovereign whose "brandished sword did blind men with his beams" and who "ne'er lift up his hand but conquerèd" (1 *Henry VI* 1.1.10, 16). Pitted against this invocation of *universitas* is the horror of the corporeal, the indiscriminate ravages of King Death that threaten to exile, not only the dead, but the unlucky survivors to the "wild Irish" country beyond the pale of English order. In the absence of a new king to ensure the continuity of the social body, there is no defence against the triumphal humiliations of Death, and the state immediately begins to crumble. It is against this background that the shocking incongruity of the Queen's onstage mourning over her lover's severed head begins to take shape as part of a nuanced and economical visual language.

Queen Margaret's lament to the severed head of her lover, Suffolk, is easily one of the most puzzling moments of the tetralogy, incongruous to the point of comedy, yet somehow retaining something of both the macabre and the pathetic. The rather startling stage direction, *"Enter the King with a supplication, and the Queen with Suffolk's head"* that opens 4.4 of 2 Henry VI, can be made meaningful in the context of these contesting discourses of idealization and corporeal disintegration. Margaret is onstage with the head for twenty-five lines of dialogue in which her lamentations for her lover interrupt the king's consultation with his council. In the time that it takes for Henry to acknowledge her presence, the severed head can only become a compelling object of fascination, asserting itself against the background of state deliberations. In its ideal manifestation, the appearance of the severed head invokes the displaying of the head, in a Perseus with the Gorgon fashion, to the assembled audience of the execution, announcing the containment of transgression by sovereign power. However, in this scene, where Margaret's asides interrupt Henry's woefully ineffectual attempts to curb the power of the Cade rebellion, this discourse of containment inadequately explains the power of this visual symbol. This is especially so since the scene ends with the Court fleeing to Kenilworth. Implicated in a complex web of allusion to the demise of the *universitas*, the severed head and the mourning Queen become images, not of closure, but of rupture.

Holding her lover's head to her "throbbing breast," the queen wonders: "But where's the body that I should embrace?" (4.4.5–6). The image of the head without a body indicates in a visual chiasmus the play's central concern with the consequences of a social body without a head. Henry, who will soon continue his pattern of absence and flee from London, offers to parley with Cade and the rebels, "Rather than bloody war shall cut them short" (4.4.12). But the heads saved in Henry's gesture of mercy are tallied up elsewhere. Henry informs the aged Lord Say that "Jack Cade hath sworn to have thy head," to which Say responds, "Ay, but I hope your highness shall have his" (4.4.19–20). It is this reference that calls to Henry's attention the lamenting Margaret who literally "has" Suffolk's head in a grotesque realization of the language of the debate. The overall effect is an image of circulating heads, charges and counter-charges, that add up, finally, to impotence.[12] As Margaret Owens observes, this impotence and the proliferation of severed heads is symptomatic of "the failure of the king to establish with any conviction his authority as the legitimate head of state" (371). For Owens, this pile-up of mutilated bodies, and especially of severed heads, marks the breakdown of established hierarchy and the creation of the "many-headed monster" of rebellion (370) whose advent produces in the play "a picture of disembodied heads jostling for power" (371). In his adaptation of the tetralogy for the Royal Shakespeare Company in 1988, Adrian Noble literalized this vision of mob violence and collapsing sovereign power when a mad, shaggy-haired Oliver Cotton as Jack Cade sat in mock triumph while the rebels danced around him with the severed heads of slain nobles on literal ten-foot poles (Rise of Edward IV). The exuberance of the dance of death around the mock-king epitomizes not only the world-turned-upside-down nature of rebellion, but the shocking realization that there is no proper king to right this carni-valesque exultation of corporeal decrepitude. Jack Cade in his macabre "court," in Noble's vision, is not merely a parody of legitimate authority, or a negative image of legitimacy, but, rather, a horrifyingly realized image of the naked violence that lies just beneath the surface of the unrealizable ideal of monarchy.[13] Ideally part of a "visual rhetoric" (Owens 367) of power and stability, the severed head in these plays is wrenched out of its ideal context in scaffold spectacle; as Owens asserts, beheading in 2 *Henry VI* becomes "a sign not of the orderly extirpation of civil dissension but of its uncontrollable proliferation" (370).

In analogous scenes in the following play, Warwick and the sons of York discover the body of Clifford, whose death in the battle has robbed them of their revenge. Warwick orders the eldest son, Edward, to cut off Clifford's head "And rear it in the place your father's stands. / And now to London with triumphant march, / There to be crownèd England's royal king" (3 *Henry VI* 2.6.85–88). Yoking through juxtaposition the severed head to the head of state, the replacement of York's head by Clifford's parallels in Warwick's speech the replacement of one king with another. Triumphant coronation is in this way contaminated with the trace of ignominious defeat. Linking coronation to abdication in this way, the scene echoes Henry's decision to entail the crown, for as a Player-King, Henry's very occupation of the throne is a sign of his defeat. Warwick's own change of heart and subsequent decision to back the Lancastrian cause likewise exhibits this doubleness. Plucking the crown, now, from Edward's head, Warwick declares that Henry "now shall wear the English crown / And be true king indeed, thou but the shadow" (3 *Henry VI* 4.3.49–50). But Henry, as the plays relentlessly demonstrate, is himself a shadow, making Edward but the shadow of a shadow. Figuring metonymically the decapitation of the body of state, the circulation of heads, both severed and crowned, articulates through a compelling visual symbol the spectre of sovereign absence defined here as a disturbing loss of individuation: king replaces king in a meaningless round.

Visually signalling the distortion of the unified social body, the grotesque "embrace" between the queen and her "lover" is part of a pattern that includes Jack Cade's obscene order to his followers to make the heads of Lord Say and his son-in-law, Sir James Cromer, "kiss" at every street corner as they progress through the city (2 *Henry VI* 4.7.120–26). This perversion of the gestures of affection and proper bodily conduct graphically symbolizes the general perversion of proper bodily signs throughout the tetralogy. The gestures of familial love become impotent gestures of revenge, for example, in Richard's desire to cut off his own hand in order to drown the dead Clifford "whose unstanchèd thirst / York and young Rutland could not satisfy" (3 *Henry VI* 2.6.80–84). Hugh Richmond asserts that, in the discourse of revenge, the play articulates a certain metaphysical order: "Virtue may be destroyed often in the world of *Henry VI*, but Nemesis always overtakes the guilty" (46). I would argue, however, in the light of the resonating images of perverse affection in the play, that revenge is symptomatic rather than curative of the disorder of the state. The scenes of revenge in these plays represent a pathological forfeiture of the *universitas* in favour of personal ambition and vendetta, figured in the image of desecrated corpses. Fleischer contends that, to the contemporary playgoer trained on the iconography of state and stage violence, such desecration "is a piece of superstitious savagery which the spectator cannot regard without rage or revulsion" (195). Embedded in the symbolism of the Passion, Fleischer asserts, the bloody abuse of the corpse activates a well-known and "timeless or eternal pattern of insult" (195). Neglecting or actively denying the rituals proper to mourning, these postmortem punishments of the flesh invariably foreground the bloodiness and ghastly horror of the dead in order to body forth, as it were, the painful absence of the larger unifying power of the social body. The evil do get their just deserts in the end, but the moral centre that might define *evil* is evacuated in the play, signalling an ultimate breakdown of the modes of knowing the social body and articulating "order."

This evacuation and concomitant breakdown is apparent in the "son that hath killed his father/father that hath killed his son" episode (3 *Henry VI*

2.5). Civil war has severed the bonds of family and caused men unknowingly to kill their own family members. This scene demonstrates the
mingle-mangle of social relations, for sons and fathers, arbitrarily renamed
enemies by the nation's political schism, no longer recognize one another.
The son, realizing that he has become a patricide, indicts the nation itself:

> From London by the king was I pressed forth;
> My father, being the Earl of Warwick's man,
> Came on the part of York, pressed by his master;
> And I, who at his hands received my life,
> Have by my hands of life bereavèd him.
> Pardon me, God, I knew not what I did.
> And pardon me, father, for I knew not thee. (2.5.64–70)

Pressed into service on the part of regional lords, the two men represent the
territory of the nation turning on itself in blind massacre. Indicted in this
speech are the traditional oaths of fealty to one's liegelord that subtend hier-
archical structures, for the values of service and loyalty that organize social
identity produce in this conflict rather a loss of identity and the dissolution
of the ground of knowledge: "I knew not thee" and "I knew not what I did."
The familial embrace is refigured in this scene, as in Richard's desire to
sever his hand to drown Clifford in blood, as self-mutilation, for father and
son unknowingly shed their own familial blood and lament their blindness
over the slain bodies on the stage. The aptly-named intestine wars are formulated here as a kind of national suicide. As mourners, then, these men become
both individuals expressing private grief and members of the social body
grieving the nation.

With its gestures toward the horrors of a state feeding upon itself, the
scene echoes on the level of the commoners the crisis of national identity
established in the very first scene of the tetralogy at the funeral of Henry V,
anticipating Dekker's own vision of the loss of identity attendant upon the
death of Elizabeth: "Oh look what an Earth-quake is the alteration of a State!
Looke from the Chamber of Presence, to the Farmers cottage, and you shall
find nothing but distraction: the whole kingdom seemes a wilderness, and
the people in it are transformed to wild men" (13). Revealing the perversion
of the bodily sign, this massacre of the family also demonstrates the precar-

iousness of the differences that justify dispute, for the terms "wild Irish" or "subtile-witted French," even "Yorkist" or "Lancastrian," can no longer safely delineate the boundaries of living, ordered Englishness. Their identities literally obscured by the blood that formerly bound them symbolically to the social body, the peasants, and by association their lords, have become "wild men" and all the nation is now a "wilderness"; the Other—the enemy— is revealed to have been the self—the family—all along.

Clutched to Margaret's breast, Suffolk's head similarly marks the return of the Other within the boundaries of the self, for his banishment and execution cannot eradicate his ability to displace the king with his erotic presence. A proxy to a death's head, Henry is upstaged once again by Suffolk's amorously coded body. That this body still holds power is apparent, for example, in the way that Margaret's elegy for her lost lover is intertwined with the deliberations of the king's council. Although she delivers these lines "apart" from the council debate, her lament is a competing focus of attention that causes a kind of hiatus in the scene, a suspension of state concerns. At the same time, this competing narrative is continuous with the news of Cade's progression to the heart of London. As in the funeral scene, the scene of state is disrupted by the entrance of Messengers with news of loss, slaughter and discomfiture. Messengers report that "The rebels are in Southwark" (4.4.27), and, a mere 22 lines later, that "Jack Cade hath gotten London Bridge" (4.4.49). Just as Suffolk's presence displaces the king from the marital bed, the penetration of the rebels into the centre of Henry's domain displaces the king to its outskirts, to Kenilworth castle in Warwickshire. This confusion of centre and margin is reiterated at the beginning of 3 Henry VI where York's troops hold Henry's traditional seat of power, London, while Henry negotiates to entail his crown and rule "but by their suffer-ance." Henry is marginalized even at the centre of power, returning to the presence chamber only to find his own absence. A strange conflation of the motherly and the erotic, the image of the queen cradling Suffolk's head emblematizes the perversion of the body's sign that is symptomatic of this collapsing boundary between self and Other, inside and outside, friend and enemy. Suffolk, who has been described as a "kennel, puddle, sink! whose filth and dirt / Troubles the silver spring where England drinks" (2 Henry VI 4.1.72–73), who has brought Margaret to England and turned Henry into a proxy in his own bed, is one of the major sites at which this infiltration and contamination are revealed. As the Lieutenant concludes in his assessment of Suffolk's role in this contamination, "reproach and beggary / Is crept into the palace of our king, / And all by thee" (4.1.102–4). Embedded in this network of images of perverse relationships, Margaret's mourning parodies the funeral's emphasis on social ties, status and position that define the *universitas*.

———

RETURNING TO COURT after his banishment, Suffolk's severed head marks the dangerous eruption of the Other whose abjection is supposed to solidify the identity of the state. Dead and in pieces, the Duke's presence is an invasion of the living English pale by the anarchy of corporeal decay. This gentle mourning of the symbol of anarchy and fragmentation is likely the source of the scene's almost comic grotesqueness, for the laugh, like the shudder of horror, is an acknowledgement that the established systems of signification, the languages of justice, power and bodily decorum, fall short. Instead of producing a narrative that, like the scars on the martial body, binds that body to the *universitas*, the queen's mourning points persistently to the collapse of continuity, dwelling obsessively not on the ideal but on the putrescence and fragmentation of both the individual and the social body.

As an individual, Margaret mourns her private loss, but as part of a narrative of social disintegration, the scene as a whole mourns the lost ideal of English life and order. The discomfort experienced by modern audiences in witnessing this scene is to some degree a product of this double focus, which to our eyes, less familiar with the complex relationship between individual bodies and the body of the state, appears as a startling, macabre impropriety. In production this impropriety can be either highlighted or dampened by the staging of the scene as either a highly public or intimately private encounter between the living and the dead. In Pam Brighton's 1980 adaptation of the three plays for the Stratford, Ontario Third Space, for instance, Margaret was discovered in a tight spotlight on the bare runway stage. She knelt before the swaddled head to utter her lamentation in choked tones while the sound of singing monks filled the dark space around her. Emphasizing the queen's isolation, the surrounding darkness disconnected her from the social context which burst in on her at the conclusion of her speech as the lights came up and the King entered with his council. While gesturing to the state of crisis that occupies the King's attention, this staging avoids the uncomfortable double focus of Shakespeare's original, since Margaret's lament for her lover does not compete with or comment on the King's ineffectuality relative to the potent, sexually coded and compelling image of the lover's severed head. Framed by darkness and the religious tones of the monks' chant, Margaret's mourning becomes a personal encounter with loss, a private moment of grief which we inappropriately overhear. Anticipating the audience's tendency to react with confusion to the interpenetration of the mourning scene and the state scene, Brighton has opted for a more modern, psychological reading, one more easily accessible to an audience reared up on the Stanislavkyian realism of the modern theatre.

The scene aptly demonstrates the queen's ultimate separation from her husband, as does the English Shakespeare Company's treatment of the confrontation. In this adaptation by Michael Bogdanov and Michael Pennington, Henry, seated on his throne, conspicuously alone in the presence chamber, bemoans his inadequacy: "Was ever King that joyed an earthly throne / And could command no more content than I?" (2 *Henry VI* 4.9.1–2). The following scene is an invented one, combining speeches from across the play. Margaret enters as his speech progresses and passes over the stage, trapped in her own grief: "Oft Have I heard that grief softens the mind" she says, " And makes it fearful and degenerate. / Think therefore on revenge and cease to weep. / But who can cease to weep, and look on this?" (4.4.1–4). This contrapuntal rhythm of lament continues, ending finally with Henry's "Come, wife, let's in, and learn to govern better; / For yet may England curse my wretched reign" (4.9.48–49). Neatly and eerily affective in its representation of the characters' inability to communicate with one another because of their solipsistic isolation, the scene, like Brighton's, emphasizes the interior over the exterior ramifications of mourning, the psychological over the social context. While Henry's final lines allude to the beleaguered state, that political upheaval is invisible, and what is left is the image of two individuals mourning in poignant isolation.

One last example will round out this brief survey. Of the three, Jane Howell's 1982 BBC production adheres most closely to the original text, placing Margaret's lament firmly in the context of the council meeting. In fact, the queen and her macabre "babe" are not isolated at the margins of the stage, but rather physically intervene in the state deliberations even as her language does so. Held in a medium close-up, the queen passes between Henry and his advisors as she delivers her speeches directly to the camera. The trick is effective, for it both shows Margaret as an individual and places her simultaneously at the heart of the social upheaval of the Cade rebellion. Thus, Howell is able to exploit the efficacies of film in order to capture the double focus that would have been possible on the broad stage of the Globe, where the queen could easily occupy the stage with the king's council and simultaneously be "apart" from them in a private space of lament. The direct address to the camera draws us into the intense psychological pain of the grieving woman, while the shifting focus of the camera to the faces of the counsellors provides a wider perspective and sense of political urgency heightened by the frantic preparations for departure to Warwickshire that take place in the background. Unlike the ESC or Stratford, Ontario productions, which, in placing the queen on a stage conspicuously bare, seek to reduce the discomfort and incongruity of her grieving, this production emphasizes it, makes it unavoidable. The effect is somewhat diluted by the tendency to see the subject in close-up as conceptually isolated, but the overall feeling produced is one of outrage: it is outrageous that Margaret should bring a severed head to the presence chamber, just as it is outrageous that she should be unfaithful to the king, and it is outrageous that he should talk appeasement while preparing to abandon the state to a gang of ruffians, whether they be Cade's or the Yorkist faction for which Cade is but a proxy.

Outrage, unseemliness, discontinuity, the plays assert again and again, are precisely the point, for, as Death's Triumph passes over the stage, we are left to contend with the "mingle-mangle" of a dissolving national identity. John Hirsch, writing his director's notes for his production of Henry VI in 1966 during the controversial Vietnam War, saw this despair at the heart of the play cycle as intensely topical. Encapsulating his approach to the adaptation of the cycle, his comments on the play are framed as questions about the hope for humanity's "progress" to greater "morality, peace, and order": "Can man ever subjugate his personal greed for status and power to the interest of the community? Will man ever be able to stifle the cruel blood-lust which is his primitive way of grabbing more life and pleasure, and a compensation for his rage against mortality?" ("Notes About the Play," n.p.). Using Yeats's "The Second Coming" to anchor his interpretation of Shakespeare's vision of civil war, Hirsch offered the play as his own brand of mourning: "Things fall apart; the centre cannot hold; / Mere anarchy is loosed upon the world."[14] Repeatedly, anarchy is the consequence when the idealizing gestures of Henry V's eulogy that opens the tetralogy are shown to be as ineffectual against the usurping power of Death and corporeal decrepitude as Henry VI proves to be against the challengers to his sovereignty. On their deepest level, the plays raise the possibility that the sovereign ideal is not merely lost, but ever was, and forever will be, unattainable for the limited, mortal humanity that must nevertheless struggle to attain its unifying power. This is why Henry V is dead at the beginning of the play, since, as an incorporeal presence, he is safely protected from the inevitable disappointments of the temporal world. This is why, too, that in rewriting the flow of history, Shakespeare's dramatic narrative of the English nation ends in the second tetralogy with Henry V's triumphant kingship, progressing from the meanness and meaninglessness of intestine wars toward a nostalgic culmination of nationalism in the providential defeat of the French at Agincourt. There, where the English suffer minimal losses to the French thousands, England is once again defined as the land of life and order against the French "royal fellowship of death" (Henry V 4.8.96), King Death's court, beyond the pale.

NOTES

1. All references to the plays are to the Pelican edition—William Shakespeare, *William Shakespeare: The Complete Works*, ed. Alfred Harbage (New York: Penguin, 1969).

2. For this reason these early histories have faced criticism for their episodic nature, for the sensationalism and seeming meaninglessness, or at best, meanness of the violence, and for the capriciousness of their focus which criticizes everyone with a moral relativity that disappoints the literary imagination looking to Shakespeare for the catharsis of poetic justice. In making his case for his adaptation of the tetralogy for the Royal Shakespeare Company in the late 1960s, for instance, Peter Hall insists that "the plays do not work in unadapted form" as they are in effect "a mess of angry and undifferentiated barons, thrashing about in a mass of diffuse narra-

tive" ("Introduction" vii). Equally strong, however, has been the desire, on the part of such critics as Hugh Richmond, David Riggs, and Edward Berry, for example, to rescue the tetralogy from such attacks, on the grounds of the close thematic relationship between plays and such sustained rhetorical and dramatic motifs as heroism and "patterns of decay." See H.M. Richmond, *Shakespeare's Political Plays* (New York: Random House, 1967) 21; David Riggs, *Shakespeare's Heroical Histories: "Henry VI" and Its Literary Tradition* (Cambridge: Harvard UP, 1971); Edward Berry, *Patterns of Decay: Shakespeare's Early Histories* (Charlottesville: U of Virginia P, 1975). These readings need not be interpreted necessarily as opposing ones, however. John Barton, Hall's partner in adaptation, admits that Shakespearean black sheep (*Titus Andronicus, Timon of Athens, Pericles*) have often been dismissed as inferior "only to be proved viable in the theatre after all" ("Adaptation" xv). Stephen Greenblatt echoes Barton's (grudging) acknowledgement of the tetralogy's of dramatic power, insisting that the second part of *Henry VI*, at least, "is more than the sum of its memorable parts.... Unflinching in its depiction of emotional and physical violence, the play examines the forms of monstrous individualism that emerge when the social identities provided by networks of kinship and feudal loyalty no longer exert their hold" (293). I tend in my own readings of the tetralogy to lean toward the latter, recuperative, critical position, not to suggest that the plays are not sensationalistic and episodic, but with an eye to reading the "mess" and "mass of diffuse narrative" as productive aspects of the plays' underlying, if elusive, cohesiveness.

3.	Ernst H. Kantorowicz, in *The King's Two Bodies: A Study in Mediaeval Political Theology* (Princeton: Princeton UP, 1957), locates the first significant use of the formula, "Le Roi est mort. Vive le Roi," to the accession of Henry VI, as the English struggled to maintain their hold on France, won at Agincourt by the hero-king, Henry V (411–12).

4.	We can see this metaphor of the politic body at work, for example, in Shakespeare's *Coriolanus*, where the First Citizen anatomizes the state, describing, "The kingly crownéd head, the vigilant eye, / The counsellor heart, the arm our soldier, / Our steed the leg, the tongue our trumpeter" (1.1.110–12). Menenius, seeking to quell an uprising of hungry peasants, appeals to an image of self-mutilation, defining "The senators of Rome" as "this good belly," and the rebelling Citizens as "the mutinous members" (1.1.143–44). At its heart, the metaphor is conservative, envisioning a body that exists according to a meticulously defined functional order.

5.	The *universitas* is concretized in and articulated through the sovereign's two bodies: the Body Natural that lives and dies, and the Body Politic, comprising the Office of monarchy, the populace and the land they inhabit, which through continual renewal and a sense of shared history, lives perpetually. It is this perpetuity that is declared, as Clare Gittings observes, in the noble funerals over which the heralds presided. The highly symbolic and carefully deployed escutcheons, family emblems and coats of arms in heraldic funerals were integral to "a display of power, intended to reinforce the social hierarchy. In a sense they were performed almost to deny that a death had occurred at all; the whole emphasis was on continuity and on the undiminished strength of the aristocracy, despite the demise of one of its members" (22). In the case of the demise of a king, the hierarchy of which he is the head remains symbolically intact, the continuity of the Body Politic being represented by the King in effigy until the coronation of the new corporeal counterpart, the Body Natural of the succeeding king.

6. If in production, these funereal cloths are constantly in view, the mourning for the individual will be seen to extend beyond this isolated event, pervading the generations of war and political unrest that follow.

7. I discuss the implications for 1 *Henry VI* of this spectacular aspect of Henry's sovereignty at length in my article, "No Rainbow Without the Sun: Visibility and Embodiment in Shakespeare's 1 *Henry VI*," *Modern Language Studies* 30.1 (2002): 137–56.

8. But the social process of mourning was not unproblematic. The late medieval practice of including effigies on funeral monuments provides an interesting example of this conceptual yoking together of, or more precisely, this conceptual turn from the temporal to the eternal. In his exhaustive study of the development of concepts of European monarchy, *The King's Two Bodies: A Study in Mediaeval Political Theology* (Princeton: Princeton UP, 1957), Kantorowicz includes several photographs of such monuments in which the effigy of the lord lies atop the monument reclining as in life dressed in his raiment of office, and below on a second level, in his mortal decrepitude, a decaying corpse naked before God (in Kantorowicz, Figs. 28–31). The images represent respectively the perpetuity of office or family dynasty, and the mortality of the now deceased incumbent. The actual mortal body is, of course, interred out of sight beneath the monument. In this way, the monument's representation of the conjunction of the two bodies of public figures is characterized by a lacuna: mortality itself is figured in stone, designed to endure, unchanging, for eternity. In the process of representing the relationship between the intangible and the eternal on the one hand and the corruption of the corporeal on the other, these monuments both acknowledge and elide the true decrepitude and transience of the human form, attesting to and evading an anxiety about the particular limitations of corporeality that resides deep within the metaphor of social embodiment.

9. John Hirsch's 1966 production at Stratford, Ontario emphasized the vacuum left by the death of Henry V through the interpolation of a Prologue in the form of Henry V's last will and testament. The will ends with Henry's injunction to the Peers: "What I have gotten, I charge you to keep it; I command you to defend it; and I desire you to nourish it" (Prologue, Promptbook n.p.). The irony of this statement is manifest, and this ironic falling off from the ideal of "one league and one unfeigned amity" (Prologue, Promptbook, n.page.) is the touchstone of the Hirsch's adaptation of the trilogy.

10. Indeed, Dekker's enumeration of "Burning Feauers, Boyles, Blains, and Carbuncles, the Leaders, Lieutenants, Serieant, and Corporalls" (31) in Death's army is a gruesome parody of the orderly hierarchy ratified in the noble funeral

parade, and the disintegration of the Court during this scene represents the transformation of order to chaos. I am indebted to Michael Neill for directing me to this passage in Dekker's text. Neill conducts a fascinating exploration of Elizabethan responses to death in his *Issues of Death: Mortality and Identity in English Renaissance Tragedy* (Oxford: Clarendon P, 1997).

11. Martin traces a pattern of disfigured civic ceremonies in his article, "Elizabethan Civic Pageantry in *Henry IV*," arguing insightfully that such fractured rituals represent junctures where Shakespeare opposes the monologic nature of civic rites "officially designed to impose a single authoritative meaning on a political or social subject" (245) with "destabilizing particularity" (251). Martin also identifies the Triumph of Death as the controlling metaphor of the scene and the first part of *Henry VI*, but does not discuss the significance of the levelling aspect of the Triumph in terms of the play's extended dilation on the relationship between individual and national identities.

12. Margaret Owens discusses the relation of the severed head to castration ("The Many-Headed Monster" 371). See also Nina Athanassoglou-Kallmyer, "Gericault's Severed Heads and Limbs: The Politics and Aesthetics of the Scaffold." While this article focusses on a later period, Athanassoglou-Kallmyer provides a pertinent discussion of the shift in popular attitudes regarding decapitation as a form of judicial punishment from the seventeenth to the eighteenth centuries, and especially through the Terror. The article also provides a pictorial history that graphically illustrates these shifts. For a good survey of philosophical developments from the Classical to the modern periods, see Gertrude Ezorsky, ed., *Philosophical Perspectives on Punishment* (Albany: State U of New York P, 1972).

13. The practice of doubling in this production further emphasizes the ascendency of corporeal decay and violence in the tetralogy, for, in addition to Cade, Oliver Cotton also appears as the seductive cuckold-maker Suffolk and, in the final of the three instalments of *The Plantagenets*, as Richard of Gloucester's venal and Machiavellian henchman, the Duke of Buckingham. Pam Brighton's Stratford, Ontario production (1980) capitalized on a similar thread of association, casting Nicholas Pennell as both Suffolk and Richard, Duke of Gloucester, both of whom are strongly associated with sensuality, decay, and a personal ambition at odds with the commonweal.

14. Hirsch's production emphasized the pervasive nature of this anarchic impulse toward national disintegration by altering Shakespeare's play to have Suffolk lynched by a mob following the murder of Humphrey of Gloucester. Moving Margaret's mourning from the Cade rebellion, and connecting it visually to the deathbed scene of Gloucester's murderer, Beaufort, Hirsch shows the vigilantism of the mob to be a direct consequence of the collapse of courtly order.

Women's Poetry of Grief and Mourning

The Languages of Lament in Sixteenth-Century French Lyric

> How to transmit to my beloved manuscript the eloquent
> mimicry of the body and the face that accompanies speech, the
> silences, the tone and music of the voice, the look filled with
> unexpressed words which are nevertheless comprehensible,
> the hands, like trays of fruit, full of mute phrases.
>
> (Marie Cardinal, *In other words* 71)

FRENCH FEMINIST THEORISTS, most notably Julia Kristeva, Luce Irigaray, Hélène Cixous, and Monique Wittig, have devoted significant attention to the question of women's language. I have often resisted the application of contemporary theory to Renaissance texts in favour of a more historical, contextualized approach. Nonetheless, my research on sixteenth-century French women poets and of the body language that permeates their writings has led me to consider early-modern constructions of *écriture féminine* in light of contemporary feminist theories.[1] My intention in this essay is to demonstrate how women poets of the Renaissance construct a language that exceeds the conventions of masculine poetic discourse. In their creation of a distinctly feminine language, they anticipated the discourse called for by theorists only within the last few decades. Dissatisfied with the limits of rational language to capture their experiences, sixteenth-century women poets turn to the forces of their bodies to express the ineffable. Poetry of grief and mourning, including works by Philiberte de Fleurs, Madeleine des Roches, Catherine de Bourbon, Gabrielle de Coignard, and Marguerite de Navarre, provides the most compelling examples of this feminine language of the body, although an analysis of women's love lyric, secular *complaintes*, or devotional compositions would also substantiate many of the ideas I propose here.

Feminist theory has probed and challenged the prospect of women producing a language that would free them from imitating the phallocentric discourse of their masculine counterparts. Many theorists question how women can inscribe themselves into a language that they have not created—one that, in fact, excludes them—and fails to communicate fully their experiences. Kristeva asserts that within masculine language "woman" refers to "that which cannot be represented, what is not said, what remains above and beyond nomenclatures and ideologies" ("La femme, ce n'est jamais ça" 135). While women function within this language that is not theirs, they sometimes fail to make themselves understood—a consequence greatly lamented by French women poets of the sixteenth century.

In "Ce sexe qui n'en est pas un," Luce Irigaray compiles the masculine complaints about the incomprehensibility of women's language, "in which [women go] off in all directions and in which [men are] unable to discern the coherence of any meaning" (353). Such criticism of women's expression implies that a gendered use of language exists, calling to mind the age-old and demeaning dichotomy between masculine Logic and feminine Irrationality. Interestingly, the source of women's language in the examples I will examine here could nonetheless be characterized as irrational: throughout history, the body has often been placed in binary opposition to the mind. Yet it is precisely the body and its irrational forces that modern feminists argue are central to women developing a language of their own. Although the idea of unmediated poetic expression implicit in this notion is troubling, the body is the dominant communicator within women's compositions of grief. In the Renaissance, non-verbal language anchored in the corporeal self—the *sanglots, criz, souspirs, gémissemens,* and *larmes* that are so prevalent in women's sixteenth-century verse—effectuates the "writing of the body" called for by feminist theorist Hélène Cixous in "Le Rire de la Meduse"(342).[2]

In her examination of *l'écriture féminine,* Ann Rosalind Jones ("Writing the Body") has questioned whether the body can in fact be the source of a new discourse. In literature of the latter half of the twentieth century, many women authors have given a voice to their bodies, and in so doing have invoked a veritable linguistic revolution, shattering rules of grammar, syntax, and punctuation. The difference between modern women authors and women poets of the sixteenth century is that today, it is generally the sexual body that is inscribed into verse. Women authors of the Renaissance sought instead to give voice to their *grieving* bodies, a revolution in itself, considering the religious condemnation and cultural rejection of such release.

Cultural beliefs concerning the notion of grief are reflected within masculine poetry of the mid-sixteenth century. A distinct movement of anti-mourning arises within masculine devotional lyric in particular.[3] Authors reject grief in a variety of ways: either by pointing to the futility, or to the selfishness, or above all to the sinfulness of such sentiment.[4] For male poets, grief is wasted emotion.

A brief look at some examples of masculine verse will furnish the contextual background for an analysis of women's poetry of grief and mourning. Eustorg de Beaulieu's "Rondeau lxj de resconforter ceulx qui se plaignent de la mort d'aultruy" provides a good point of departure. His poem is intended to deliver a comforting message to those in mourning, but serves instead as a harsh reminder of the impermanence of life and of the utter vanity of all efforts to deny death:

> C' est faict il faut passer par la
> Tout homme est né affin qu'il meure
> Et face eternelle demeure
> En joye, ou pleur de par dela,
> D' alleguer cecy, ou cela,
> Vous n'amendriez point d'une meure
>   C' est faict.
> Cessez de plourer, sus hola?
> Priez Dieu en temps & en heure
> Qu'au residu ayde & sequeure,
> Car que y feriez vous plus? Veez la
>   C' est faict. (Ciiij–b)

Beaulieu's expression of supposed consolation reflects the stoic resolve encouraged by many religious thinkers of this period. The fundamental message, "C' est faict," repeated at crucial points within the poem, conveys the poet's own mastery of emotional indifference to loss. There is no point in wasting tears over the inevitable.

Bergedé echoes this view wholeheartedly. His "Pleurer les mors" is even more obdurate than Beaulieu's *rondeau*. The imagery of his composition moves beyond the abstractions of Beaulieu's preaching to form a ridiculing portrait of the mourner:

> Tu rompz ta barbe & tes cheveux,
> Tu remplis de larmes tes yeux:
> De plaintifz tu rompz ton visage,
> Douloureux par le dur outrage,
> De tes ongles ensanglantez,
> Pour y avoir este plantez.
> Crois-tu pourtant faire revivre
> Celuy que Dieu ne veult plus vivre,
> En dueil pour les deffunctz se mettre,
> N' est sinon mal sur mal transmettre. (Ma–b)

With disdain, the poet details the physical manifestations of grief in a manner that recalls medieval and biblical depictions. He mocks the self-abuse and bitter outrage that result from the confrontation with death and its unavoidable finality. The pain the mourner experiences, Bergedé suggests, is not the result of absence, but stems from having been "planted" here unwillingly, forced to remain while a loved one has been released. All displays of grief are therefore in vain; there can be no beneficial purpose to such behaviour. Mourning serves only to divulge a sinful defiance of spirit. Bergedé's message echoes that of Beaulieu: submission to God's will is the only reasonable way to confront loss.

The most remarkable example of this belief is found in Marot's *Deploration sur le trespas du feu messire Florimond Robertet* (1534). Even Marot, who makes every effort to elicit tears in the beginning of the poem, completely rejects the notion of grief by the time he reaches the end.[5] The turning point takes place as Marot considers the foolishness and hypocrisy of mourning. He affirms that such behaviour is not befitting to believers in Christ, and that the torments of grief should be left as punishment to the pagans who fail to believe in the eternal life begotten by His sacrifice:

Parquoy bien folle est la coustume humaine
Quant aulcun meurt porter et faire dueil
Si tu crois bien que Dieu vers luy le meyne
A quelle fin en gettes larmes doeil:
Veulx tu le vif tirer hors du cercueil
Pour a son bien mettre empesche et deffence:
Qui pource pleure est marry dont le dueil
De Dieu est faict jugez si cest offence.
Laisse gemir et brayze les payens
Qui nont espoir deternelle demeure
Faulte de foy te donne leurs moyens
Dainsi plourer quant fault que aulcun meure
Folie cest de mener dueil a lheure
Hypocrisie en a taille lhabit
Dessoubz lequel tel sa mere pleure
Qui bien vouldroit de son pere lobit. (Lb)

A more personal effort to avoid indulgence in grief can be found in Jacques de Billy's Sonnet spirituel XLVII "De la misere de cette vie." In this example, Billy tries to comfort himself over the loss of his brother.[6] He confesses his grief through a vehement rejection of it:

Pourquoy t'affliges tu de dueil & de tristesse
Pour ton frere Prunay? Son sort n'est il heureux,
Quand, ayant combatu d'un bras fort valeureux,
Meurt, la foy soustenant, qui a salut s'adresse?
    Quicte donc tels regrets, telles pleurs & detresse.
Ne regrette celuy, qui d'un coeur genereux,
Par un illustre mort ayant fendu les cieux,
Jouist ores des biens, dont avons la promesse.
Mais bien deplore toy, les maux considerant
Ausquels resté tu es, & quau monde adherant

Quelque jour te sera de sentir necessaire.
Chetif & miserable, & plein d'aveuglement,
Quel profit te revient de vivre longument,
Sinon voir plus de maux, plus en souffir, ou faire? (189)

There should be no sadness for the one who has died, for he has gained a new and better life of bliss and eternal repose. Billy attempts to stifle the voice of mourning by turning his thoughts away from the one he has lost to contemplate instead his own miserable condition.

It is especially by contrast to such fervent suppression of grief and mourning in poetry by male authors that the difference women authors brought to the poetic tradition of grief in the sixteenth century becomes apparent. This feminine poetic and transgressive response to grief is all the more remarkable given the religious and cultural restraints, as well as the prominence and recognition afforded masculine poetry. The status of mourning itself put sixteenth-century women poets in an exceptional category that entitled them to commit their literary acts of grief.

As many scholars, such as Margaret King, Constance Jordan, and Ruth Kelso have argued, widows, in particular, found themselves in an unusual situation during the Renaissance, as they gained a social and financial autonomy uncommon to most women of the period.[7] The pleasure some widows took in their independence resulted in occasional bouts of societal suspicion concerning the authenticity of feminine grief.[8] At the same time, a tension developed between cultural expectations of how women should display their grief and the simultaneous ideal of silence imposed upon widows, and on women in general for that matter.[9]

In his "Ornamenti della gentil donna vedova," for example, Guilio Cesare Cabei proposes a list of widows' virtues, the third and fourth of which seek specifically to silence the widow's voice: "She will speak sparingly and without raising her voice.... She will observe silence, except on being questioned" (qtd. in Kelso 130). Despite the deprecation of the widow's voice, widows throughout literary history have refused to be silenced.

Christine de Pisan, for example, represents the paragon of feminine literary grief in her *Cent ballades*, which are fundamental to the tradition. Pisan is almost defiant in her literary lament and writes her grief with an exemplary authority of voice, generating self-portrait after self-portrait to capture the intensity and singularity of her grief.[10] In the following excerpt from Ballad VI, Pisan enumerates her woes through a rapid succession of substantives and descriptives that register the limitlessness and ineffability of her pain:

> Dueil engoisseux, rage desmesuree,
> Grief desespoir plein de forsennement,
> Langour sanz fin, vie malheürée
> Pleine de plour, d'engoisse et de tourment,
> Cueur doloreux qui vit obscurement,
> Tenebreux corps sus le point de perir,
> Ay, sanz cesser, continuellement;
> Et si ne puis ne garir ne morir. (7)[11]

The physicality of Pisan's grief, the fundamentally corporeal expression of her despair, foreshadows feminine depictions of grief during the sixteenth century. At the same time, it announces a double transgression that will take place within women's poetry: the turn to the body as a means of expression and the act of grieving that is accomplished through the refusal of silence.

The tradition of poetic mourning is not only developed by major women poets such as Marguerite de Navarre, but it also resonates uncannily in the works of more obscure authors of the sixteenth century. Philiberte de Fleurs, the virtually unknown author of the *Soupirs de viduité* (1585), collected in *Oeuvres*, is representative of the minor poets who were influenced by the grief tradition. The few extant passages of her five hundred verses (devoted to her dead husband Le sieur de Marteray) reproduce the body language devised in the poetry of Christine de Pisan. For both authors, writing becomes a translation of the body's indomitable force of grief. Unbridled tears play the central role in the interpretation of grief: "je ne saurai restreindre / l'oeil fontaineux, ruisselant cette humeur, / Qui ne permet recéler ma douleur," de Fleurs confesses, hoping God will grant her the restraint of which she knows her body to be incapable (117).

The grammar of grief consists of apostrophic and exclamatory cries, moans, sighs, screams, and sobs. But tears—gushing and all-consuming—like those in the previous passage, provide the foundation for women's body language. The following stanza taken from Madeleine Des Roches's first sonnet in the second collection devoted to her husband François Eboissard, is also exemplary of the type of lachrymal lament one finds in women's poetry:[12]

> O douloureux regrets! O triste pensement
> Qui avez mes deux yeux convertis en fontaine!
> O trop soudain depart! O cause de la peine
> Qui me fait lamenter inconsolablement! (174)

In sonnet II, Des Roches reiterates the ceaselessness of her suffering, turning a second time to the Jeremiac fountain of tears. The whole body is overcome and overwhelmed by its own ungovernable language:

> O miserable estat ou je me voy posée,
> Dont j'ay tousjours au cueur un amer souvenir
> Qui me fait le cerveau fontaine devenir,
> Dont l'humeur par les yeux n'est jamais espuisée. (175)

The notion of the uncontrollable body of grief, as portrayed in the works De Fleurs and Des Roches, is universal in sixteenth-century women's laments. There is a constant battle to dominate the flesh and its inconstancies. At the same time, in moments of some subversive indulgence, women almost seem to take a private pleasure in their grief, or at least in the writing of it.

Michel de Montaigne addresses the relation of grief to the process of writing in the Essais. In the opening lines of "De l'affection des peres aux enfans," Montaigne explains to Madame d'Estissac:

> C'est une humeur melancolique, et une humeur par conse-
> quent très ennemie de ma complexion naturelle, produit par le
> chagrin de la solitude en laquelle il ya quelques années que je
> m'estoy jetté, qui m'a mis premierement en teste cette resverie
> de me mesler d'escrire. (Vol. II, 56)

Although he insists that melancholia counters his natural disposition, Montaigne raises the fundamental point that suffering, "le chagrin de la solitude," brought about by loss, is what drew him to writing in the first place.[13] Montaigne is an exception among male authors. His words, in fact, are more representative of the feminine experience of the call to writing. In her article on the significance of grief in the work of Montaigne, Françoise Charpentier argues that writing "est déjà un premier geste de désendeuille-ment, manifestant 'le travail du deuil'" (829).[14] The expression of grief through the written word can play a crucial and highly effective role in the mourning process.[15]

The notion of writing as "travail du deuil" is compelling in light of sixteenth-century women's poetry of grief and mourning. While women share Montaigne's shame and resistance to mourning as literary motiva-tion, their works, at the same time, thrive on grief: it is the heart of their literary creativity.[16] Women, nonetheless, make every effort to suppress their grief as is expected of them, but their bodies refuse to be silenced.[17] Marguerite de Navarre writes in La Navire about her grief over the death of her brother François I: "Le corps me vient contraindre / A regretter, à pleurer, à crier; / Et le dehors ne peult le dedans faindre" (407).

In Chanson II "Autres pensées faites un mois après la mort du roy," Marguerite de Navarre transforms her whole Self into lamentation. Rational language is abandoned; the poet, empty of any mindfulness of God or social expectation, gives herself over entirely to her tears and her cries:

> Esprit et corps de dueil sont pleins,
> Tant qu'ilz sont convertiz en plainctz:
> Seul pleurer est ma contenance.
> Je crie par bois et par plains,
> Au ciel et terre me complains;[18]
> A rien fors à mon dueil ne pense. (9–10)

The onomatopoeic quality and echo-effect of "pleins," "plainctz," "plains," "complains" deftly accentuates the image of the poet physically overcome with grief, unable to think or speak of anything else. In La Navire, Marguerite de Navarre turns again to wailing and screaming in an attempt to push out the grief that binds her: "Criez, ma voix, jusqu'à sa demourance; / Pleurez mes yeux, jusqu'a saillir dehors..." (423).

The scream imparts tremendous linguistic power to women's poetic laments. Catherine de Bourbon, for example, viewing language as an obstacle to the conveyance of her suffering, instinctively turns to her body as an alternative, and perhaps more reliable, means of expression: "Quelque fois, mais en vain, de parler je m'essaye, / Pour te dire mon mal, mais ma langue begaye, / Et ne peut prononcer un mot de ma douleur, / D'esprit donc et de coeur a toy, Pere, je crie" (208).

Like Catherine de Bourbon, Marguerite de Navarre is deeply troubled by the limitations of language to translate her experience. She is resistant to verbal codes into which she cannot, or perhaps does not wish to, transcribe her grief, for the resulting depiction could never be an accurate one. As she explains in Chanson XLII: "Mon parler n'a couleur / Pour monstrer ma douleur" (119). The body, therefore, becomes the source of women's language and rhetoric.[19] In the very first of the *Chansons Spirituelles*, the "Pensées de la royne de Navarre, estant dans sa litière durant la maladie du roy," Marguerite de Navarre claims she will be unable to write her grief, unable to render visible her pain "par escrit," "par parole." She asserts that language or, more precisely, "[s]on parler" is defeated before she even begins.[20] Unable to find sufficient words to give voice to her grief, her body provides her with the necessary means:

> Mes larmes, mes souspirs,[21] mes criz,
> Dont tant bien je sçay la pratique,
> Sont mon parler et mes escritz,
> Car je n'ay autre rhétorique. (4)

There is nothing that can more directly express the inarticulate "douleur de [son] esprit" than her body (3).[22]

One final example will illustrate the significance of women's body language. Gabrielle de Coignard's Sonnet XXIV in *Oeuvres chrétiennes* provides a particularly cogent example of verbal language submitting to the expressive forces of the body. Unlike Marguerite de Navarre, Gabrielle de Coignard does not explain her use of body language as the result of a distrust of verbal language; rather, in her grief, she simply experiences a loss of contact with language:[23]

> Mon Coeur estoit de douleur oppressé,
> Je n'avois plus parole ny langage;

Mon estomach ressembloit à l'orage,[24]
Qu'eleve en mer Aquilon courroucé.
Mille sanglots vers le ciel j'ay poussé,
Vrais tourbillons eschelans ce nuage. (169)

Coignard relays the intensity of her grief through a description of its physical manifestations. Using hyperbolic, metaphorical water imagery to convey the internal experience of grief, Coignard successfully renders what she considers to be indescribable. The storm in her stomach compels her to cry out toward the heavens, driving out her pain in the only language she has: "mille sanglots."

The so-called irrational forces of the body, the emotions of the grieving "hysteric," are omnipresent in women's poetry. I have discussed only a few among the many examples that deserve further analysis and consideration in what should be a discussion of the history of women's language. As the poems examined here undeniably suggest, the development of a feminine language has a long and nuanced history.

As Madeleine Lazard, in *Image Littéraires de la femme à la Renaissance*, has already observed, women poets rarely focus their compositions of mourning on the one who has died; they choose instead to expound upon their own suffering that is the result of their loss.[25] Their inspiration is purely selfish, in the most positive sense of the word. Their writing provided the private space to grieve denied them by social custom. As a result of their awareness of the failures of language, women turn to their bodies of grief and indeed refuse, through the rejection of rational discourse and the construction of their own language, the patriarchal control over the feminine body that feminist theorists today continue to discuss.

Although there is substantial evidence that women hesitated as they shed their grief in writing, the plethora of examples in their works reveals the transgressive act they committed through their poetic mourning. Self-criticism pervades their literary expressions of grief because they are required to deal with the contradictions between their private needs and the expectations of society. Women advance, within their poetic sanctuaries, from emotional restraint and self-denial to moderation in their grief and, then, still unsatisfied, to justifications of their grief and confrontations with the cultural codes that seek to silence them. As sixteenth-century Italian poet

Vittoria Colonna reveals, women's grief poetry can transcend its own literary purpose to fulfill the more intimate, emotional needs of the author where the process of poetic composition replaces the outward act of mourning:

A bitter weeping, not a sweet song,
and melancholy sighs, not a clear voice,
make me vaunt not my style but my grief. (Love Poem I, 129)

NOTES

1. In my research on French women's literature of the Renaissance, I have been repeatedly surprised to discover how women writers of the sixteenth century struggled with some of the same linguistic and literary problems that many modern women authors and critics contend with today. Considering the work of Renaissance women authors with an awareness of the perspectives of modern feminist critics can better illuminate their linguistic challenges and literary goals. While I would not go so far as to suggest that there is a universalist quality to women's writing, the ideas of contemporary feminist critics can serve as an enlightening gloss on women's writing of the past.

2. Cixous writes: "Women must write through their bodies, they must invent the impregnable language that will wreck partitions, classes, and rhetorics, regulations and codes, they must submerge, cut through, get beyond the ultimate reserve-discourse."

3. There was a formal tradition of poetic weeping, which actually stands as a paradox to religious opposition to grief, that was established during the middle ages and was greatly popularized during the sixteenth century. The genre, known as the *déploration funèbre*, refers to literary tributes to individuals who have died. The *déploration* most often follows a conventional schema (e.g. lamentation, eulogy, prayer), is written by request, and is rarely inspired by personal loss. In many cases they chronicle controlled meditations on Death itself and turn to realistic descriptions of the decomposition of the body, drawing on the vanitas tradition or the ars moriendi, etc.—all notions that have received extensive critical attention. For a solid history of the *déploration*, see Christine Martineau-Cenieys's *Le thème de la mort dans la poésie française: (1450–1550)* (Paris: H. Champion, 1978).

4. For Catholic believers, grief was a sin; mourning suggested, without exception, in submission to God's will. Nothing and no one outside the relationship with God deserved to hold any significance. Penitential grief alone was permitted. All other feelings of despair were deemed corrupt and disobedient. Consider Paul's words in 2 Corinthians 7:10: "For Godly grief produces a repentance that leads to salvation

and brings no regret but worldly grief produces death." Although this statement is taken out of context (Paul is writing to comfort the Corinthians who have at last been moved to repent after a temporary lapse in faith), it nonetheless parallels the problem of grief associated with mourning, since this latter emotion is so clearly grounded in the terrestrial experience.

5. The opening lines of the poem describe the difference between affectation and authentic grief as the poet attempts to feel the pain of loss:

> Mais quant la mort a faict son malefice
> Amour adonc usc de son office
> Faisant porter aux vray amys le dueil
> Non point ung dueil de fainctes larmes doeil
> Non point ung dueil de drap noir annuel
> Mais ung dueil tainct dennuy perpetuel
> Non point ung dueil qui dehors apparoist
> Mais qui au coeur sans apparence croist
> Voyla le dueil qui a vaincu ma joye
> Cest ce qui faict que tout rien que je oye
> Me donne ennuy; c'est ce que me procure
> Que couleur blanches a loeil me soit obscure
> Et que jour cler me semble noir nuyct
> De tel facon que ce qui tant me nuyst
> Corromp du tout le naif de ma muse
> Lequel de soy ne veult que je mamuse
> A composer en triste tragedye
> Mais maintenant force mest que je dye
> Chanson mortelle en stille plain desmoy. (Aija–b)

This excerpt of the initial movement of the *déploration* is presented as a lesson in the proper expressions of grief. At the same time, the passage reveals the efforts on the part of the author to convince his reader that he is indeed sad over the death of Robertet. As modern readers, it is difficult to perceive any sincerity in his expression. The poet uses conventional rhetoric and imagery to capture a grief that is not his own. The end result, as is often the case with official poetry of circumstance, is a failure to convey an authentic sense of despair.

6. The meditation is inspired by Saint Gregory of Nazianus's *oraison funebre* on the death of his brother Cesarius. Billy notes after his own sonnet how he was moved by the words Saint Gregory said to his mother and father. He translates:

> De combien Cesarius no us a-t-il desadvance: Combien encores
> pleurons nous son deces? N'allons nous pas en diligence en une
> mesme demeure? N'entrerons nous pas en bref soubs la mesme
> pierre? Ne serons nous pas incontinent mesme pouldre? Tout le

proffit que ferons en ce peu de jours, qu'aurons encores a vivre, ne
sera-ce pas, partie de voir plus de maux, partie d'en souffrir, partie
aussi, paraventure, d'en faire, & puis apres payer le commun tribut,
a la loy de nature? (191)

7. See Constance Jordan, *Renaissance Feminism* (Ithaca: Cornell UP, 1990), Ruth Kelso,
    Doctrine for the Lady of the Renaissance (Urbana: U of Illinois P, 1978), and Margaret
    King, *Women of the Renaissance* (Chicago: U of Chicago P, 1991).

8. Widows were often suspected of feigning their grief and fabricating illusions of
    melancholy for the sake of appearances. Masculine disbelief of feminine grief is
    reflected in many Medieval and Early Modern texts. Aside from two exceptional
    pieces by Benoît Alizet ("Consolation des Vefves") and Nicolas Le Digne ("Sonnet
    pour les vefves"), the predominant literary image of the widow from the 12th
    through the 16th centuries, in works spanning from Chretien de Troyes to Michel
    de Montaigne, is one that portrays her as full of deceitful tears and false regret. In
    "De trois bonnes femmes," Montaigne, refusing to be duped by the trickery of the
    widow, maintains that the women of his century:

    réservent plus communement a estaller leurs bons offices a la vehe-
    mence de leur affection envers leurs maris perdus, cherchent au
    moins lors a donner tesmoignage de leur bonne volonte. Tardif
    tesmoignage et hors de saison! Elles preuvent plustot par la qu'elles
    ne les aiment que morts.... S'il y a quelque honneur a pleurer les
    maris, il n'appartient qu'a celles qui leur ont ry; celles qui ont pleure
    en la vie, qu'elles rient en la mort, au dehors comme au dedans.
    Aussi ne regardez pas aces yeux moites et a cette piteuse voix;
    regardez ce port, ce teinct et l'embonpoinct de ces joues soubs ces
    grandes voiles: c'est par-la qu'elle parle franc;ais. Il en est peu de qui
    la sante n'aille en amendant, qualité qui ne sc;ait pas mentir. Cette
    ceremonieuse contenance ne regarde pas tant derriere soy, que
    devant; c' est acquest plus que payement. (II, 35, 406–07)

    See also Heather Arden's "Grief, Widowhood, and Woman's Sexuality in Medieval
    French Literature," in *Upon My Husband's Death: Widows in the Literature and Histories of
    Medieval Europe*, ed. Louise Mirrer (Ann Arbor: U of Michigan P, 1992), 305–19.

9. Juan Luis Vivés's council concerning the appropriate manner of the widow's grief
    promotes this paradoxical code of conduct, one which suggests that the widow
    reveal some evidence of her grief so that others can be assured of her femininity,
    but that she limit herself to avoid over-indulgence in her expression, which would
    attract unseemly attention. "Floods of tears and bitter laments," he writes "are
    allowable to her, even to be recommended; not to weep at all is a sign of a hard
    heart and unchaste mind. ...Let a widow therefore bewail her husband, if not for

one reason then for another, but with due measure, not crying out or beating herself to display her grief to others" (qtd. in Kelso 127–28).

Moderation was the key to appropriate grieving or to any emotivity for that matter, which was so often associated with feminine weakness. From a medical point of view, the physical difference of the woman—her physiology and humours—was thought to contribute to her supposed emotional "instabilities." According to Ian Maclean, the physician Mercado believed that melancholia, list-lessness, and irrational behaviour, among other hysterical illnesses, were caused specifically by the female reproductive system (41). Maclean explains that women's assumed physical frailty, for sixteenth-century thinkers, "is accompanied by mental emotional weakness" (43). "For all this, woman is considered to be inferior to man in that the psychological effects of her cold and moist humours throw doubt on her control of her emotions and her rationality" (46). Grief, therefore, with its associa-tions to irrationality and lack of emotional control, became linked in the minds of men with a feminine madness to be avoided at all costs. Marguerite de Navarre herself contributes to this kind of thinking, referring to her *fol pleurer* in *La navire* (386). The association of grief with madness would explain the issue of anti-mourning raised earlier. In "Accoustumance," Bergedé distinguishes the appropriate masculine response, or rather lack thereof in the face of adversity: "Cueur *viril* ne doibt lamenter / Lorsque luy survient infortune" (published under the name Nicolle Bargedé de Vezelay, Kiiij–a, emphasis added).

10. See in particular Ballads I, V, and VI.
11. A comparison of Pisan's poem with Madeleine des Roche's Sonnet VIII written over a century-and-a-half later, reveals the fundamental role of the body in the experience and rather morbid expression of grief.

> Pleurant amerement mon douloureux servage
> Qui tient mon corps mal sain, mon esprit en souci,
> Le coeur comble d'amer, le visage transi,
> Cachant l'ombre de vie en une morte image,
> Je cherche vainement qui l'esprit me soulage; (127)

The series of "plaintes" in Ode IV further illustrates the physical extreme to which Madeleine Des Roches experiences her grief:

> Du chef jusques a la plante
> Une humeur froid se plante
> Par le millieu de mes os
> Dont la douleur trop pressante
> M'oste repas et repos. (102)

12. For Des Roches's primary grief poems, see Sonnet XXXVI in the first collection, her *Ephitaphe de Feu Maistre François Eboissard, Seigneur de la Villée, son Mary*, and the first

and second sonnets of the second collection. At the same time, Madeleine des Roches experiences a certain guilt over allowing herself this kind of release—much like Gabrielle de Coignard. Compare Des Roches's sonnet VII and Coignard's sonnet LXXXIII. See also Catherine de Bourbon's "Stances de Madame, Seur du Roy."

13. In Françoise Charpentier's words: "Les *Essais* sont enfants du deuil et de la melancolie" ("Ecriture et travail du deuil" 828).

14. Despite the opposition to grief expressed in "De la tristesse," Montaigne undeniably experiences and writes about the pain he suffers over the loss of his friend, Etienne de la Boetie. His doleful remembrances of the union they once shared inevitably suggest that he is overcome by the grief he so despises. In "De l'amitie," writing provides the ideal opportunity for Montaigne to honour the beauty of his friendship with La Boetie and to mourn their separation.

15. Charpentier elaborates:

> Ecriture du deuil, c'est aussi dire, célébrer l'objet perdu, et décrire ce qu'il en est de cette perte. C'est une démarche qui oblige celui qui ecrit a aller chercher en lui l'objet de sa célébration, dont il a intériorisé l'image puisque la réalité lui en refuse désormais la recontre; cette image est devenue un modèle, auquel il s'identifie, puis que l'objet du deuil est un objet d'amour.... [L]'écriture du deuil, c'est aussi élaborer et dépasser le deuil, c'est une therapie; elle permet de mettre à distance cet objet perdu et dangereusement introjecté. (829)

16. The shame women associate with their grief is the result of societal pressures to silence it. In *La navire*, François I attempts to goad Marguerite out of her misery, prompting: "Laisse ton pleur, laisse ton soupirer, / Laisse le deuil qui tant d'ennuy te donne, / Qui ne te sert sinon que d'empirer" (411). Briçonnet's missive to Marguerite in September of 1524 is intended both to comfort Marguerite after the loss of her niece and to criticize her excessive indulgence in her grief:

> Si mes dernières lettres concluent et vous persuadent n'estre à plaingdre feu nostre bonne dame et royne, qu'il a pleu à Dieu appeller a luy, plus doivent pour sa bonne fille, qui chantera, suivant l'aigneau, quelque part qu'il voyse, le cantique qui n'est permis à sa bonne dame et mere, la royne. Innocence l'a conduicte au domicille de l'innocent aigneau sans macule. En la plorant l'on desplaist non seullement à Dieu, comme contrevenant ou desirant (sinon obvier) ne se contenter de son vouloir, mais aussi a elle, luy substrayant, par nostre inconsideré à desir, la felicité incommuable, et ce pour une folle amour, que cuydons avoir en elle. (264)

17.   Gabrielle de Coignard, endeavouring to overcome her personal struggles with grief, epitomizes the predicament of women authors in Sonnet LXXXIII.

> Non je ne veux aucunement me plaindre,
> Non je ne veux mes ennuis racompter,
> Non je ne veux mon esprit contenter,
> Pour en parlant faire ma douleur moindre.
> Je veux plustost dissimuler et feindre,
> En me taisant ma langue surmonter,
> Il faut ce corps severement dompter
> Par la raison qui se doit faire craindre. (240)

The series of anaphorae that opens the composition reflects the persistent efforts of the author to avoid surrendering herself to lamentation. The repetition of "Non je ne veux" resounds as a mantra that she chants in order to mould her will to the behaviour she considers appropriate. Coignard aspires to bear her burdens with austere resolve. To complain, to "racompter [s]es ennuis," would allow for a release of her pain, which would, as she suggests, diminish it. "Taire [s]a langue" would symbolize her ultimate triumph over the body, to deny the natural forces of grief would be the utmost proof of her devotion. Coignard moves from expressing what she does not want in the first stanza, to a forceful statement of what she does want, trying to comply wholeheartedly with Christian acceptance and endurance of pain as punishment. She is resolute that reason will conquer her instinctive need to express her pain in order to avoid losing herself to it entirely.

    The irony in the passage is that by the expression of her desire not to complain, Coignard carries out her complaint indirectly. By mere mention of it, she makes her suffering known, thereby permitting at least a partial release. Despite this, Coignard reveals her profound determination to overcome the body, to mortify the concrete with abstract reason (in this case, faith). Colette Winn clarifies the thought process at the root of Gabrielle de Coignard's refusal: "L'auteur refuse de s'épandre sur ses maux, de décharger son coeur afin de trouver réconfort dans l'acte d'écriture. Point ne suffit de diminuer la peine. Il faut apprendre à la dominer pour se render maître de son corps et de soi" (*Oeuvres Chrétiennes*, Introduction 41).

18.   As this example illustrates, women poets often turn to nature to create and secure private space in their compositions for the release of emotions. Gabrielle de Coignard also employs this tactic. See for example, sonnet LXXIX.

    Poetic composition becomes the sanctuary where grief is savoured in a few stolen moments: "Quand nul ne voy, l'oeil j'abandonne / A pleurer," admits de Navarre, "puis sur le papier / Un peu de ma douleur j'ordonne; / Voilà mon douloureux mestier" (Chanson I, 6).

19.   Chanson II also describes the physical toil that grief has taken on her, bringing her to the point of death, leaving her with nothing but her voice. Despite her feeble state, Marguerite succeeds in developing a rare strength of voice:

Tristess, par ses grans efforts,
A rendu si foible mon corps
Qu'il n'ha ny vertu ny puissance:
Il est semblable à l'un des morts,
Tant que, la voyant par dehors,
L'on perd de luy la cognoissance.

Je n'ay plus que la triste voix,
De la quelle crier m'en vois
En lamentant la dure absence.
Las, de celuy pour qui je vivois,
Que de si bon Coeur je voyois,
J'ay perdu l'heureuse presence. (8–9)

20.   Si la douleur de mois esprit
Je povois monstrer par parole
Ou la declarer par escrit.
Oncques ne fut sy triste rolle;
Car le mal qui plus fort;
Par-quoy n'ay rien qui me concole,
Fors l'espoir de la douce mort.

Je sçay que je ne dois celer
Mon ennui, plus que raisonnable;
Mais si ne sçauroit mon parler
Atteindre à mon dueil importable:
A l'escriture veritable
Defaudroit la force à ma main;
Le taire me seroit louable,
S'il ne m'esoit tant inhumain. (3)

Within the first two strophes of the poem, despite her lack of confidence in her ability to write and function within language, there is a marked refusal to silence herself. She describes her grief as "raisonnable," which is not necessarily in opposition with the "mal…qui [l]'affole." Marguerite admits that this inordinate pain she bears brings about an irrational response within her, but claims simultaneously that her reaction is not irrational, that it is perfectly normal, in fact, considering the tremendous loss she endures. The poem serves as a defence, a discreet riposte against anyone who might reproach her voice of grief. For although language is inadequate, and despite the fact that it would be praiseworthy for her to silence herself, Marguerite de Navarre boldly claims her right to mourn.

21.   In the *Complainte pour un detenu prisonnier*, de Navarre argues for the superiority of the sigh over verbal language in expressions of pain: "Et les souspirs sont plus certain

message / De tes douleurs, que ne fait ton langage" (*Marguerite de la Marguerite des Princesses* [Ed. Ruth Thomas. Paris: Mouton, 1970] 452).

22. In the Chapter entitled "The Rhetoric of Tears" in his study of Marguerite de Navarre's religious poetry, Robert Cottrell describes the dilemma the poet faces, clarifying exactly what the turn to lachrymal language representation means:

> In the opening three stanzas, Marguerite returns to a double-edged theme that runs through her poetry: although she recognizes the utter inadequacy of fallen language, she cannot remain silent; she is compelled by inner necessity to go on writing. Whereas for Humanists copiousness was a sign of man's fertile mind and inexhaustible creative energy, for Marguerite it signals an ontological flaw. Since the Fall, man has been condemned to language. Marguerite continues to speak, although (or at least claims to know) that words are useless.... Declaring that she finds no solace in language, Marguerite asserts that her chansons are not linguistic structures at all. They rely not on the artificial code of language and textuality, but on the natural code of tears, sighs, and sobs. Weeping is the non-linguistic discourse of the heart. (*In The Grammar of Silence: A Reading of Marguerite de Navarre's Poetry* [Washington DC: Catholic U of American P, 1986], 195–97).

23. Madelein des Roches describes this experience in similar terms. In her physical grief, she discovers that she is stripped of language: "Par le repos perdu j'ay la raison blessée, / J'ay le discours rompu" (Sonnet VIII, 128).

24. Cf. Job 30:27: "My stomach seethes, is never still, / for every day brings further suffering."

25. "La poésie du veuvage ne s'attache guère à rappeler le bonheur enfui, se complait rarement à évoquer la figure de disparu ou sa tendresse protectrice. Elle se détourne du passé pour s'appesantir sur la tristsse présente" (*Images littéraires de la femme à la Renaissance* 58).

Mourning, Myth, and Merchandising

The Public Death of Princess Charlotte

THE OUTPOURING OF PUBLIC GRIEF over the death of Princess Diana of Wales in 1997, and the widespread and often frankly commercial public activities of mourning that were mounted for her, eerily recalled the circumstances nearly two centuries earlier surrounding another Princess of Wales, Charlotte Augusta, in the wake of that princess's untimely death in November 1817. Looking back at that earlier phenomenon through the lens of 1997's events reminds us of the stabilizing and even restorative nature of public mourning rituals. In both cases the activities of mourning, while they of course celebrated and memorialized the object of grief, performed a larger social function in enabling the mourners to participate in the actual and symbolic worth (or import) of the object of those activities. Mourning becomes in these circumstances a public performance in which the distinctions normally separating the elite object of mourning from both the common individual and "the people" collectively are reduced or even nullified and the mourned individual is fused symbolically with the "common" public. The performance of these rituals of mourning is therefore an inherently democratizing one. Moreover, because so much of this mourning activity involves physical objects and artifacts, it is grounded in—and mediated through—a culture of commodities that is driven by commercial consumerism. In such cases, mourning may then often be seen as a ritualized cultural practice by means of which an individual or a social unit "purchases" the gratification that is the unstated object of its acts of empathetic identification with the particular mourned person.

She was Princess of Wales, a highly visible public figure whose appealing manner and fairy-tale marriage had endeared her to a populace increasingly weary of a royal family (and royal establishment) upon whose official behaviour they frowned and for whom their affection had eroded in proportion to the increased stresses produced at home by economic instability and class antagonism and abroad by Britain's uncertain place in the emerging new world order. Her sudden and unexpected death shocked and dismayed the nation, and "England's Hope" (as she was often popularly styled) was transformed overnight into "England's Grief." Especially in death, she seemed "the people's princess," as if the nation had collectively taken her not just into their hearts but into their families. Apostrophized widely in the popular culture as "Albion's Rose" (a term of endearment only partially indebted to the emblematic rose denoting her station as Princess of Wales), she was memorialized within days of her death in prose and verse, in song and visual image, and in a remarkable variety of consumer goods. These latter included print materials like memorial cards, "instant" biographies, and poems, lyrics, and sermons; commemorative ceramic and textile goods imprinted with her image; and metalwork and sculptural artifacts produced with astonishing rapidity. Everywhere schemes took shape to commemorate her virtuous life (and death), her domestic charms, her philanthropy, and the promise of benevolent power and influence that death had cruelly truncated. Her funeral, an elaborately scripted, staged, and choreographed affair, occasioned unprecedented outpourings of heartfelt sympathy from the throngs of mourners who lined the route of her funeral procession. It seemed to many that the nation itself had in some sense perished.

The Princess in question was not Diana, Princess of Wales, whose death and public mourning in 1997 I have deliberately tried to suggest in the preceding paragraph without altering the facts. Rather, she was Princess Charlotte Augusta of Wales, granddaughter of George III and the only child of the Prince of Wales. Her wholly unexpected death on 6 November 1817 as a complication of giving birth to a stillborn son plunged the nation into an orgy of mourning—as well as a crisis of royal succession.[1] The Prince of Wales—then serving as Prince Regent while his royal father wandered the hallways of Windsor Castle, blind and mad, until his death in 1820 elevated the Prince to the throne as George IV—would have no other legitimate child, in consequence of his messy public separation from his royal consort, Caroline of Brunswick. Famously unpopular with the general public, the Prince Regent could by late 1817 scarcely venture out without being subjected to indignities ranging from hisses, groans, and catcalls to hurled potatoes.[7] The disreputable and discredited Caroline, by 1817 already packed off to the Continent and made the subject of elaborate hypocritical inquiries into her conduct, was scarcely more popular—except as she could be paraded physically or symbolically in public or press as a further humiliation to the despised Regent.

Charlotte, on the other hand, was warmly embraced by the British public by 1816, when she married Prince Leopold of Saxe-Cobourg, the uncle of Albert of Saxe-Gotha who later wed Queen Victoria. Perhaps the couple's warm reception was simply a matter of the British public's choosing what today would be called "family values" in preference to the seeming moral vacancy of the ruling members of the royal family. Certainly the model of domestic accord and model citizenship presented by Charlotte and Leopold at their royal villa at Claremont played a large part in the rise in England of the new sort of companionate marital relationships that soon became—at least in principle—the model for the emerging bourgeois family. This paradigm, which assigned the woman the organizing, nurturing function that Coventry Patmore later called "the angel in the house" in counterpoint to the man's role as provider and disciplinarian, seemed in 1817 to promise a less combative domestic arrangement that many hoped would in some manner also domesticate and "civilize" the nation's behaviour and wean it from the appetite for warmaking it had fed for nearly a quarter century following the French Revolution.

The politically unstable climate in England in the years following Waterloo (June 1815) gave rise to growing public disenchantment with the government and its titular leaders as the English increasingly perceived a crippling lack of national direction or priorities in the wake of the great wave of British nationalism that had crested in the later eighteenth century. The populace was therefore naturally eager for some physical sign of hope. They found it, seemingly, in the Princess Charlotte, who was believed to suffer much: she was denied an establishment appropriate to her position as the Regent's only child, frequently banished from his glittering social functions at Carlton House, denied all but minimal contact with her mother, and denied too the friends and confidants any daughter might desire. The people came, not surprisingly, to see in Charlotte's apparent plight a measure of their own, and because unlike both her parents she was attractive physically and socially, they found it easy to invest her with what we may recognize as essentially *mythic* qualities that reflected their own aspirations as well as their idealistic nationalistic views of "Englishness": liveliness, extroversion, independence of mind and spirit, and an easy commerce with the public generally. Charlotte seemed to break the prototype of the aloof, elitist royal, crossing the traditional gulf (frequently to the astonishment, embarrassment, and dismay of the elite who wished to preserve that gulf) separating the nobility from the rest of society.

How Princess Charlotte's death in 1817—like Princess Diana's nearly two centuries later—became the occasion for elaborate public rituals of mourning, and how those rituals functioned as public *performances* (often in the wholly theatrical sense which that word suggests), reveals much about the cultural dynamics of the two historical moments. At the same time, the remarkable similarities exhibited in these two sets of mourning performances suggest that some aspects of public mourning change very little with time and circumstance. Indeed, it is their stabilizing and even restorative nature that makes the rituals and performances of mourning so effective and so desirable, not just for the mourners but also for those who stand to benefit most from the sedative effects these ritual performances produce. Thus the various public responses to an event like the princess's death can tell us a great deal about how that public is constituted, about what are the sources and applications of its governing values, and about what are its responses to the changing relationship among the private and family-oriented individual, the politically-conscious public citizen, and the members of the royal establishment, viewed both as symbolic figureheads for the government and as "real people." A traumatic public event like the princess's death provides a dramatic *levelling* of social and societal strata, one that in 1817—and again in 1997—furnished fertile ground for writers, publishers, artists, artisans, and other commercial entrepreneurs across a broad social, political, economic, and intellectual spectrum.

One result of such levelling is a democratizing of experience: the princess is perceived to be also a woman, a woman who falls victim to that most common of Regency women's experiences, death in childbirth. Because people in general (and women in particular) relate immediately to this experience as one that intersects with their own, the shared phenomenon serves also to *elevate* the otherwise undistinguished, common person. Something of the same sort occurred in the case of Diana, whose death resulted from the common event of a traffic accident (its extraordinary circumstances notwithstanding). A prominent aspect of the public rituals of mourning involves the transformation of the dead from the status of private individual to public icon. Indeed, the more elevated (and presumably visible) that dead individual happens to be, the more her or his transformation becomes over-coded with mythological status, and the more she or he is consequently invested with the qualities of myth. In the cases of Charlotte and Diana, this mythologizing of history in both personal and public/political terms is apparent in the remarkable profusion of artifacts in all the media that appeared immediately and during the months (and years) following their respective deaths. In 1817, these items, which ranged in price from the very cheap to the very costly, document one of the earliest and most telling examples of the *commodification* for a variously constituted mass audience of historical events and their central figures. The commodification of Diana followed a remarkably similar path in the media-driven modern global community.

Prose works treated the events surrounding Charlotte with great interest. "Historical" works—would-be memoirs, biographies, and the like—manage at once to mythologize *and to politicize* those events. A prose account sold by a radical publisher like William Hone, for instance, relates the "facts" in an entirely different fashion than does one by a pious Tory writer like Thomas Green. Perhaps the most overtly didactic purposes to which the deaths of Charlotte and her child were immediately put are visible in the remarkable number of sermons that were rapidly composed, preached, and published. Chief among the sermonic literature's themes is that of the fragility of human life, coupled with the terrible uncertainty of the human situation, in which one may be plucked suddenly from the comfort and bliss of domestic tran-quillity (as particularly epitomized in culturally-sacred tropes of motherhood) by Death. It is no "mere" woman who is thus snatched in this case, though, but the royal princess, key to the royal succession. Deprived at once of the stillborn male heir and the woman who might otherwise be expected to successfully deliver some future heir and/or assume the throne herself, the *nation* is at once instructed and *chastised*. This latter point was stressed by many authors of sermons who read in Charlotte's death yet another mythic significance: her death became the most terrible of warnings to the nation over its failure as custodian of liberty, freedom, benevolence, and virtue.

Anthologies of extracts from the sermons preached throughout England on the day of Charlotte's funeral and in the days following appeared as well. A good example is Robert Huish's collection, A Sacred Memorial of the Princess Charlotte Augusta of Saxe Coburg Saalfeld (1818), which, in common with the vast quantity of commemorative consumer goods produced on the occasion, capitalized on the general public outpouring of sympathy by connecting the princess's death to the larger universe of human experience, reading it metaphorically as "a link in that vast chain by which thrones, and kingdoms, and nations, are encircled and limited and bound" (vi). This is not to suggest that collections of this sort were without their ulterior motives. In addition to collecting these sermonic extracts, for example, Huish also wrote a long memoir of the princess (Life and Memoirs). The copy in the Royal Archives at Windsor Castle includes a letter from Huish to Sir Benjamin Bloomfield, who had presented the Prince Regent with some sort of petition on Huish's behalf.[3] Huish points out in his letter the extent to which he has put his own "spin" (to use the currently fashionable media term) on history so as to support and promote "the Interests and Dignity of the royal Family." In short, Huish painted a flattering picture of the Regent and his circle precisely because (as the linkage of events in Huish's letter makes clear) it was in his personal interest to do so. Others used Charlotte's death for more avowedly political purposes: a particularly remarkable example is P.B. Shelley's Address to the People on the Death of the Princess Charlotte, composed rapidly in two days and linking Charlotte's death with the executions of the Derbyshire rebels Brandreth, Ludlam, and Turner (victims of government entrapment) in a rhetorical tour de force culminating in an apocalyptic transformation that metamorphoses Charlotte in the figure of an entirely different princess, Liberty, whose death and implied resurrection conclude the essay. In both these instances, the authors manipulate the emotions and the intellects of individual readers whose interest in the facts and circumstances of Charlotte's death provided fertile ground for the cultivation of favour or special interest. Central to this transaction with the audience—whether it be Huish's letter to the Prince Regent or a clergyman's sermon to his congregation or Shelley's radically subversive political pamphlet—is the appeal to shared experience that makes the rituals of mourning so cathartic. Your loss is my loss and my loss is your loss, the public performance of the ritual implies; more important, it is our loss and it therefore unites us in and through this performance.

Indeed, it is the *performance* of the mourning ritual, more so than the mere reflection on the person or qualities of the dead individual, that activates the peculiar sedative function of mourning.

The greatest quantity of responses to Charlotte's death took the form of commemorative poems that number into the hundreds in surviving copies and that appeared in the periodical press, in slim volumes, on broadsheets, and as memorial cards and other devices intended for purchase by even the poorest members of society who were assumed (correctly, it appears) to be willing to part with a penny or two for a memento of the dead princess. Their modest investment inserted these humble purchasers into the general community of sentiment, sympathy, and suffering whose individual social, economic, political, religious, and class differences were for the most part transcended through their joint participation in the shared consumer activity of public mourning. This, too, involves a sedative effect, in that it is naturally more difficult to maintain one's antipathy—however justified and longstanding it may be—to another whose grief (and ritualized mourning) so clearly parallels one's own. This is one reason why the Prince Regent was not averse to the elaborate staging involved with Charlotte's funeral procession at Windsor, a performance that involved a torchlight procession attended by throngs of spectators/mourners. Whatever their ill will toward to Regent (and his unsteady government), their own participation in this public performance unavoidably made them *de facto* co-mourners with the Regent, the royal establishment, and the nation as a whole. Of course, the Prince Regent—foolish, but no fool—appreciated this fact and willingly capitalized in just this fashion on the death of his only child.

The memorial poetry occasioned by Charlotte's death takes several forms. Some treat the princess's death as at once a national catastrophe and a powerful warning to England. As in the sermonic literature, this warning is multifaceted: admonition for perhaps celebrating too well—and feeling too secure—in the aftermath of Waterloo, *memento mori*, and commemoration of the personal and public virtues embodied both in the actual person of the princess and in the image of her that had been fostered among the public. In the poems, the dead princess is repeatedly represented in what quickly come to be stock images like the rose—nipped in the bud or, more often, severed from its stem, along with a bud emblematic of her stillborn son— or a star in the night sky (alluding at once to her place in heaven and her nighttime death). Widely apostrophized as "Rose of England," Charlotte is also "England's (or Britannia's) Hope," now blasted—like the people's hopes with which she had been popularly identified—by her sudden and unexpected death.[4]

As has happened in the past several years with details that have been related in competing authorized and unauthorized biographies of Princess Diana, the element of competition among authors to outdo one another in their tributes to Princess Charlotte also contributed to the creation of myth. Many "prize poems," for instance, resulted from competitions on the subject of her death (as had been the case also with her marriage the previous year). Inevitably, poets drew ever more ambitious rhetorical and figurative pictures of Charlotte, her life, and her national significance, linking her with the conventions of "high" art including the epic and, perhaps surprisingly, the pastoral (drawing upon details of her married life at the royal couple's home, Claremont). These poets invested Charlotte with the symbolic, allegorical, and mythic attributes associated with the epic and pastoral traditions, in the process merging artistic and mythologic/iconographic tropes and traditions with temporal public events.

The range of sentiment expressed—and the range of readerships addressed— in the poems on Charlotte's death are reflected also in the postures assumed by their real and invented authors, which range from clergymen and university dons and students, through public figures of one sort or another, to poets who identified themselves variously as "an old seaman," "a shepherd," or the ubiquitous "A Lady." At the same time, the titles of many of these poems betray their didactic intent, as is apparent from titles such as "The Princess's Tomb: A Dialogue for the Nursery" or "Hymn, sung at the Asylum for Female Orphans." Over and over, poems dwell on the theme of greatness missed, of hopes dashed, of promise abruptly truncated:

> Could wisdom soar through time's domain[,]
> Know what will be, and what had been,
>   Had Charlotte liv'd to sway;
> How chang'd would find the course of things,
> The fates of Kingdoms and of Kings,
>   Fix'd on her mortal day[.]
>
>   (H. C. *Elegy* l. 30–35)

The common thread in all such elegiac discourse is that the princess is irreplaceable, and that her death leaves the world irreversibly diminished. This concentration of signification in the persons of a few public luminaries reflects an important shift in eighteenth-century European thinking about affectivity. Previously, affectivity—the power to express, or to generate expressions of, powerful feeling—was diffused widely among members of society, whereas by the early nineteenth century that affectivity was coming to be concentrated on a few select individuals, who were consequently regarded as "exceptional, irreplaceable, and inseparable" (Ariès 472). In this respect, as in many others, the responses to Princess Charlotte's death are strikingly reliable indicators of significant changes at work in the cultural dynamic of a nation—and a national consciousness—that was undergoing a self-refashioning in the wake of both the Enlightenment and the destabilizing social, political, and technological revolutions to which it gave birth.

One poem that was frequently quoted and excerpted in print was *Sincere Burst of Feeling!*, which was also broken up into three sections when it was included in one of the major anthologies of memorial poetry, John Gwilliam's *A Cypress Wreath*, where the thirteen-page poem is called "a little piece of great poetic merit" (100).[5] The poem, which comprises eight stanzas of various length filled with exclamation points, proceeds in three movements, each beginning with the apostrophe "Daughter of Joy!" The first movement, which explicitly links Charlotte's marriage and her death, features rhetorical questions of the sort common to the memorial poems: "Hath Hymen dug, alas! thy tomb, / And widowed COBURG's Princely bed?" "Is CHARLOTTE dead?" (5) Rejecting those poets who would memorialize Charlotte for "venal passion" (hence the title's declaration that this poem is a *sincere*— not a merely opportunistic—effusion), the speaker observes that "Poesy's a sorry thing, / Unless inspired from Heaven!" and calls therefore for a Muse to "touch the Lyre with seraph-might, / In soothing condolence!" or, in order to assuage grief temporarily, to "tell how Rapture paused awhile, / Till Beauty grac'd the Throne!" (7):

For she was sprung of Royal Blood,
    And more than Royal mind!
With heavenly excellence endued,
    That gloried to be kind!

In Charlotte's widely reputed kindness ("Delighting to do good!"), the speaker emphasizes one of the many domestic virtues for which Charlotte is made to stand in the memorial testaments. Moreover, the poem quickly shifts to the royal couple's domestic bliss, which the public had found so attractive:

> Then pure felicity for Them
> > Had still increasing charms—
> For *Home* was both the Diadem,
> > And motto of their Arms! (9)

But the end of the first movement marks the death first of "CHARLOTTE's Son" and then of the "Hope" that had been left behind in her briefly surviving body, "leaving none / To chear [sic] the Patriot mind!" (10). In thus rhetorically fusing the speaker's mourning posture with a patriotic impulse, the author implies that just as Charlotte's role was both domestic (private) and national (public), so is the performance of grieving both individual (private) and communal (public) and therefore equally patriotic.

The second movement again presents the princess's public attributes within the context of her personal and matrimonial qualities:

> Daughter of Joy! With Spirit pure,
> > And beauteous royal Form –
> Thy loveliness might not endure
> > Affection's tender storm!
> ...
>
> And LEOPOLD was thy maiden choice –
> > Unbiassed by controul:
> He shunned with thee unmeaning toys,
> > For Sympathy of Soul[.] (11–12)

Here are only thinly veiled references to Charlotte's earlier notorious (and publicly popular) rejection of the marriage with the young Prince of Orange her father had attempted to arrange, as well as to the couple's lack of interest in the ostentation and "toys" popularly associated with the Prince

Regent and his circle. From here it is only a short step to a passage that demonstrates the levelling effect I have already mentioned upon people whose social status is entirely unlike Charlotte's but whose experience as human beings is wholly comparable:

> For Sympathy the Soul hath bound
> In universal woe;—
> The haughty, meek, obscure, renowned,
> One face of feeling show.
> The matron, while her sorrows flow,
> With intermittent sigh—
> Bewails, a Mother thus should go
> On giving birth to vanished joy!
> And maiden beauty there is seen
> To dread the troth she gave—
> And weep how short a space between
> The Altar and the Grave! (14–15)

This movement then concludes with the assembled mourners committing the dead princess to her grave; trusting in God and in the salvation "promised to the Just" by his Son, they pray,

> "And with such Hope in MERCY's Throne,
> We yield this virtuous, blessed ONE,
> With sorrow to the dust!" (16)

The final, and briefest, movement (a single stanza), is at once retrospective and predictive:

> ...what avails Devotion's tear
> On lost Affection's awful bier!
> Thy MEMORY will live for ever—
> In other hearts than those of favour;
> For fondness will the theme prolong
> In tender tale, and plaintive song. (17)

Note the significant point made here about who will keep alive the memory of the princess *and the values for which she stood*: those who are "out of favour" and whose art forms are the "tale" (i.e., oral literature) and the "song" (another medium still associated particularly with the common people). In other words, she will be—in her death, in the rituals of mourning, and in the hearts of her mourners—the *people's* princess, just as work after work had styled her as "A Nation's Hope" (5). This point is underscored in dramatic fashion in the poem's concluding lines. Referring to his (or her) own inspiring Muse, the speaker exclaims:

> She [the Muse] gloried in thy Spirit high,
> With all a Freeman's ecstacy!
> And poured this tributary theme
> With all a Patriot's pure esteem –
> Lamenting much, with all forlorn,
> Thy Death, in Beauty's blooming morn
> She drops the pen, most truly Thine,
> THOU FAIREST, FADED HOPE OF BRUNSWICK'S ROYAL LINE! (18)

The pointed linkage of terms like "Freeman" and Patriot" here at the end, in such a prominent position, gives a powerful political and social charge to the poem's conclusion. It renders the entire poem—and the consolidated consciousness of the implied community of mourners who participate in its sentiments through their individual and collective acts of reading and therefore of "performance"—very much a populist manifesto. In this poem, as in so many other literary and extra-literary artifacts that were produced on the occasion, there is an implied democratization at work, one that appropriates the princess, her life, her experience, and her symbolic significance for the majority of the populace rather than for the elite coterie ("other hearts than those of favour") at the same time that it extends to her the eminently human, domestic values which that majority embraces and which differentiate her (and them) from the despised court society whose misshapen values her presence served to emphasize.

While there is of course much bad verse among the many tributes to Princess Charlotte from authors who are today largely unknown to us, there exist nevertheless poems of real accomplishment, poems that are interesting technically as well as intellectually, poems whose sincerity and eloquence transcend the seemingly exhausted rhetoric and the figuration of postured sentimentality and exaggerated grief. It is worth noting, too, that publicly visible poets like Anna Letitia Barbauld, Leigh Hunt, Felicia Hemans, and Robert Southey published noteworthy poems on the occasion, while others like Byron incorporated Charlotte's life and death into poems on quite other subjects (like Canto IV of *Childe Harold's Pilgrimage*). Because memorial poems were so numerous, and because they continually reworked familiar iconographic and rhetorical tropes, they inevitably began to have about them the repetitiveness of ritual expression, which helps to explain how and why they reflected the immediate cultural response to Charlotte's death even as they inevitably helped to shape that response. And, of course, all this reiteration served a performative function in that the reading activity itself produced for the readers a sedative and restorative stability, with each reiteration (and variation) augmenting the consoling, communitarian nature of a shared activity, even when that activity was carried out in physical privacy.

Treatments of the death of Princess Charlotte in the extra-literary arts—including the decorative arts—offer other interesting opportunities to examine the cultural diffusion of a popular mythology as part of the public performance of the rituals of mourning. Of particular interest are visual works intended for popular consumption. The many memorial paintings, drawings, and engravings that followed Charlotte's death build upon a tradition of portraiture that included the iconographically interesting early portrait of the infant Charlotte by Richard Cosway (engraved by Bartolozzi and published in May 1797) and the delightful portrait of the young Charlotte by Sir Thomas Lawrence (1806). Of course, the memorial prints emphasize what is inherent also in the literary works, and what is epitomized in the two-line inscription on Richard Corbould's 1817 engraving:

She was a nation's hope—a nation's pride;
With her that pride has fled—those hopes have died!

Corbould's engraving features a disconsolate Britannia weeping over Charlotte's tomb and funerary urn, surrounded by suggestive iconographic details that include her shield and helmet and a lily, while above her hovers a rose-garlanded bust-portrait of Charlotte, surmounted with a halo-like ring of stars from which light radiates downward. Still more extravagant commemorative engravings exist, like the *Apotheosis* by "Lieutenant Read" (1818) whose iconographic program was explicated by a printed key. In other prints both the pose of Charlotte and her child and the iconography of the scene are unmistakably indebted to the Renaissance visual tradition of (Roman Catholic!) Madonnas. In drawing in this fashion upon a visual tradition for their central image, they injected into the Charlotte mythology yet another element that conferred upon her at least an allusive relationship with the Mother of God—a point that, despite its religious heterodoxy— was not without political significance for nationalistic British citizens who had grown accustomed to regarding themselves in terms of the New Israel.[6] Moreover, in creating these images intended for public circulation rather than for wholly private consumption, producers of these goods kept in the public view both the *object* of the mourning and the performative aspects of the mourning rite. A modern analogy exists in the many postage stamps commemorating Princess Diana; while many of these are of course aimed purely at private stamp collectors, the many such stamps that enter the mail serve to keep alive the image(s) of—and therefore the process of mourning for—the perished princess.

Charlotte was also depicted on many other sorts of consumer goods, from transfer-printed ceramic pieces (like tea services) to commemorative coins, textiles (printed scarves and ribbons were especially popular, the Regency counterparts to silk-screened Princess Diana T-shirts and the like), and sculptures like the lavish monument at St. George's Chapel, Windsor, which was financed by individual subscriptions of no more than a pound and whose installation in the relatively inaccessible chapel at Windsor angered the subscribers (who may have been "paid off" in the form of rather unsatisfactory engravings of the sculpture installed *in situ*). That many of these commemorative items were also produced in forms which the general public could readily afford further reinforced the sense among the people that the princess was "one of them" in a way that her father could not—and would not—be; in possessing commemorative items they seemed to possess *her*, in a manner analogous to the way in which the auditors of the classical epic came to "possess" the epic hero and his or her cultural significance by virtue of the simple fact of their listening to the epic poet's song. In the process of thus "possessing" Charlotte, the people found that they gained also a measure of dignity; this was perhaps particularly so for the women, whose proximity to Charlotte's experience was inevitably reinforced by the memorial items.

As one examines the extraordinary wave of myth-making that attended Charlotte's public life and death in various segments of Regency English culture, one begins better to appreciate the intellectual, spiritual, and cultural impulses that drive the mythologizing of a popular subject through the rituals of public mourning in times of domestic instability and crisis. One comes, too, more clearly to recognize the public function of popular mythology, which overlays the events of history with additional layers of theatricality (or "performance" and spectacle), ritual behaviour, and moral and spiritual earnestness.

This theatricality is readily apparent. Over and over the death of the princess is "staged," for instance, as a melodramatic deathbed conversation in which the young princess admonishes her dashing young husband, Prince Leopold (who was not in fact present when she died) to bear his loss with fortitude and to play his appropriate role in this great moral drama. The heart-wrenching (or heart-numbing) sentimental excesses that typify these deathbed scenes are directly related both to the rising popularity in British theatre of melodrama (especially the domestic sort) and to the overt theatricality of Regency culture generally as we see it reflected in figures like Beau Brummell, Lord Byron, Lady Caroline Lamb, and of course the Prince Regent himself. But we need to consider also the growing cultural value placed upon "the domestic virtues."

In the "domestic virtues" which the public increasingly associated with Charlotte; in the "romantic" nature of her storybook marriage to Leopold of Saxe-Coburg; in the couple's serene retirement to rural domesticity at Claremont (whence she might emerge to distribute bibles or to express concern for local children); and in her pregnancy and imminent motherhood the public glimpsed a reaffirmation of life and domesticity not unlike what late twentieth-century culture has called (not without trouble) "family values" or "traditional values," and which was already in 1817 becoming central to the emerging bourgeois family ethic that would form so large a portion of Victorian culture.[7] The happy union, played out both in the Edenic confines of their retreat at Claremont and in the popular mythology of the press and the popular arts, presented the British people with an alternative to the excesses of the Prince Regent and his circle epitomized in his fantastic Royal Pavilion at Brighton, his luxurious existence at Carlton House (while his poor mad father walked the halls and terraces of Windsor), and his own spectacularly failed marriage. Charlotte's pregnancy, which was followed eagerly in the press, brought her nearer both the sentimental hearts of the people and the actual experience of British women generally. Her wholly unexpected death was devastating, both to the hope that had been constructed around her figure and to the associated sentimental mythology that had been generated—in no small part at the prompting, even the deliberate manipulation, of those who had already recognized the potential for profit that lay in the commodification of the princess.

The dead princess is presented repeatedly in poetry and prose as a moral exemplar. But the significance of her exemplary life is magnified by the fact that she was not just a woman but also the princess and the woman who might be queen. Indeed, it was in this double role that Princess Charlotte came to bear such significance—and such symbolic utility—for writers and rhetoricians of all parties. The astonishing focus on the domestic details of her life and death, and in particular the emphasis on her marriage, her pregnancy, and her death specifically in childbirth, help us now, at the distance of nearly two centuries, to recognize in the public treatment of her experience the beginnings of an ideology of woman and of family that would become the defining one for Victorian and post-Victorian England— and indeed for much of Western culture generally. In his introductory remarks in *A Sacred Memorial of the Princess Charlotte Augusta of Saxe Coburg Saalfeld*, Huish locates in the person of the princess "an epitome of all the virtues that could adorn the woman, or the Christian" (iv) and it is appropriate to observe the rhetorical structuring of his comment. For while the ostensible focus of the sentence in which these words appear is the figure of Charlotte, their position at the very end of a long and much-modified sentence gives them the added rhetorical force of summation and culmination. Significantly, it is not in her public role as princess that Charlotte is last seen here, but rather in her *rhetorical function* as "epitome" of all those virtues. Moreover, the rhetorical structure of the sentence directs us not to Charlotte herself but rather to "the woman" and "the Christian." In other words, Huish's rhetoric is directed less toward Charlotte than toward the reader, who is provided in these introductory remarks with a sort of ideological "filter" through which to pass the excerpts that make up the body of

Huish's anthology. Huish is, in effect, invoking both the dead princess and her pious eulogists in the construction of a new ideological model of the feminine, of woman.

Indeed, deflecting the mourner's attention away from the physical reality of the dead princess's body and instead toward her abstract, emblematic attributes is entirely consistent with western attitudes toward the death of women. As Elisabeth Bronfen has observed, because the fear of death is so strong in European culture, the physical corpse—especially of a woman— has largely been made a taboo, so that any depiction of female death is fraught with contradictions, not the least of which is the frequent recurrence of "narratives about experiences of the sublime at the sight of a corpse." Bronfen locates the resolution to this contradiction in an important shift in aesthetics that becomes apparent during the Romantic period in England, when the artist (or indeed the public memorialist generally) draws on the "fact" of the dead beloved for the inspiration that leads to the production of a "textual copy of the beloved" that provides a vicarious experience for artist and audience alike while at the same time creating a psychological and *aesthetic* distance between the spectator's experience and the physical, bodily reality of the dead princess (60, 365).

In his prefatory remarks, Huish goes on to stress "the personal character, and the domestic virtues of the amiable and beloved object of our regard" (iv). The language Huish uses here specifically casts Charlotte as "viewed object," as the object of a universal cultural gaze that at once objectifies and consumes her by translating her personal (or physical) being into a set of abstractions that are then categorized and prioritized by the very language Huish himself employs. This phenomenon strikingly anticipates Bronfen's point that "what is plainly visible—the beautiful feminine corpse—also stands in for something else" (xi) so that in a paradoxical fashion we are enabled to "read" in the visible that which is not visible. Indeed, remarkably little of the writing that appeared after her death *really* focuses on her actual private, personal character, however many the details and anecdotes about Charlotte that it includes. Rather, and especially in the sermons, this writing consistently uses personal details as points of departure for observations and exhortations that have more to do with defining and directing the *social* (or societal) character of English readers and the collective *national* character of English citizens. Moreover, Huish's word, "amiable"—a word that recurs countless times in both the titles and the main texts of sermons, poems, and other written memorials—ascribes to Charlotte both a pliability and an attractiveness of character that is not entirely in keeping with facts.

To some, Charlotte may indeed have been amiable, but to others she was headstrong, opinionated, and transgressive. Wellington, for instance, regarded her death as "a blessing to the country," and Lord Holland had accused her of "a love of exaggeration, if not a disregard of truth [and] a passion for talebearers and favourites" (Hibbert 102). Therefore, for Huish to render her "amiable" by means of language was to subjugate and "civilize" her (and her behaviour) for rhetorical purposes. This was, after all, an age not much inclined to respect or admire eccentricity and fierce independence in the women it cast as its objects of regard or affection. Wild eccentrics like Caroline of Brunswick (or Lady Caroline Lamb, for that matter) may have held a certain charm for a public appreciative of oppositional spectacle, as the Queen Caroline affair would demonstrate, but that public tended not to install such images of womanhood in its common estimate of the domestic circle—as wife, as mother, as sister, or as daughter.

Further still, the princess's public function as icon is made manifest here and elsewhere in the use of telling phrases like Huish's reference to her as the "beloved *object* of our regard" (my emphasis). For one thing, the expression denotes a one-way street: regarded by the public gaze, the princess is herself rendered silent, objectified, depersonalized. Only in words, in images, in rhetoric, and in the myth that is being manufactured by those intent upon commodifying her, is Charlotte kept "alive." And anything that she may have to "say"—any "speaking" that she may do—is ventriloquistic subterfuge: it is the voice of others who attribute a form of "speech" to her in the guise of actions and significations which they themselves assign to her dead body and her living image.

Hence the significance of Huish's remark that "the character of this illustrious and virtuous Female should be handed down, as the brightest pattern of moral excellence, of conjugal affection, and of strict conformity to the dictates of her God" (v). Huish refers not to the princess (nor does the remainder of the paragraph contain any such reference) but to the generalized and capitalized "Female," who is exhibited, *seriatim*, as an exemplar of "moral excellence," proper wifely behaviour, and absolute obedience to authority. These traits would come in the Victorian period to be precisely those that characterized the exemplary "angel in the house" as the dominant patriarchal culture would define them and as they would be objectified in the arts, in the home, and in more broadly public social and political institutions.

The cultural needs that encourage and nurture popular mythologies of the sort that sprang up around Princess Charlotte are grounded in personal needs that govern the hopes and aspirations of individuals in their personal, often isolated and alienated, lives. These needs are projected in the form of public cultural idols that are then invested with characteristics that reflect those of the private individuals themselves. The public figures play out, at the level of popular myth, the largely unrealized desires and aspirations of the public(s) to whom the avenues to power, influence, heightened experience, and adventure are largely closed. At the same time, in the misfortunes, reversals, and even the deaths of those public icons, the private individuals are able to trace the lines of their own experiences and in the process draw comfort from the narrowing of the gap that separates the mythic figure from the mortal individual. Paradoxically, the result is that both are dignified and valorized by the process. This is one reason why the exercises of mourning for Princess Diana that received such prominent coverage in the media in 1997 were both so widespread and so seemingly spontaneous. Studying the circumstances of Princess Charlotte's life and death nearly two centuries ago helps us appreciate more fully why this is so and, in the process, enables us better to understand both the continuing cultural impulse to mythologize historical phenomena and the diverse but inextricably interrelated contexts in which that mythologizing activity occurs within the formalized public performances of the rituals of mourning.

———

THE PARALLELS BETWEEN the exercises of public mourning for these two princesses are indeed many. When John F. Kennedy was assassinated in 1963, cultural historians and popular journalists alike itemized numerous parallels with the assassination of Abraham Lincoln almost exactly a century earlier: Both presidents were killed by shots to the head, each was succeeded in office by a man named Johnson, etc. History, it would seem, does indeed have an eerie way of repeating itself. In the cases of the Princesses Charlotte and Diana, their deaths were followed by public mourning that included sharp criticism of the Royal Family, who were in each case criticized for apparent failures to appreciate, respect, and nurture the young princess properly. In each case loud public outcries accompanied the apparent miscarriage of official plans for appropriate public memorials: each princess was promised an easily accessible public monument (for which individual small contributions were solicited and accepted) and yet the principal memorial was in each case appropriated by the princess's family and erected in that family's private space. The circumstances of the two deaths were of course worlds apart: one died early in a happy marriage as a result of unanticipated complications of childbirth, while the other's death followed her marriage's failure and her own breakneck midnight attempt to outrun the relentless *paparazzi*. Oddly, the widespread public grieving proved in each case to be comparatively short-lived. By 1819 England was on to other, more pressing domestic crises that culminated (politically) in August 1819 in the "Manchester Massacre" (or "Peterloo") and, soon afterward, the death of George III in January 1820 and the carnivalesque spectacle of the attempted return of "Queen Caroline" for George IV's coronation in July 1821. Post-Diana Britain also moved on fairly soon to other matters: Northern Ireland remained unresolved, the nation became involved militarily in places like Bosnia, celebrations (and then mourning) for the Queen Mum transpired, and Elizabeth II celebrated historic milestones and made peace with the public concerning Diana. Perhaps it was their very *popularity*—their immediate and palpable connection to *ordinary* citizens—that ensured the relatively rapid passing of the two princesses from the front page. Even as the twenty-first century dawns uncertainly, the general populace—and their cultural icons—continue to observe history more from the sidelines than from the forefront.

NOTES

1. The commodification of the dead princess has not until recently been sufficiently appreciated, either by traditional historians or by contemporary cultural historians.

Esther Schor's discussion in *Bearing the Dead: The British Culture of Mourning from the Enlightenment to Victoria* (Princeton: Princeton UP, 1996) goes farther than even the several modern biographies of Charlotte—see Thea Holme, *Prinny's Daughter* (London: Hamish Hamilton, 1976); Alison Plowden, *Caroline and Charlotte: The Regent's Wife and Daughter, 1795–1821* (London: Sidgwick and Jackson, 1989)—and members of her family, but Charlotte still receives only a chapter's notice there, and Schor's focus is largely upon the verbal arts. For the fullest discussion of the subject see Stephen C. Behrendt, *Royal Mourning and Regency Culture: Elegies and Memorials of Princess Charlotte* (London: Macmillan, 1997).

2. Marc Baer discusses the potato incident in his introduction to *Theatre and Disorder in Late Georgian London* (Oxford: Clarendon Press, 1992). Though its subject is seemingly distant from that of the present essay, Baer's study of the performative theatricality of public group behaviour during the Regency offers an interesting analogy to the group behaviour that is explored in what follows here.

3. The letter quoted here is inserted in the Royal Archives copy at Windsor Castle, classification number III 3 D / 1052522a.

4. See the dramatic visual presentation of this metaphor in the memorial print by P.W. Tompkins, *The Royal Rose*. Inscribed "London. Published Dec. 16, 1817, by P.W. Tompkins, 53, New Bond Street." In the inscription at the bottom of the print, Tompkins (who is credited with engraving the print "from the life by Henning") is called "Engraver to Her Majesty." A copy of this print is in the Royal Archives at Windsor Castle.

5. Although the title page of *A Cypress Wreath* furnishes no author's name, I have attributed the collection to Gwilliam because many of the poems in the volume are identified with his name and because he is also the only poet whose name is mentioned prominently on the title page. This volume is not to be confused with one that was roughly contemporary, *The Cypress Wreath*.

6. On the currency of this notion, see Linda Colley, *Britons: Forging the Nation, 1707–1837* (New Haven: Yale UP, 1992).

7. Indeed, already in 1812 Felicia Hemans, the poet whose works would unfortunately become inextricably linked by many of her contemporaries and successors with the very essence of what were purported to be women's sentiments (indeed with woman's very soul), had published a volume bearing the telling title of *The Domestic Affections* (London: T. Cadell and W. Davies, 1812).

Adam's Mourning and the Herculean Task in *Adam Bede*

THIS PAPER EXPLORES and delineates the work of mourning as it is depicted in George Eliot's *Adam Bede*. Adam's robust and energetic work is reflected by Adam himself as he reminisces, reflects and articulates his transformative processes; by Elizabeth, his mother, as she reveals the complexity of the family dynamic; and by the collective community as it reacts to and offers commentary on the accidental drowning of the Bede family patriarch. To further illuminate the intricacies of this bereavement, this essay will consider the impact of Hetty's deception and the Captain's defection on Adam as his sorrow is further exacerbated and his resolve more vigorously challenged.

The relationship between Mary Ann Evans's grief at the death of her father, Robert Evans, and the creation of *Adam Bede*, as well as the connection between the author's mourning and that of her protagonist, will be explored, raising the issue of the links between the textual work of mourning and biography. The contributions of contemporary grief counsellors about the nature of healthy grief in relation to pathological grief speak directly to Adam's "case." In bringing their observations and prescriptions to bear upon the ambiguous nature of Adam's mourning, the evolution and resolution of Adam's sorrow will be examined more fully, resulting in a finer appreciation of the muscularity of his struggle.

George Eliot fashions a stalwart hero, moulds him out of the sturdy stuff of the Saxon peasantry, and sets him a task of Herculean proportions. His work is to mourn the father that he did not love and to mourn him with vigour. For Adam Bede, on finding his father's sodden body in the brook beneath the willow, is required to do combat; he is called to face whatever is base, whatever is ignoble in his soul, and to engage it. And it is upon this grim contest that the novel rests.[1]

To Eliot the work of mourning is no light matter. It is through mourning that Adam learns to see himself with awe-full clarity and it is through grief that he is both cursed and blessed. For mourning, like the angel who comes to wrestle Jacob, bestows both a gift and a wound. The gift is conferred neither for passive enjoyment nor for solitary reflection. Like Jacob, Adam is expected to respond with energy and verve. Now that the veil has been lifted and Adam's sight has been rendered keen, the old terrain that he was wont to travel appears strangely altered. He must learn to negotiate his life's path anew pebble by irksome pebble. It is his work.

Neither must Adam neglect the wound for it is left to him to excavate its nethermost regions, to identify its core, and to dislodge the shrapnel that retards its healing.[2] The man is not meant to hide away and lick his wounds. He is called to action. If grief has laid its silver talents at his door, Adam will bury them at his peril. For it is not merely the relationship with his father, Thias, that he is called to tackle but also the hardness that will come to poison his perception of his beloved, Hetty, and later drive him to denounce his childhood friend and comrade, Captain Donnithorne.

But grief is more than gift, and it is more than process. Once neatly codified, it becomes chimeric. It is greater than the sum of its parts for Adam tells that "there's things go on in the soul, and times when feelings come into you like a rushing mighty wind, as the Scripture says, and part your life in two a'most, so as you look back on yourself as if you was some-body else" (177). As the tale is spun, mourning is productive—for Adam is not simply made giddy by emotion; he becomes, as he laments, a man who will never meet life again on the same terms. In latter days, when he encounters a yet more formidable adversary, we hear him cry, "God help me! I don't know whether I feel the same towards anybody: I seem as if I'd been meas-uring my work from a false line, and had got it all to measure over again" (306), and we know that he is one who has "not outlived his sorrow" (467–68). We perceive that mourning's task is to groom and to coach, and to mould and equip him for the soul-feat yet to come. Adam must prepare himself for metamorphosis—the heart of stone that now inhabits his breast must be rejected and routed out, and the heart of flesh, that he has caused of late to wither, must be nourished and cultivated so that it will grow and thrive and swell into that place.

We begin to see the protracted nature of Adam's mourning as we watch it meander through the hills and the hollows of his benighted life. And once introduced to the dimpled[3] Hetty at work pressing her cheeses, to the trusted friend who will savage the maid and to Stoniton prison where Adam's heart will break at the news of Hetty's fate, we will comprehend the connection between Adam's early grief and the misfortunes yet to befall him. We will then return, in the fullness of this mourning circle, to the grove where Adam takes Arthur's soft white hand in his hearty grasp, and in forgiving, experiences the re-emergence of boyhood affection (451): "sorrow lives in us," claims the narrator, "as an indestructible force, only changing its form, as forces do, and passing from pain into sympathy" (468).

Having succeeded in persuading us to wind our collective heart strings around the wretched Adam, the narrator obliges us to watch the pain-filled progression of his ensuing metamorphosis. Knowing the intensity of feeling to which he thrills as the gentle maid of the Hall Farm links her trusting arm in his, we stand aghast as the "sweet odour" of Adam's affection (214–16) begins to reek and putrefy with the slow and tortuous apprehension of her treasonous behaviour. Not merely bereft at her loss, not merely wounded by her rejection, Adam contrives to turn his heart to stone. And here—impenetrable, adamantine, immovable—he comes to rest. But here he will not stay for though he has cast her off, and shut up his heart against her, Adam cannot withstand the horrors of Hetty's abandonment at Stoniton prison. Becoming increasingly distraught at the spectre of her isolation and the torment of her execution, his tears begin to fall, and by virtue of his mourning, the man is granted a heart of flesh.

A similar metamorphosis plays itself out in Adam's rigid rejection of the Captain. Tenderness gives way to repulsion when Adam discovers the baseness of Arthur's behaviour towards Hetty in the wood and its terrible ramifications—for with mind unbalanced and heart broken, the simple maid decides to expose her babe to the elements. Adam is called, once again, to do battle with what is uncompromising and unmalleable in his nature, and it is only when—after the passage of time—he encounters a broken and contrite Arthur, and a haunted and chastened Arthur, that he allows himself to embrace, once more, the older and dearer affection that still lodges within his breast.

In plying her craft, Eliot frames the novel with Adam's illumination and binds it with the concrete stuff of grief. For it is the same Adam who, at the opening of the novel, stands at the water's edge with his mind rushing back over the past in a flood of relenting and pity that we meet again at the end (54). He has been moved to pity the young Arthur in the same way that he came to pity his father:

> It's true what you say, sir: I'm hard—it's in my nature. I was too hard with my father, for doing wrong.... I've known what it is in my life to repent and feel it's too late: I felt I'd been too harsh to my father when he was gone from me—I feel it now, when I think of him. I've no right to be hard towards them as have done wrong and repent. (450)

And as if to underscore the muscularity of Adam's struggle, the narrator sees fit to interject: "Facile natures, whose emotions have little permanence, can hardly understand how much inward resistance he overcame before he rose from his seat and turned toward Arthur" to offer the hand of friendship (450).

What is characteristic of the mourning of Adam Bede is the protagonist's struggle with the hardness that is in his soul. It is a battle that Adam must fight again and again—for his impatience with those who are errant seems to rear its ugly head at every turn. The reader can but sympathize; surely he is provoked beyond bearing. Does not Hetty, the "pink and white" posey of Adam's fragile heart, demonstrate her inconstancy when she deserts her loyal swain without a backward glance? Does not the youthful Captain, the trusted friend of Adam's boyhood, prove himself immoral, self-centred, and woefully irresolute when he seduces the maid and decamps for parts unknown?

Adam is woefully beset by ambiguous relationships so that even his mourning is tainted. George Eliot fashions for Adam Bede a father figure who, though once a respected member of the Hayslope community, turns in his latter years to drink and debauchery. When his lifeless body is discovered beneath the willow, the reader assumes—along with the general population of Hayslope—that Thias has died "in his cups." The village mourns, not for the errant father, but for the beleaguered family who is, by all accounts, "well rid." The wayward Thias has not only shamed the Bede name but also managed to undermine the family economy. When we first encounter Adam, we find him harried with fatigue and frustration but working, nonetheless, all through the night, to finish a coffin his father has promised for daybreak but not yet begun. We watch him simmer and seethe and work off his rage while Seth, not unsympathetic to Adam's bouts of righteous indignation, prays in the kitchen with Lisbeth for "the poor wandering father, and for those who were sorrowing for him at home" (47).

The ambiguity of the relationship is further compounded by the Bede matriarch who, though devoted to her darling Adam, still sees fit to upbraid him:

> I know thee dost things as nobody else 'ud do, my lad. But thee't allays so hard upo' thy feyther, Adam. Thee think'st nothing too much to do for Seth: thee snapp'st me up if iver I find fault wi' th' lad. But thee't so angered wi' thy feyther, more nor wi' anybody else.

> That's better than speaking soft, and letting things go the wrong way, I reckon, isn't it? If I wasn't sharp with him, he'd sell every bit o' stuff i' the yard, and spend it on drink. I know there's a duty to be done by my father, but it isn't my duty to encourage him in running headlong to ruin.... But leave me alone mother, and let me get on with my work. (42–43)

While Eliot characterizes Lisbeth as a whining, manipulative woman whose heart, nonetheless, is in the right place, the reader remains uncertain of her integrity. It is only when the evidence provided by the assorted denizens of Hayslope reveals a Thias who has "done little this ten year but make trouble for them as belonged to him," and is considered by the knowing Mrs. Poyser, at least, to be "better out o' the way nor in" that we come to appreciate the pain of Adam's position (94). For has not Thias been the cause of Adam's reluctance to ask for Hetty's hand? Has not Adam been forced to use his meagre earnings to pay for Seth's substitution in the army? Has he not been forced to buy the precious stock of wood that keeps the business thriving—the same wood that his father would sell for drink if Adam did not remain wary? How, when he has been compelled to assume the position of family patriarch, can he begin to mourn a parent who is little more to him than a recalcitrant child?

There is biographical basis for the fictional depiction of life in the Bede cottage. In the Evans family, it was Mary Ann who was considered to be the recalcitrant child. Years before her father died, an "uneasy truce" was said to have obtained in the household (Adams 10) much like the truce that obtained in the Bede cottage before Thias met his death beneath the watery willow. Ambiguous familial relationships besieged Mary Ann as she grew into womanhood, asserted her independence, and lived to mourn the father she had once so vehemently defied. We can but wonder if the acute pain she experienced in her dealings with the unforgiving Robert Evans informed and shaped the torment she later visited on Adam, and if, in fact, the Herculean task she set Adam to perform was the one she could never, herself, master. Was she, in framing this pathetic tale, working out her own salvation?

We know from her letters to Miss Sara Hennel that while Mary Ann was gratified to find herself in the position of nurse to the dying Robert, she also found him to be a trying patient and confessed that she tried to "look amiable in spite of a constant tendency to look black; and speak gently though with a strong propensity to be snappish" (Paterson 26). Such peevish behaviour, brought on no doubt by worry and fatigue, does not—under normal circumstances—warrant self-reproach, but when our sensitivities are heightened by the death of a loved one, even imagined offenses loom larger than life, and we can only wonder if Mary Ann was given to self-castigation over such momentary lapses. Adam surely was.[4]

Yet we fail to appreciate the narrator's intent if we allow ourselves to dismiss, as of little moment, the propensity for self-reproach that bedevils Adam as he mourns. It is not meant to be taken as evidence of a mere passing fragility or an over-tender conscience. Eliot delineates with care and sensitivity the terrible tension that tears at Adam's internal equilibrium. It unfolds with painstaking clarity as the reader becomes privy to the intricacies of the father-son relationship, for we are told that Adam cannot forget "the night of shame and anguish when he first saw his father quite wild and foolish, shouting out fitfully among his drunken companions.... He had run away once when he was only eighteen, making his escape in the morning twilight" (49). He had returned just as quickly, however, after contemplating the hardships to which he had, by his cowardly defection, consigned his mother and brother, and had come to the conclusion that even though his father would be a sore cross to bear for many a long year to come, he had the health and limbs and spirit to bear it (49–50). We learn as well that the Bede cottage, once a haven of harmony and bliss, came to harbour bitterness and suspicion, for as Adam wended his way homeward at eventide to the waiting Lisbeth who took such pleasure in his coming, he was heard of late to call in a fit of petulance and temper, "Where's father?" (201). Even the Rector, Mr. Irwine, seems to have the true measure of Thias Bede, for when he hears the news of his misadventure, we hear him exclaim: "Poor Old Thias!... I'm afraid the drink helped the brook to drown him. I should have been glad for the load to have been taken off my friend Adam's shoulders in a less painful way. The fine fellow has been propping up his father from ruin for the last five or six years" (62). It is clear that Thias's loss is seen rather as a blessing than as an occasion of deep sorrow for the Bede family. Sympathy obviously rests with Adam, not because he has been bereaved, but because he has carried an impossible load and borne it without complaint. The offer of solace, even from the rector, does not seem to be a priority. Adam, we observe, is made to wait while Irwine and Donnithorne take their luncheon in leisurely fashion and plan a detour to the Hall Farm so that Arthur can see his pups and peek in on Hetty, and so that Irwine can "have another look at the little Methodist who is staying there" (62). As we continue to eavesdrop, we find that the conversation soon shakes off its sombre tones and returns, without missing a beat, to its former note of jocularity.

Adam's equilibrium is not so easily restored, however, for the spectator can neither appreciate nor apprehend the task that this grieving son is obliged to undertake. It requires no effort, on the part of the observer, to dismiss Thias as the load that has been lifted, but Adam must yet reckon with the father who, in happier days, used to boast to his fellows about his little chap's "uncommon notion o' carpentering," the father that once made the wonderful pigeon-house at Broxton parsonage, the father whose side he once so proudly and affectionately ran beside (48–49). As the memories flow thick and fast, Adam's work is to acknowledge and redeem them as he grieves.

No evidence of this subterranean exertion appears visible either to the village or to the grieving son's more intimate comrades, for little is offered to Adam by way of condolence. There is, in fact, a marked absence of anything resembling sympathy. Even though allusions are made to visits to the Bede household, the narrator does not make us privy to the conversations that ensue. It is assumed that Lisbeth will both require and welcome the tender ministrations of the gentle Dinah, but her sons, it seems, are left to their own devices.

The work of mourning, in this Victorian setting, appears to be the work of women—at least in its outward manifestations—as Dinah feels compelled to come to Lisbeth in her grief "in the place of a daughter" when she realizes that the widow is bereft, not only of a husband, but also of female kin (108). While Dinah proceeds to commiserate with Lisbeth and to busy herself about the kitchen, we note that both Seth and Adam are inwardly soothed by her presence. This seems to be a secret that we share with the omniscient narrator, however, for it becomes apparent that the male members of this grieving household are not to have their emotional needs pandered to in any overt fashion though we watch them wander listless and silent through the melancholy rooms of the now-wretched Bede family cottage.

We must not be misled at this point, however, by what appears to be the uninhibited keening of the women and the tight-lipped reserve of the men, for though the outward trappings suggest a rigidly gendered grief,[5] Eliot has not merely sculpted an artless stereotype nor treated us to a Victorian "slice of life." The menfolk may appear to be resigned and the women inconsolable, but it is of no particular significance for we come later to appreciate that Adam's efforts at restraint are every bit as taxing as Lisbeth's outpourings. Adam, though we may not mark it, has already embarked upon the excavation of his soul; he is engaged in covert operations, and as readers we must not allow ourselves to be deceived by facile comparisons.

The general mood of the Hayslope community fails to alert us to Adam's true state. It appears to carry on in cheerful oblivion while volcanic activity erupts with regularity beneath his carefully controlled exterior. Neither, it seems, does the demeanour of those who would be wont to sympathize serve as a cue, for though the men of Hayslope touch their hats and stand respectfully by while Thias is laid to rest by the White Thorn, we soon learn that Bartle Massey—Adam's trusted friend and mentor—is conspicuous by his absence and that the young squire has taken himself off on a fishing trip. Even as Adam walks over to the night school to determine the reason for Bartle's absence—and we note that it is Adam who feels the weight of this responsibility—the condolences he receives are noticeably restrained, if not curt. Ascertaining that it was the mere whelping of his bitch that kept Bartle away, Adam begins, "I was afraid you must be ill for the first time i' your life. And I was particular sorry not to have you at church yesterday." Bartles responds: "Ah, my boy, I know why, I know why.... You've had a rough bit o' road. But I'm hopes there are better times coming for you. I've got some news to tell you. But I must get my supper first, for I'm hungry, hungry. Sit down, sit down" (231). Thias's demise appears to be of so little moment that the subject is dismissed pre-emptively, and Bartle Massey, we suspect, harbours no suspicion of Adam's internal torment. As Adam continues to groan inwardly under the chafing burden of his grief, he does so in solitary fashion. It is only later, when Adam suffers the excruciation of Hetty's imprisonment, that Bartle emerges as loyal friend and comrade. But at this particular juncture, Adam knows no companion in his anguish, and we can but remember the tender solace offered to Lisbeth and mark the inequity.

It must be admitted that Lisbeth invites succour—her tears flowing without check and her plaints and cries seemingly unceasing while Adam, even as he tugs at the sodden body, remains mute, awe-struck. No clear sign of torment is visible save the dishevelled appearance and the oppressive weariness. He does not quarrel and challenge; he does not reminisce and upbraid. He does not, like his mother, find comfort in "Incessant movement, performing the initial duties to her dead with the awe and exactitude that belong to religious rites" (142). For Lisbeth brings out the little store of bleached linen which she had been holding in reserve for her own funeral, she being the eldest by two years, and noticing at the same moment a "long-neglected and unnoticeable rent in the checkered bit of bed curtain" begins to mend it, "for the moments were few and precious now in which she would be able to do the smallest office of respect or love for the corpse, to which in all her thoughts she attributed some consciousness." It seems, the narrator interjects, that "our dead are never dead to us until we have forgotten them" and Lisbeth is soothed by the belief that Thias, although he can be injured and wounded still can also know all her penitence, all her aching sense that the place he left is empty, and can feel all the kisses she bestows on the smallest relic of his presence (102). We are left in no confusion as to the state of Lisbeth's mind. She wears it openly. She keens, not in ambiguity, but in simple heart-wrenching sorrow. For it was never Lisbeth who found it difficult to love the errant Thias. Her regrets, we observe, are irrational, fanciful and short-lived. She reproaches herself for lying snug abed while Thias lay struggling just outside her window, and she bewails the fact that she has been denied the chance to nurse him into a good and proper death. She also reflects affectionately that when "I'd gotten my old man I war worreted from morn till night" but "now he's gone, I'd be glad for the worst o'er again" (110).

Adam, in marked contrast, remains a closed book to those who both know and love him. His back remains confoundedly upright and his manner cool and deferential. The harried state soon passes—Adam turns his attentions once again to the Hall Farm and his precious Hetty and returns to work for he maintains that, "there's nothing but what's bearable as long as a man can work...the best o' working is, it gives you a grip hold o' things outside your own lot" (113). Adam appears, in fact, to return to normality—his self-recriminations at the river bed being nothing more than an aberration not to be repeated in saner moments. If Adam is undergoing inner turmoil, the narrator goes to great lengths to put us off the scent. Having briefly witnessed the macabre scene at the swollen brook, we find ourselves transported to the sleepy village of Hayslope where the narrator begins her introductions. She manages to draw our attention away from the mourning Bedes and into the elegant living room of Broxton Parsonage to meet the Rector, Adolphus Irwine, and the self-indulgent women who inhabit his world. We become captivated by his protégé, the dashing Donnithorne, and follow him gladly to the riotous Poyser household where the lovely Hetty flirts unabashedly in the cool redolence of the farm dairy. We are easily charmed by this vain little creature, and by the time we have been introduced to the young Methodist preacher, all memory of Thias's death and the family's sorrow has been lost to us. Before the action moves full circle and Dinah, learning of Lisbeth's loss, determines to visit her, we become privy once more to the romantic machinations of Hetty's girlish imagination and to the provoking irresolution of Arthur.

Even the funeral is eclipsed by the denizens of Hayslope who, like Hetty, treat the occasion more like a wedding than a funeral. The humour insinuated into the Sunday promenade by the antics of the precocious Totty and her rosy-cheeked brothers—dressed for the event in fustian tail coats and knee-breeches—does not prepare us for the deep rumblings that are about to sound in Adam's simple soul.

It is at this sorrowing moment, nonetheless, with his emotions so keenly compromised by the proximity of his beloved Hetty, that we see the man begin to wrestle, and he wrestles in earnest in his grief work. While considerable time may seem to have elapsed for the reader, for Adam the death was but yesterday. With his voice so hemmed in that he cannot join in the strains of the funeral psalm, we watch Adam become increasingly over-wrought because the "chief source of his trouble and vexation" is forever gone out of his reach and what has been broken can never, now, be mended. He regrets most deeply not having been able to "press his father's hand before their parting," and to say, "Father, you know it was all right between us; I never forgot what I owed you when I was a lad; you forgive me if I have been too hot and hasty now and then!" As the service progresses, Adam's thoughts continue to run on "what the old man's feelings had been in moments of humiliation, when he had held down his head before the rebukes of his son" (195). And the narrator sees fit to interject—if "when our indignation is borne in submissive silence, we are apt to feel twinges of doubt afterwards as to our own generosity, if not injustice; how much more when the object of our anger has gone into everlasting silence, and we have seen his face for the last time in the meekness of death!" (196). While Lisbeth placates herself with happy reminiscences that run on the affection her Thias showed while she, still but a girl-bride, lay weak and frail in childbed—reminiscences that bring her happiness, Adam continues to torture himself with scenes that occasion regret, as he reflects to himself,

Ah, I was always too hard.... It's a sore fault in me as I'm so hot and out of patience with people when they do wrong, and my heart gets shut up against 'em so as I can't bring myself to forgive' em. I see clear enough there's more pride nor love in my soul, for I could sooner make a thousand strokes with th' hammer for my father than bring myself to say a kind word to him. And there went plenty o' pride and temper to the strokes, as the devil will be having his finger in what we call our duties as well as our sins.... It seems to me now, if I was to find father at home to-night, I should behave different; but there's no knowing—perhaps nothing' ud be a lesson to us if it didn't come too late. It's well we should feel as life's a reckoning we can't make twice over; there's no real making amends in this world, any more nor you can mend a wrong subtraction by doing your addition right. (196)

As the narrator observes, "This was the key-note to which Adam's thoughts had perpetually returned since his father's death, and the solemn wail of the funeral psalm was only an influence that brought back the old thoughts with stronger emphasis" (196). While Adam's inner deliberations appear, to the reader, to be both genuine and cathartic, they do not touch on what we know to be reality, for Adam—while excoriating his pride and confronting his "hardness"—does not allow himself to dwell on the fact that Thias was truly wayward. And Eliot, in her rendering of Adam's torment, does not permit a single drop of grace to cool his fevered brow. While the villagers file out of Hayslope church, some of them smiling and winking at their companions, and while the rector intones the "sublime words" of the final blessing—"The peace of God which passeth all understanding" (197), we watch the Bedes wind "their way down to the valley and up again to the old house, where a saddened memory had taken the place of a long, long anxiety—where Adam would never have to ask again as he entered, 'Where's father?'" (201), and in our mind's eye, we see him wince at the very thought.

At this point in Adam's mourning process it appears as though his grief, although still in its earliest stages, is tending towards pathology. Adam cannot rid himself of the notion that he has been too hard. He has begun to brood. We divine, as well, from a previous exchange with Lisbeth, that the Bede family has a dangerous dynamic at work for the narrator has allowed us, once again, to eavesdrop while Adam, thinking of nothing more than his mother's tender feelings, plans to have his father's coffin built in the village out of sight and sound of her hearing. When Lisbeth's learns of the plan, she is defiant: "Nay, my lad, nay...thee wotna let nobody make thy feyther's coffin but thysen?...I wonna ha' nobody to touch the coffin but thee." And as if to underscore her point, she persists: "Nay, nay...I'n set my heart on't as thee shalt ma' they feyther's coffin.... Thee was often angered wi' they feyther when he war alive; thee must be the better to him now he's gone. He'd ha' thought nothin' on't for Seth to ma's coffin" (119). While Lisbeth dotes openly on her beloved Adam and considers Seth to be no more than a soft lad with his head "full of chapellin," it is Adam, nonetheless, who is the target for her wrath (44). And if we were not made a party to much that goes on in the Bede household, it would be easy to misconstrue this interaction for Lisbeth is not dismissing Seth, not treating him as a nonentity, but chiding her *elder* son for his prodigality in matters of the heart, and it is on this same sad note that she persists in pricking him. Seth will continue to remain the one whose affections are taken for granted—the son who can be trampled upon without fear of reprisal or defection. It is Adam, the stalwart, Adam the outwardly upright who is being challenged, at this crucial juncture, to prove his familial affection. By Lisbeth's reckoning, it is time for him to atone. And we come to realize that it is she alone who can plumb his depths and find the canker in his soul.

If Adam is to remain resident in the Bede household, he will be accosted daily by Lisbeth's skilfully manipulative jibes. He will be made to flinch and to shrink as she probes and pokes, with neither conscience nor license, into the deepest and most vulnerable crevices of his wounded psyche. Adam, we perceive, will not be restored to balance and well-being by those who love him. Seth, though he reveres his elder brother to a fault, will dare to neither cross nor challenge him. And Lisbeth shows neither mercy nor good sense.

This being his context, Adam would be placed in a high risk category by psychologists like Lewis R. Aiken who contends that when those who are grieving experience an acute lack of social and emotional support, they are more likely to find their mourning process tending towards pathology (249). Have we not already observed that the familiars of Hayslope both disregard and misread the significance of Adam's turmoil and choose to turn their attention to brighter and better things? On the one hand, Adam's grief is dismissed out of hand and on the other, it is complicated and exacerbated. If that were not enough to signal trouble, Aiken numbers accidental death and unresolved conflicts—including shame—amongst the chief factors that contribute to pathological grieving (249). Adam, we might conclude, has three serious strikes against him.

To further compound Adam's position, it must also be recognized that some grief counsellors place father-son relationships in a separate and distinct category when attempting to elucidate the many subtleties that pertain in the grieving process. In his work in *The Orphaned Adult: Confronting the Death of a Parent*, Rabbi Marc D. Angel places considerable emphasis on the final meeting—be it a deliberate farewell or a chance encounter—that occurs between a parent and an adult child when death is imminent. The image of the last days becomes indelibly engraved on the memory particularly if the farewell has been a hostile or disturbing one and will not be dislodged until time has done its healing work. In his interviews with adult orphans, Rabbi Angel discovered that final words and gestures were reviewed over and over again apparently in the hope of eventually finding consolation: "Every detail," in fact, "seemed to have its own mysterious significance" (68). For those who were burdened, like Adam, with the unbearable guilt that had attached itself to last encounters, Rabbi Angel discovered that a "realistic approach" was the most efficacious—the "lifelong relationship between the parent and child," was to be considered "ultimately far more important than the short period preceding the parent's death" (68). The same raw memory that causes us to wince in the early days of our mourning has the potential to soothe and to heal and console when it is allowed to meander freely through the halcyon days of childhood affection and unencumbered love. And Adam, for all his agonies over the disturbing departure of Thias, for all his regrets over the humiliation he rained repeatedly upon the recalcitrant man-child that was his father, has already travelled this far in his journey. For has he not begun the difficult task of sorting through the past, both recent and distant, and has he not discovered the surprising joy of gentle juxtaposition? We may watch his tears burn hot and heavy at the galling memory of his recent hardness, but we are also made privy to his reminiscences—we are also permitted to watch him frolic in playful pride beside the man he once revered, the parent whose presence he once gloried in, and in our watching, we find hope.

But how are we to understand the guilt that still plagues him? Is Adam tending toward pathology or is he not? David Carroll, in his 1985 treatment of ambiguous grief, claims that "When we brood on what might have been, things get worse psychologically until we become enveloped in a cocoon of recriminations. "Guilt," he contends, "is one of the most insidious effects of grief." Admitting and venting one's anger towards the deceased serves as a "kind of purging mechanism" and is an integral part of the mourning process, especially if the relationship has been a troubled one (344–46). The type of idealization that Adam appears to be engaged in, that produces a "false all-positive portrait of the deceased" (346), will lead inevitably to pathology and not, as we might hope, to health. Elizabeth Kübler-Ross claims that when a traumatic loss has not been fully faced up to and resolved, it can result in various forms of cancer, ulcerative colitis, and depression. "Working it through" is paramount in importance if the grieving one is to avoid later psychosomatic damage (47).

As an antidote, J. Wm. Worden suggests the "reality test": "An inability to face up to and deal with a high titre of ambivalence in one's relationship with the deceased inhibits grief and usually portends excessive amounts of anger and guilt which cause the survivor difficulty" (53). In his therapeutic approach, Worden sets up an empty chair in his office and invites the bereaved to talk directly to the deceased about their thoughts and feelings (74).

But Adam seems to need no intervention—no empty chair in the office— for his internal conversation with the poor drowned Thias has long since flowed without check. Just as the cadence of Joshua Rann's rendition of the psalm rose and fell: "Thou sweep'st us off with a flood: We vanish hence like dreams," so too did the son's outpourings (195).

Adam has made his peace with Thias. He has admitted his hardness, laid bare his soul, and asked for forgiveness. But is that enough? Has he not missed a crucial step? For Adam has not yet articulated Thias's failings. He has not vented. We have not heard him confront the wayward father—to his face—about the defection, the drunkenness, the thievery, the sloth. Worse still, Adam has maintained his guilty stance and guilt, we have been told, can lead to repressed anger and anger to depression and physical illness.

Had we not come upon Adam, in the early pages of the tale, seething against the reprobate that was his father, we might be tempted to entertain the notion that the Adam who later grieved Thias's grisly demise was indeed given to bouts of unhealthy, unhealing, idealization. But such is not the case. We have heard Adam vent, and we have watched him rage and once made privy to that painful scene, we will not forget.

George Eliot understood that engaging in idealization and entertaining feelings of guilt might actually, in circumstances such as Adam's, be both healthy and productive. If we do not allow such a process to take its natural course, if we enter the arena prematurely and declare it to be an unsound practise, if we consider that it is requisite rather to "work through" feelings of ambiguity, then we may well block or at worst disrupt the work of sorrow.

For it lives in us as "an indestructible force, only changing its form, as forces do, and passing from pain into sympathy—the one poor word which includes all our best insight and our best love" (468).

The mourning that Eliot fashions for Adam falls like a grace-filled shower—the very moment Thias is plucked from the brook—annihilating in an instant all that had previously provoked Adam's indignation and imbuing him with pity and tenderness. It works to distill from the father-son relationship whatever, as the narrator of the Epistle to the Philippians suggests, was once true and honourable; whatever was right and pure; whatever was lovely and of good report; whatever was excellent and worthy of praise (ch. 4, v.8), and it enables Adam, as in former times, to dwell on these (117). Having eradicated all bile and bitterness, it serves to illuminate for the grieving son the poisoned part that he has come to play in the Bede family drama. In his retrospection, Adam becomes keenly sensitive to his pride, to his overweening sense of duty, and to his hardness. As the willow wand once rapped smartly at the door of Adam's workshop to alert him to the life and death struggle that was playing itself out in the swollen brook (50), so it raps now at the door of his soul. And this time Adam responds with alacrity, for mourning becomes a provocateur that catapults Adam into the subterranean depths of his being and demands excoriation and transformation.

We see Adam now in his "becoming." He has discovered that "by getting his heart strings bound round the weak and erring, so that he must share not only the outward consequence of their error, but their inward suffering," he can extend enough charity and patience towards his "stumbling falling companions" to enable him to walk with them in the "long and changeful journey" (204). It is with this end in mind that George Eliot has conceived the Herculean task. She believes that humankind must learn to accept and extend the hand of patience and good will towards those fellow mortals who can neither "straighten their noses, nor brighten their wit, nor rectify their dispositions; and it is these people—amongst whom your life is passed—that it is needful you should tolerate, pity, and love." For these are the "real breathing men and women" of our world, and they can be either "chilled by your indifference or injured by your prejudice" or "cheered and helped onward by your fellow-feeling, your forbearance, your outspoken, brave justice" (172). These are the familiars of Hayslope, and indeed of the

Bede family. Although they may be "more or less ugly, stupid, inconsistent people,"—the narrator cries, "Bless us, things may be lovable that are not altogether handsome, I hope?" (172–73).

It is towards refinement of character and renewal of spirit that George Eliot impels her hero. Adam must come to recognize what is ignoble in his soul and work to purge and conquer it. The narrator reflects that

> Deep, unspeakable suffering may well be called a baptism, a regeneration, the initiation into a new state. The yearning memories, the bitter regret, the agonised sympathy, the struggling appeals to the Invisible Right—all the intense emotions which had filled the days and nights of the past week, and were compressing themselves again like an eager crowd into the hours of this single morning, made Adam look back on all the previous years as if they had been a dim sleepy existence, and he had only now awaked to full consciousness. It seemed to him as if he had always before thought it a light thing that men should suffer; as if all that he had himself endured and called sorrow before, was only a moment's stroke that had never left a bruise. Doubtless a great anguish may do the work of years, and we may come out from that baptism of fire with a soul full of new awe and pity. (409–10)

It is not to forge a tougher, more resilient Adam that sorrow is at work, however. It is to forge an Adam who no longer walks so decidedly erect and with such surety of purpose, an Adam who now meanders slowly with his hands thrust into his side pockets and his eyes resting chiefly on the ground (446), an Adam who can no longer suppress a sob at the first approach of sympathy (384), for the products of Adam's mourning are a broken and a contrite heart and an increased capacity for love.

The Adam who is reputed to have a will as well as an arm of iron has used the metal's might against himself. It is not the narrator's intent to change the essence of Adam's character; though his heart strings have been more finely tuned, he remains a man of firm resolve: "for what have we got either inside or outside of us but what comes from God? If we've got a resolution to do right, he gave it to us, I reckon, first or last; but I see plain enough we shall never do it without resolution, and that's enough for me" (178). While we note that Adam's reflections are framed, in this chapter, by a broader discussion of Christian theology, we recognize a complementary sentiment in Feuerbach's work on *The Essence of Christianity*—a text to which the author would have turned just as readily as to the Scriptures for instruction (Myers 25).[6] Feuerbach asks rhetorically:

> When love impels a man to suffer death even joyfully for the beloved one, is this death-conquering power his own individual power, or is it not rather the power of love?...When though sinkest into deep reflection, forgetting thyself and what is around thee, dost thou govern reason, or is it not reason which governs and absorbs thee? ...when thou suppressest a passion, renouncest a habit, in short, achievest a victory over thyself, is this victorious power thy own personal power, or is it not rather the energy of will, the force of morality, which seizes the mastery of thee, and fills thee with indignation against thyself and thy individual weaknesses? (4)

Surely Adam has been both governed and absorbed and has come to gain mastery over himself as his troubles have been compounded. He cries out to Bartle when on the day of Hetty's trial he learns that the Poyser family has deserted her: "They oughtn't to cast her off—her own flesh and blood. We hand folks over to God's mercy, and show none ourselves. I used to be hard sometimes; I'll never be hard again," and the narrator adds, "There was a decision in Adam's manner which would have prevented Bartle from opposing him, even if he wished to do so" (413).

Mourning has done its work. It has bestowed a gift and a wound. It has regenerated Adam and initiated him into a new state. He has evolved into compassion (Bonaparte 185). The mourning that began with Thias's drowning, that followed Adam like the solicitous hound of heaven through the fields and prisons and groves and great houses of Hayslope, has—even as the story draws to a close—yet to spend itself:

> For Adam, though you see him quite master of himself, working hard and delighting in his work after his inborn inalienable nature, had not outlived his sorrow—had not felt it slip from him as a temporary burthen, and leave him the same man again. Do any of us? God forbid. It would

be a poor result of all our anguish and our wrestling, if we won nothing but our own selves at the end of it—if we could return to the same blind loves, the same self-confident blame, the same light thoughts of human suffering, the same frivolous gossip over blighted human lives, the same feeble sense of that Unknown towards which we have sent forth irrepressible cries in our loneliness. (467–68)

So it is with Adam who—after he has wrestled with the angel that is mourning—demands, like Jacob, a blessing, and so the son who once despised his father emerges from "that baptism of fire with a soul full of new awe and pity" (409), now supple in spirit and well endowed with love.

NOTES

1. An equally justifiable reading of the myth that lies concealed behind this tale is Knoepflmacher's contention that the novel is Eliot's reinterpretation of the fallen and redeemed Adam of Milton's epic (qtd. in Johnstone 25). The Herculean parallel is meant to do nothing more than underscore the immensity, complexity and muscularity of Adam's tasks.

2. Given that Eliot has chosen to use metaphorical language in her depiction of Adam's mourning processes, I have chosen to echo these figures of speech in my attempts to delineate the protagonist's burgeoning self-awareness. The language of clinical psychology will also be employed when grief counsellors and therapists are included in the discussion as it pertains to Adam's prolonged sorrowing and struggle with guilt.

    In reference to the "shrapnel" that Adam is taking, an assumption has been made that battle is already in progress before we turn the first page of *Adam Bede*. Johnstone contends that "By the time Adam's story opens, his shame has turned to rage which shows itself in his propensity for fighting and in his severity towards his father" (86).

    In reference to the "core" of Adam's wound and his attempts to "excavate" this tender place, Staudacher has observed that "There is only one way to grieve. That way is to go through the core of grief. Only by experiencing the necessary emotional effects of your loved one's death is it possible for you to eventually resolve the loss" (qtd. in Doka 161).

3. Hetty's "dimpled" countenance is of singular significance. Eliot, in introducing this youthful maid to the reader, takes pains to repeat such coquettish descriptors and has been much maligned by critics for her callous caricature of this vixen-child. For

our purposes, it is important simply to note that Hetty's inconstancy and self-absorption exacerbate and complicate Adam's grieving. In so doing, they also bestow a gift, for Adam is challenged to confront, once again, his hardness and to renew his efforts to dismantle and disarm it. For an expanded discussion on the nature of Eliot's caricature of Hetty see Johnstone 26ff.

4. For an expanded discussion on Mary Ann's volatile but affectionate relations with her father and their impact on the nature of her protracted mourning and resultant depression see Frederick R. Karl, *George Eliot Voice of a Century: A Biography* (New York: W.W. Norton, 1995) 53–54; 96–101.

5. Eliot's insights into and observations of the gendered nature of grieving are to be commended. For a concise and pertinent depiction of the unique ways in which men and women mourn see Doka on "Masculine Grief" 161–71.

6. For a detailed account of Mary Ann's movement away from the Christian tradition, in which she was raised, and into secular humanism see Karl 48–64.

"Hieroglyphics of Sleep and Pain"

Djuna Barnes's Anatomy of Melancholy

> "grief concealed strangles the soul."
> ROBERT BURTON

Anatomy of Melancholy

Djuna Barnes's *Nightwood* is an unfinished work of mourning. The ongoing critical debate about whether incest occurs between the main character Nora Flood and her grandmother testifies to this unfinished mourning because her memory of their relationship is rendered in a "hieroglyphics of sleep and pain" (56) that conceals as much as it reveals. Something hidden remains outside Nora's conscious memory of her grandmother. But if what Freud calls the "work of mourning" fails, then the interiorizing and idealizing work of memory we perform upon the death of the other is the only testimony we have of what has been lost. And if Nora's hieroglyphic figure resists the interiorizing and idealizing powers of language, because she cannot find the right words to express her pain, then neither Nora's, nor Barnes's, nor the reader's mourning work is finished.

Critics have not yet considered their debate as a re-enactment of the fictional text's own refusal to represent the issue of Nora's incest in a decidable way. As long as Nora's grief remains concealed and uncommunicated, she will suffer the narcissistic wound of melancholy. The reader or critic who attempts, and inevitably fails, fully to explain the significance of the grandmother suffers a similar wound and therefore participates in this interminable act of mourning, or melancholy.

Since the significance of the grandmother remains beyond our full comprehension, just as it does for the main character Nora Flood and Barnes herself, she obstructs our desire to complete the mourning process, a process of interiorizing and idealizing the lost figure through language. Inasmuch as we are unable totally to comprehend the significance of the grandmother, she remains for us a thoroughly linguistic, yet hieroglyphic, figure waiting to be deciphered. We mourn what remains of her to be understood.

The appeal to biographical evidence has not made the hieroglyphic any easier to decipher. Recently, for instance, Philip Herring's controversial biography of Barnes, *Djuna: The Life and Worls of Djuna Barnes* (1995), questions the evidence of incest between Barnes and her paternal grandmother, Zadel Barnes. Despite the prominence of incest as a theme and the hieroglyphic dream symbols used to convey Nora's relationship with her grandmother in *Nightwood*, most critics have been cautious in applying a Freudian interpretation to the text because of its reductive male bias, while others see the text as a parody of Freudian psychoanalysis. Recent revisions of Freud, however, provide a way of understanding the causes of psychological resistance to meaning that are indispensable in helping to translate such cases as Nora's hieroglyphic dreams. The psychoanalytic theory of mourning and melancholy in the writings of Nicolas Abraham and Maria Torok, and specifically in "Mourning *or* Melancholia: Introjection versus Incorporation," offers a technique of revealing the psychological processes that lead to concealment in language, especially through their analysis of melancholy as an illness of mourning, an inexpressible or cryptic mourning.

Furthermore, Jacques Derrida's extensive writings on Abraham and Torok allow us to understand mourning not just as something negative but as the affirmative ethical structure that underlies the subject's relation to itself and the other. Derrida points out that the inability to finish mourning the lost object has the ethical advantage of not integrating, assimilating, and effacing the other in memory. In this respect, "failure succeeds" (*Memoires* 35) since to fail to assimilate the other in mourning permits one to respect the other as an other. Derrida calls this contradictory state of incorporation, where a lost object is taken within the self, but left outside the self in the crypt, "impossible mourning" (*Memoires* 34). For instance, Nora's hieroglyphic dream of the grandmother that is left undeciphered remains a foreign body within the self, an outside on the inside, an other affirmed as other. While the failure to assimilate her grandmother signifies Nora's pathological illness of mourning, she hopes to repeat this failure in some analogous way since the contradictory structure of impossible mourning which builds the crypt may succeed in preserving the uniqueness of her love for Robin, allowing the singularity of Robin to remain, unassimilated, in memory.

For Barnes and her main character Nora, then, *Nightwood* is ostensibly a work of mourning over a lost love. What complicates the relationship between Nora and her lover Robin Vote is the intrusion of Nora's feelings for her deceased grandmother. In comments Barnes has made about Robin Vote's historical counterpart, Thelma Wood, readers are, by analogy, encouraged to see Robin and the grandmother as deeply imbricated figures in Barnes's, as well as in Nora's, psyche. Herring, for instance, alludes to a memoir in which Barnes says that she had "fallen in love with Thelma Wood because she resembled her grandmother" (59). In a letter to her friend Emily Coleman dated May, 1936, Barnes writes, "I am up to my neck here in my lost life— Thelma & Thelma only—& my youth—way back in the beginning when she has no part in it & yet she is cause of my remembrance of it" (qtd. in Plumb, "Revising *Nightwood*" 158). What critics have overlooked in this admission by Barnes is its significance not for the psychoanalytic "talking cure," but for the theory of the illness of mourning. With the entry of Robin Vote into her life, Nora feels that she can begin to decipher the hieroglyphic of her dreams about her grandmother, complete her mourning, and end her melancholy. In other words, through the relationship between Robin and Nora, Barnes can surmount the things that obstruct the expression of her childhood grief and write her anatomy of melancholy.[1]

"A Second Anatomy of Melancholy"

Many have noticed that one of Barnes's favourite books was Robert Burton's seventeenth-century book *The Anatomy of Melancholy*, one friend of Barnes even going so far as to call *Nightwood* a "second *Anatomy of Melancholy*" (Herring 204).[2] Her interest in Burton's text includes both the form and the content, for *Nightwood* is marked by the traits of the novel and the anatomy. As Plumb points out in the introduction to her splendid new edition, one of the titles Barnes originally considered for *Nightwood* is "Anatomy of the Night" (viii).[3] If, as Northrop Frye states, anatomies present us with a "vision of the world in terms of a single intellectual pattern" (310), then in *Nightwood* that pattern is melancholy.

Barnes employs a number of linguistic techniques to show that Nora's melancholy hinders her attempts to mourn her grandmother (and Robin) by telling their story. Barnes's techniques may also indicate that she is hiding something from herself through these techniques that include hieroglyphic dream language, a discontinuous narrative, as well as themes and images representing, ironically, the problems with communicating and eating. The problems of communicating and eating are, as we will see, associated, but it should be noted here that the "devices turning on the difficulty of communication" (Frye 234) attest to another convention of the anatomy genre in Barnes's text. Louis Kannenstine has already commented incisively on the narrative discontinuity in *Nightwood*, citing most notably O'Connor's remark "I have a narrative, but you will be hard put to it to find it" (82). Yet Kannenstine does not mention Frye's observation that "violent dislocations in the customary logic of narrative" (Frye 310) are a recurring feature of the anatomy genre. The discontinuity is produced by the presence of digressions and epigrammatic statements in O'Connor's speech, qualities that Kannenstine notes (113–15). Digressions are "endemic in the narrative technique of satire," but never more often than in Menippean satire, which Frye renames the anatomy genre (311).[4]

Drawn from the writer's creative powers of "subconscious association" (Frye 275), the riddles of Barnes's imagistic style contribute, to borrow Kannenstine's word, to the "obscurity" (90) proper to an anatomy of "night." While we, as readers, share this obscurity with the characters, we also share a desire for luminaries that will serve (in the words of another great anatomist) to light us on our way in this night of our obscurity.[5] For psychoanalysis, words and images are the luminaries that bring unconscious memories to light. When we carry out the work of mourning successfully, we replace the lost object with another. The "ideal" replacement or substitute is language.

Frye takes his name "anatomy" for the genre of Menippean satire from Burton's *Anatomy of Melancholy* without commenting on the influence the object of Burton's text may have had on the formal approach to that object. If we accept the Freudian model of mourning and melancholy rather than Burton's humoral psychological model, some of the resemblances to the anatomical method are strikingly similar. Frye explains that the "word 'anatomy' in Burton's title means a dissection or analysis, and expresses very accurately the intellectualized approach of his form" (311). From a psychoanalytic perspective, to anatomize is to suffer a melancholic withdrawal of our attachments "bit by bit" from the lost objects that we have identified with and will eventually take within ourselves.

When, for example, Dr. Matthew O'Connor attempts to display his "exhaustive erudition" (311), or what we now refer to as the attempt to "totalize" a given object of study, he reaches a limit and fails to exhaust anything but himself or his reader. The refusal to mourn the loss of his romantic Faustian dream marks O'Connor as a figure known as the *philosophus gloriosus*, the ridicule of which is a constant theme in Menippean satire (Frye 311).[6] O'Connor occasionally acknowledges his failures such as his sexual impotence: "'Tiny O'Toole was lying in a swoon'" (111); and his narrative impotence: "'I've not only lived my life for nothing, I've told it for nothing'" (136). If O'Connor and Nora, out of pride or pain, deny their loss or its importance, they may begin to attack their object and take on a satirical disposition toward it. As we shall see, this attack corresponds to Freud's notion concerning the "work of melancholia." The satirical tone of *Nightwood*, Barnes's "Anatomy of Night," may itself be a symptom of her state of mind during the production of her text. *Nightwood* may, indeed, be motivated by Barnes's need, like Nora's, to anatomize the "black choler" of her own long, dark night of melancholy.

"'Red Riding Hood and the Wolf in Bed': A Fantasy of Incorporation"

The "work of mourning," as Freud describes it in his classic essay "Mourning and Melancholia" (1917),[7] consists in the withdrawal of libido, or psychic energy, from its attachments to a lost object, whether that object is a person or "some abstraction which has taken the place of one, such as country, liberty, an ideal, and so on" (243). The distinguishing features of melancholia are "a profoundly painful dejection, cessation of interest in the outside world, loss of capacity to love, inhibition of all activity, and the lowering of the self-regarding feelings to a degree that finds utterance in self-reproaches and self-revilings, and culminates in a delusional expectation of punishment" (244). In both mourning and melancholy, the withdrawal of libido from the object is carried out "bit by bit" during which time the "existence of the lost object is psychically prolonged" (245). Unlike mourning, which comes to an end, melancholy is pathological because of the "open wound" (253) that persists in the subject.

Abraham and Torok's elaboration of Freud's distinction between mourning and melancholy in their article, "Mourning or Melancholia: Introjection versus Incorporation," proceeds from the ambivalence the subject may feel toward the lost object (135–37). The causes of this ambivalence in melancholia are many, but the struggles in which "love and hate contend with each other" make it impossible for the melancholic person to decide whether to cling to the lost object or detach from it, as Freud notes in "Mourning and Melancholia" (256). One important aspect of the ambivalence is that it accounts for the "work of melancholia" (255) which entirely absorbs the subject, but is hidden internally. In fact, Freud asserts that where mourning is a conscious process, melancholy is not. He qualifies this opposition, saying that even if a melancholic person is aware of the loss that has given rise to the melancholia, it is "only in the sense that he [sic] knows *whom* he has lost but not what he has lost in him" (245).

A similar observation is made to Nora by O'Connor who, despite being a parodic Freudian figure and a *philosophus gloriosus*, also shows himself to be a person of genuine insight. He says to Nora, "'be careful who you love— for a lover who dies, no matter how forgotten, will take somewhat of you to the grave'" (122). O'Connor is referring to Nora's final rejection of Robin for her continued infidelity, but his comment applies equally well to Nora's melancholy over her grandmother. O'Connor warns Nora that the loss of her emotional investment, the loss of what Freud calls "cathexis," must be dealt with as much as the loss of the object itself. As Freud states, "In mourning it is the world which has become poor and empty; in melancholia it is the ego itself" ("Mourning and Melancholia" 246). Rather than withdraw her attachment from the object of her affection and displace it onto another object as in normal mourning, Nora has withdrawn her libidinal energy into her ego by identifying with that object. The difficulty Nora faces, however, is that her identification with Robin has been preceded not by the typical displacement of, or identification with, her grandmother found in normal mourning, but by the fantasy of sharing a divided self with her grandmother.

Unable to give up the lost object of her grandmother, Nora has allowed the ensuing alteration of identity to influence her relationship with Robin, particularly the manner in which she relates it. To explain how a melancholic person can avoid consciously identifying with a lost object by including it in the ego as another, separate identity, Abraham and Torok return to Freud's concept of incorporation. Freud regards the substitution of identification for the love of an object as a regression to an earlier form of narcissism. Like a child during this period of "primary narcissism," a melancholic person who desires an object external to his body will identify and abolish its separate existence by incorporating or devouring it. In Freud's words, "The ego wants to incorporate this object into itself, and, in accordance with the oral or cannibalistic phase of libidinal development in which it is, it wants to do so by devouring it" ("Mourning and Melancholia," 249–50). The symptoms of the conflict that the melancholic subject has with incorporating the object will, therefore, take place in the mouth.

Freud exemplifies this oral dysfunction characteristic of melancholia with the refusal of nourishment (250), but Abraham and Torok extend the dysfunction to words in the mouth, speech ("Mourning or Melancholia" 128–29). For Abraham and Torok, normal mourning takes part in the larger process of "introjection," or "throwing within" the self an external object in order to preserve it in our memory. Desire for an object gives way to identification with it. Like Freud, Abraham and Torok believe that successful introjection means replacing a lost object with another: "Learning to fill the emptiness of the mouth with words is the initial model of introjection" (128). In the initial model, the satisfactions of the mouth filled with the mother's breast are replaced by "satisfactions of a mouth now empty of that object but filled with words pertaining to the subject" (127). The psychoanalytic claim for the remedial effects of language in mourning finds support in Barnes. When one hears of a sudden death, the narrator of Nightwood calls it a "death that cannot form until the shocked tongue has given its permission" (137). But how long will the tongue deny its permission?

"Incorporation" is the name Abraham and Torok give to the melancholic's refusal to mourn, when the shocked tongue denies the subject permission to speak of death. Where Freud often uses incorporation and introjection interchangeably, Abraham and Torok see the two terms as opposed to one another because incorporation for them is a denial that anything has been lost: "Incorporation is the refusal to reclaim as our own the part of ourselves that we placed in what we lost" ("Mourning or Melancholia" 127). To accomplish this denial, incorporation, as if by magic, carries out "literally something

that has only figurative meaning" (126). In order to avoid having to intro-
ject or "'swallow' a loss, we fantasize swallowing (or having swallowed)
that which has been lost, as if it were some kind of thing" (126). The
paradox of swallowing to avoid swallowing conveys the subject's desire to
resist introjection or identification and yet to identify with the object at the
same time by hiding it. This "endocryptic identification" (Abraham and Torok,
"Lost Object" 142), a hidden fantasy of identification, reveals itself as Nora
moves beyond her melancholy. Furthermore, what makes incorporation,
the reversion from words back to imaginary food, relevant to Barnes's representation of Nora's recovery from melancholy, is the presence of cannibalistic
metaphors which, ironically, Abraham and Torok say, act as a measure of
prevention against incorporation.

The most explicit use of cannibalistic metaphor occurs when the reader
encounters Robin during her unhappy marriage with Felix Volkbein. Associated
with death and memory, Robin's image in Nightwood will live on the border-
line between introjection and incorporation. Robin is the kind of woman
who is "the infected, carrier of the past—before her the structure of our
head and jaws ache—we feel that we could eat her, she who is eaten death
returning, for only then do we put our face close to blood on the lips of our
forefathers" (Nightwood 36). The narrator's notion that "we could eat" Robin
evades incorporation and anticipates Nora's identification with Robin because
the narrator and Nora knowingly articulate the loss. They replace the lost
object with language, just as the act of cannibalism itself replaces the fantasy
(Abraham and Torok, "Mourning or Melancholia" 130). Robin's power to
stimulate memory seems paramount, but why she is "the infected, carrier
of the past" is not readily apparent. Perhaps, as "eaten death returning,"
Robin's image, while being eaten itself, is infected with a previous, unidentified
death that has already been "eaten" through the concealed fantasy of incorporation, and that only through its association with Robin returns to conscious
memory. Robin is the infected carrier of Nora's incorporated memory of
her grandmother.

Another passage, below, confirms the memorializing effect of Robin's
image. Her image—to invoke Jacques Derrida—carries the "force of mourning."
The image's force of mourning is its potential to be, despite death or not
being. Its force is its ability to dwell in that ghostly state of "being" between
life and death, "a spectral power of the virtual work" ("By Force" 175) of the

possible. The image possesses the power to be life-like, like life in death, a spectral power which carries "the force, *to resist, to consist and to exist in death*" (176).

The passage below deserves to be quoted in full since it illustrates so well what Derrida calls the "pictorial vocation, namely, to seize the dead and transfigure them" (185). On Robin's pictorial vocation the narrator states:

> The woman who presents herself to the spectator as a "picture" forever arranged, is for the contemplative mind the chiefest danger. Sometimes one meets a woman who is beast turning human. Such a person's every movement will reduce to an image of a forgotten experience; a mirage of an eternal wedding cast on the racial memory; as insupportable a joy as would be the vision of an eland coming down an aisle of trees, chapleted with orange blossoms and bridal veil, a hoof raised in the economy of fear, stepping in the trepidation of the flesh that will become myth; as the unicorn is neither man nor beast deprived, but human hunger pressing its breast to its prey.
> (Nightwood 36)

As a "picture" or "image," Robin assumes the memorializing function of the picture and image in general, which Derrida indicates "makes the absent present" ("By Force" 183). She makes a "forgotten experience," an unconscious memory, available to conscious memory again in the form of an image. The image, or picture, though "forever arranged" in memory, is a danger to the "contemplative mind" because it does not present itself with a clear meaning to the understanding as a concept. Nevertheless, the "insupportable" image of the eland in the "eternal wedding" wearing a "bridal veil" clearly conveys a scene of desire. Foreshadowing the ambivalence Nora feels toward her grandmother in her dreams, the scene is mixed with an "economy of fear" because of a predatory presence of "human hunger pressing its breast to its prey."

Despite being described as a woman "who is beast turning human" (Nightwood 36), Robin is not necessarily the predator of the visionary scene. Robin's sexual promiscuity during her relationship with Nora does mark her as sexually aggressive. Her relationship with the young girl Sylvia suggests the plundering of sexual innocence. It is the narrator, however, who resembles Nora in wanting to "eat" Robin—a display of both desire and oral aggression. Nora's reaction to O'Connor's transvestism reveals a similar fusion of desire and oral aggression when she says, "'God, children know something they can't tell; they like Red Riding Hood and the wolf in bed!'" (69). Jane Marcus in her admirable analysis regards the wolf as a metaphor for Nora's grandmother, a role played here by O'Connor (245–46). This reading places Nora in the role of Little Red Riding Hood who is about to be devoured sexually by the grandmother. Nora's observation that children "like" or desire sexual contact with the wolf is ironically consistent with modern interpretations of the traditional fairy tale, particularly Charles Perrault's sexually suggestive version written in French.[8] Doubtless, twentieth-century critics have been influenced by Freud's case history of the "Wolf Man," "From the History of an Infantile Neurosis" (1918), where he explicitly links the child's fear of being eaten by the wolf with the wish for sexual satisfaction from his parent (35–36). But no one has seen the allusion to the fairy tale as Nora's effort to get beyond her interminable mourning when she will no longer have to hide her identification with her grandmother in the fantasy of incorporation.

We can, I believe, see the structure of the relationships in the fairy tale acting as a governing scene for many of the relationships in the text, beginning with Nora and Robin's. For Barnes, the fairy tale is the "trepidation of the flesh...become myth." The fairy tale structures the two dreams that Nora cannot explain even though she knows that they are intended for her. After her second dream, she goes to O'Connor who, she hopes, will make the dreams understandable to her: "'What was that dream saying, for God's sake, what was that dream?' For it was for me also" (124). What the tale of Little Red Riding Hood reveals is that the imposition of the unequal grandmother-child relationship upon the lesbian relationship pervades the text.[9] Furthermore, the ambivalent feelings of desire and fear that would attend Nora's incestuous feelings toward her grandmother are evinced in the literal and metaphorical meanings of the word "wolf," the rapacious canine, and the sexually rapacious (traditionally male) person. The ambivalence is also evident in that children "can't tell" others about their secret love. Abraham and Torok's theory of incorporation focusses on subjects, like Nora, who cannot even tell themselves.

One of the things that Nora cannot tell herself is what motivates her to tell the story she is telling, with great difficulty, of her own sexual predation. What motivates her sexual predation is her hidden identification with her grandmother. In terms of incorporation, there is no reason to object to the wolf's oral consumption of the grandmother and Little Red Riding Hood as a sexual metaphor in Nora's cryptic comment. But what requires explanation in the tale, especially the Grimms' version, is the relationship of the wolf's disguise as grandmother to Nora's fantasy of incorporation. The comparison of Red Riding Hood suggests itself to Nora when she sees O'Connor wearing a "woman's flannel night gown" (69). Like the wolf, O'Connor dresses like a woman so that he may be identified as a woman, if only to himself. Judging from their mutual embarrassment, O'Connor's transvestism has remained hidden up to this point. The allusion to Red Riding Hood may refer not only to a narrative of desire, but also to one of hidden identification.

Rather than identifying merely with Little Red Riding Hood, then, Nora is also the wolf disguised as the grandmother because she has eaten her grandmother through the fantasy of incorporation. However, we should be careful not to confuse Nora's conscious reference to the story with the unconscious fantasy that precedes it. Since she refuses to mourn the loss of her grandmother, she avoids swallowing the *reality* of the loss by resorting to the unconscious *fantasy* of swallowing what is lost in the form of an object, such as food, real or imagined. She need not adjust to the painful reality of her grandmother's death through the process of introjection while the fantasy of incorporation enables Nora to deny the loss even occurred. Nora encrypts or hides the shameful secret of their incest to protect the idealized vision she has of her grandmother, or in psychoanalytic terms, her "ego ideal." When she says the "children know something they can't tell," she may be referring to her own childhood repression of the unspeakable act of incest with her grandmother. Her interest in the narrative of Little Red Riding Hood does signal that Nora is beginning to remember what she has hidden from herself.

"'Findings' in a Tomb": The Crypt and Its Decryption

As Esther Rashkin points out, the melancholic cannot speak the trauma of loss and must develop a "rhetoric of hiding" (42), or what Abraham and Torok refer to as a "cryptonymy."[10] To keep their secret love for their grandmother from themselves, Barnes and Nora develop precisely this "rhetoric of hiding." But Barnes does not use simple cryptonyms or words that hide a trauma in words. Barnes's rhetoric of hiding consists mainly of "hieroglyphs"—a combination of words and images or scenes—of memories that appear in dreams and sometimes behavioural habits reconstructed in a discontinuous narrative. The very discontinuity of the narrative, with its imagistic and aphoristic style, guarantees that the point of the story will be either difficult to recover or, at times, lost altogether. The hieroglyphs resist meaning, but Nora's dreams of her grandmother imply that she is performing the work of melancholia, or in Abraham and Torok's contradictory phrase, her "melancholic mourning" ("Mourning or Melancholia" 137).

The paradoxical experience of melancholic mourning in *Nightwood*, given that Abraham and Torok set the two terms in opposition to each other, is possible only if Nora can keep a secret from herself and then be seen to reveal it, if not to herself, at least to others. The "*intrapsychic secret*" ("Mourning or Melancholia" 131) that Nora keeps from herself is, however, not kept in her unconscious, but in an "artificial unconscious" ("Topography" 159) constructed in the ego that Abraham and Torok denominate the "crypt" ("Mourning or Melancholia" 130).[11] The walls of the crypt are built by the contradictory feelings of love and hate represented in the cryptonyms, the words that hide. Whereas introjection assimilates the lost object of love to the self, incorporation swallows and preserves the lost object in the crypt as a living, though foreign, presence within the self.

Inexpressible mourning erects a secret tomb inside the subject. Reconstituted from the memories of words, scenes, and affects, the objectal correlative of the loss is buried alive in the crypt as a full-fledged person, complete with its own topography. The crypt also includes the actual or supposed traumas that made introjection impossible ("Mourning or Melancholia" 130). The crypt is a wound left by the loss of the love-object that the melancholic tries to isolate and hide. Nora's melancholic mourning signifies the destruction of the crypt.

Destroying the crypt releases Nora's buried desire for her grandmother and the memories associated with her. In her past, Nora may not have been able to articulate certain words, utter certain phrases, so, in fantasy, she took into her mouth "the unnamable, the object itself" ("Mourning or Melancholia" 128). The unresolved trauma of incest, along with any other abuses, real or imagined, may have made Nora's grandmother a toxic object impossible to assimilate, but her grandmother remained a person whom Nora "loved more than anyone" (*Nightwood* 123). Melancholics, Abraham and Torok suggest, cherish the memory of their lost object as their "most precious possession, even though it must be concealed by a crypt built with the bricks of hate and aggression" ("Mourning or Melancholia" 136). They add an important point in understanding melancholy:

> It should be remarked that as long as the crypt holds, there is no melan-
> cholia. It erupts when the walls are shaken, often as a result of the
> loss of some secondary love-object who had buttressed them. Faced
> with the danger of seeing the crypt crumble, the whole of the ego
> becomes one with the crypt, showing the concealed object of love in
> its own guise. ("Mourning or Melancholia" 136)

By remembering her dreams, Nora begins to understand that her "ego becomes one with the crypt, showing the concealed object," her grandmother. Whether or not Robin constitutes the secondary love-object whose loss shakes the walls of the crypt, Nora identifies Robin's love with entombment soon after their first encounter. Robin's entombment consciously repeats Nora's unconscious entombment of her grandmother and therefore offers a means of healing Nora's psychic wound.

Robin's role in Nora's melancholic mourning initially appears merely as a displaced repetition of the grandmother, as a conscious reminder that something else has been buried. If Nora's grandmother, undeveloped in *Nightwood*, is based on Zadel Barnes and her philosophy of free love (Herring 58), then Robin's promiscuity may have evoked a recollection of her grandmother not just in Nora but, through the autobiographical allegory of the novel, in Barnes herself. For in Robin, "love and anonymity...were so 'haunted' of each other that separation was impossible" (49–50). Nora mourns in advance the loss of her love, anticipating the end of their relationship from its earliest stages:

> Love becomes the deposit of the heart, analogous in all degrees to the "findings" in a tomb. As in one will be charted the taken place of the body, the raiment, the utensils necessary to its other life, so in the heart of the lover will be traced, as an indelible shadow, that which he loves. In Nora's heart lay the fossil of Robin, intaglio of her identity, and about it for its maintenance ran Nora's blood. (50–51)

The analogy between Robin and Nora's grandmother goes further than placing desire for a lover in the tomb of memory. The prohibition against the desire joins the two women in Nora's mind. The social stigma against homosexual love, significantly for incorporation, the "love that dare not speak its name," receives explicit notice by O'Connor, but little from Nora. Surprisingly, Nora portrays her love for Robin as incestuous, the same prohibited desire that she feels for her grandmother and that her secret crypt commemorates.[12]

Nora's endocryptic, or hidden, identification with her grandmother differs, nonetheless, from her identification with Robin in that Nora is not aware that she assumes the identity of the former object as it breaks through the walls of its crypt. Nora complains to O'Connor that she cannot lose Robin because "'She is myself'" (108). But, in Robin's case, the loving assimilation of Nora's lost object is fully conscious and expressed in the displaced object of words. Nora's identification with her grandmother stays hidden and unspeakable until melancholic mourning permits the object partially to reveal itself through the hieroglyphic of dreams. Nora's role as grandmother compels her to infantilize Robin and designate their love as incestuous. In a desperate attempt to understand Robin, Nora haunts the cafes to meet Robin's lovers, learning only that "'others had slept with my lover and my child. For Robin is incest too'" (129). All of Nora's claims that she must go "'against nature'" and that her love for Robin is "'forbidden'" (129) agree with the feelings Nora's melancholic fantasy might ascribe to her grandmother, the lost object's ego.

Nora exhibits another significant melancholic feature when she reproaches herself for her treatment of Robin. By representing her love for Robin as incestuous, Nora foists the history of her family's dysfunction upon her. Cheryl Plumb sums up the issue from an autobiographical perspective when she weaves together two questions from Barnes's unpublished notebooks: "'Did your grandmother ever try to make love to you' which Barnes labeled 'monstrous family questioning' and the plaintive question 'I have yet to be forgiven for being abused?'" ("Revising *Nightwood*" 158). The two questions are inextricably related. However, the latter question may be distinguished as accentuating the conflicts that the melancholic person must undergo as a witness to something about which she feels desire yet fears to testify. Since it is her conflicting role as witness which makes her mourning impossible, we must first attend to the symptoms that signal Nora's melancholic self-reproach, and then, in the last section of the essay, turn to the courtroom of conscience where the mourner is called as a witness and where the only testimony to the crime she can give, even to herself, is the ghostly presence of the other that haunts her in the act of mourning.

Plumb feels these two questions represent the "hidden theme" of child-hood betrayal and abuse recaptured in Robin, Thelma's fictional other ("Revising *Nightwood*" 158). Nora does regard both of the dreams she has of her grandmother as "something being done to Robin" (56). She tells O'Connor in their long exchange concerning her grief over losing Robin that "'there's something evil in me, that loves evil and degradation'" (113) and later asks if she is Robin's "'devil'" (121). These reproaches are more intelligible in relation to the dreams if we take them as being directed at the grandmother who has been secretly preserved in Nora's crypt.

Abraham and Torok confirm Freud's speculation that the melancholic's self-reproaches "loosen the fixation of the libido to the object by disparaging it" (Freud, "Mourning and Melancholia" 257). They go further than Freud, however, who shows surprise that the "melancholics show no shame at all the horrible things for which they blame themselves" (Abraham and Torok, "Mourning *or* Melancholia" 136). Abraham and Torok explain that melancholics "stage the grief attributed to the object who lost them" (136) not simply in a "public display," but in a display whose magnitude is a measure of the object's love for the subject, which in *Nightwood* is the grandmother's love for Nora:

the more suffering and degradation the object undergoes (meaning: the more he [sic] pines for the subject he lost), the prouder the subject can be: "He endures all of this because of me." Being a melancholic, I stage and let everyone else see the full extent of my love object's grief over having lost me. (Abraham and Torok, "Mourning *or* Melancholia" 136)

Robin refers to Nora as her "Madonna" (122) who by comparison makes her feel "dirty" (120), yet Nora is hardly guilty of anything more serious than loving the wrong woman too much. On the other hand, the grandmother-child structure of their bond with which Nora reproaches herself almost takes on the archetypal dimension of original sin in *Nightwood* because of the implied incest and the unequal union of lovers. The archetypal dimension of this unequal union of grandmother and child is especially clear in Nora's rivalry with Jenny Petherbridge over Robin.

The satiric figure of the elder sexual predator embodied memorably by Jenny Petherbridge, a "'squatter' by instinct" (60), reflects the grandmother's relation to Nora, and Nora's own perceived relation to Robin. Jenny mirrors Nora's feeling of possessiveness toward Robin. Furthermore, Jenny's role as a toxic grandmother figure is clear from the moment she is introduced. Although middle-aged, the narrator describes Jenny as advanced in years and yet, to use an animal metaphor consistent with Barnes's satiric style, always "in heat": "She looked old, yet expectant of age; she seemed to be steaming in the vapours of someone else about to die, still she gave off an odour to the mind (for there are purely mental smells that have no reality) of a woman about to be *accouchee*" (58). Her mimetic rivalry with Nora for the affections of Robin—for they each desire the desire of the other—will be repeated when she competes with yet another of Robin's lovers, the "child" (62), Sylvia.[13]

The significance of the rivalry with Sylvia stems from Jenny's public confession of her feelings of guilt, which resemble Nora's melancholic feelings of self-reproach. Jenny wants to be rid of the young girl whom Robin has abandoned; and, when she takes steps to do so, she is seen by others as manipulative: "'You can't blame me, you can't accuse me of using a child for my own ends!'" (98). Jenny's remark implies that it is Robin who has used the young girl for her own ends, but the denial of blame is a partial admission of guilt. This is not the first love triangle that Jenny has created. It is, after all, the "squatter's instinct," her mimetic desire to possess the object of another person's desire, that made her Nora's rival. Jenny's equivocal confession of guilt anticipates Nora's own regrets concerning her possessiveness toward Robin. Nora's regret is further compounded by the ghostly presence of her grandmother who compels Nora to act, unawares, like her grandmother and the predacious Jenny. The dreams of her grandmother evoke the feeling in Nora that she has been caught in a love triangle long before Jenny raises the spectre of one again in her life. Through Jenny, and then through Nora, Nightwood repeatedly expresses the melancholic self-reproach that Barnes feels and, ironically, publicly stages. This occurs, not in order to show the extent of her grief over the loss of her grandmother, but of the grandmother's grief over having lost her.

When Nora shows her self-reproach to O'Connor concerning her treatment of Robin, his acceptance and acknowledgement of the grandmother's love for Nora facilitate Nora's mourning. O'Connor fulfills the function of the analyst who, as Abraham and Torok see it, is not only meant to recognize the love object behind the disguises of hate and aggression, but also to accept the melancholic's "narcissistic bliss at having received the object's love despite dangerous transgressions" ("Mourning or Melancholia" 137). After hearing only the second dream, O'Connor exhibits his astute skills at listening, for his response affirms Nora's desire for her grandmother, whom we know she loved more than anyone. His reply, "'It's my mother without argument I want!'" (Nightwood 124), could be interpreted as an acknowledgment of Nora's "incestuous" love for Robin, but the incestuous desire he declares for his mother applies equally well to the grandmother as the intended target of his sympathetic response. When the melancholic obtains this acknowledgement from the analyst, the crypt gradually gives way to "genuine mourning and the fantasies of incorporation can be transferred into introjections" (Abraham and Torok, "Mourning or Melancholia" 137). Having found another means to repeat safely the initial trauma of incest, Nora may continue to perform the work of melancholia she has already begun by falling in love with Robin.

That Nora associates Robin with the cure and not the illness of mourning is evinced in Nora's own acknowledgement of Robin's memorializing function that we have called, after Derrida, her "pictorial vocation." Since the desire for the grandmother is an encrypted desire, the desire is completely forgotten in the sense that it is repressed memory, though a special kind which creates the crypt and is referred to by Abraham and Torok as "preservative repression" ("Mourning *or* Melancholia" 133–34). In another psychoanalytic paradox, Nora can only forget what she has already secretly forgotten (because it is preserved in the crypt) when she does the work of mourning and knowingly remembers her encrypted desire for her grandmother through the return of the repressed memory in such symptoms as slips of the tongue and dreams. The narrator recounts Nora's unusual heightened awareness surrounding the first dream:

> She nodded and awoke again and began to cry before she opened her eyes, and went back to the bed and fell into a dream which she recognized; though in the finality of this version she knew that the dream had not been "well dreamt" before. Where the dream had been incalculable, it was now completed with the entry of Robin. (54–55)

Without any mention of the content of the dream, Nora links Robin to her enhanced ability to recall a recurring dream which until now remained uncertain, or "incalculable," in its significance.

In the dream, Nora finds herself and Robin in her grandmother's room "which was impossible," the narrator tells us, "because the room was taboo" (55). The contradictory experience of desire and fear associated with the feeling of transgression in the room expresses itself in various ways throughout the dream. Nora hears herself invite Robin into the room, indicating a desire to be there, but she feels "anguish" when she hears her own voice (55). Despite being the object of desire, Robin, who has entered the dream in another part of the house, shows the "smile of an 'only survivor,' a smile which fear had married to the bone." Robin's frozen smile expresses the "painful love" that pushes her "further away," as if Robin and Nora were a "pair of opera glasses turned to the wrong end." Like the architecture of the crypt itself, the grandmother's room is described as a contradiction, for while it was her room, it was at the same time "the absolute opposite of any known room her grandmother had ever moved or lived in, was nevertheless saturated with the lost presence of her grandmother, who seemed in the continual process of leaving it" (55–56). However, what Derrida calls the "contradiction within desire" ("Fors" 69), a contradiction that builds the crypt, also destroys it—not only because the sheer effort of maintaining the secret of the desire can lead to failure, but also because the conditions that prohibit the melancholic from speaking of it can change. Nora's fear of losing the memory of Robin in mourning her so resembles the forgotten, encrypted desire for her grandmother that Robin triggers in Nora an intense desire to remember which breaks down the walls of her crypt.

The first dream brought to completion by Robin dramatizes a scene of desire with the grandmother that Nora has until this time partly hidden from herself. Recalling a childhood memory of her grandmother, Nora's dream is rife with ambivalent emotion: "—the grandmother who, for some unknown reason, was dressed as a man, wearing a billycock and a corked moustache, ridiculous and plump in tight trousers and a red waistcoat, her arms spread saying in a leer of love, 'My little sweetheart!'" (55). The lasciviousness in the "leer of love" suggests that the grandmother's sexual gesture is unwelcome. The sexual advance may bear directly on the way Nora portrays Robin's objectified role in the memory: "—her grandmother 'drawn upon' as a prehistoric ruin is drawn upon, symbolizing her life out of her life, and which now appeared to Nora as something being done to Robin, Robin disfigured and eternalized by the hieroglyphics of sleep and pain" (56). A lost object of desire uncovered in Nora's encrypted, unconscious memory, the grandmother is aptly described as a "prehistoric ruin." A memory is a ruin that can be "'drawn upon'" even though it is prehistoric, or buried in the past of the unconscious before it can be recorded by historical, or conscious memory. For the melancholic, the special emphasis given to the phrase "drawn upon" connotes, more than simple recollection, identification.

The endocryptic identification upon which Nora has drawn has reincarnated her grandmother, and it is the phantom of the grandmother in Nora that determines the structure of her relationship with Robin. Now that Nora is becoming aware of the identification in her melancholic mourning, the grandmother does symbolize "her life out of her life." The grandmother still directs her behaviour from the crumbling crypt, allowing the influence to appear as "something being done to Robin." In the dream, one critic states, "Robin thus becomes like the child Nora, seduced by the grandmother" (Kaivola 90). Cast in Nora's childhood role by a dream, Robin is "disfigured and eternalized by the hieroglyphics of sleep and pain." Robin is eternalized by the dream, a lover's memorial to her, in much the same way that her grandmother is eternalized by Nora's crypt.

However, by the time of the second dream Nora regrets the commemorative effect and its inevitable attachment to loss and death. She regrets it because, as Abraham and Torok argue, the illness of mourning makes the sufferer feel guilty for the crime of repressing an illegitimate desire ("Illness" 122). Nora wants to be free of her interminable mourning for her grandmother by unmasking the crime of repression and identifying the victim she has buried. Recounting the burial of her grandmother, and her father's grief, Nora appears to remember the moment when the repression of her encrypted memories is lifted:

> And I woke up and still it was going on; it went down into the dark earth of my waking as if I were burying them with the earth of my lost sleep. This I have done to my father's mother, dreaming through my father, and have tormented them with my tears and with my dreams. For all of us die over again in somebody's sleep.— And this I have done to Robin; it is only through me that she will die over and over, and it is only through me, of all my family, that my grandmother dies, over and over. (124)

Clinging to the memory of a beloved lost object may reassure the melancholic Nora by making the absent present, but clinging to the memory of the lost object also repeats the loss which is always attended by the pain. The paradox faced by the mourning subject is that to finish mourning is to forget the beloved other whom you have sworn never to forget.

"Book of Concealment": Impossible Mourning and Mourning the Impossible

Nora seems to accept the possibility that her mourning for Robin may never be finished, and that something of Robin will remain outside, unknown, and beyond the interiorizing memory. Nora experiences what Derrida poignantly calls the "tender rejection" (Memoires 35) of impossible mourning: "Only the impossible lasts forever; with time, it is made accessible. Robin's love and mine was always impossible, and loving each other, we no longer love. Yet we love each other like death" (Nightwood 116). To understand how "the impossible lasts forever," we as readers must share Barnes's and Derrida's passion for the impossible, a paradoxical experience that joins and separates the mourner and the mourned.

"With time," Nora believes that the impossible is made accessible through her mourning. But to gain access means to approach the impossible, not to possess it. With time, the work of mourning allows Nora to approach the love of Robin, but like death, that love cannot be possessed. Nora will never know Robin's love in its completeness, any more than she will know the illegitimate love she felt for her grandmother. Nora's mourning is the only evidence of the impossible relationships she shared with Robin and her grandmother, the only way she can dress "the unknowable in the garments of the known" (114). The impossibility of Nora's desire for the two women does not therefore make her desire for them a mistake. O'Connor raises the issue of impossible love in relation to his feeling that his gender orientation is a "permanent mistake," saying to God, "I will not be able to stay permanent unless you help me, oh Book of Concealment!" (111). O'Connor also faces the "impossible that lasts forever" in his relationship with God as a "Book of Concealment," a relationship in which God appears to be absent, and any knowledge of God or God's love is concealed. Still, the metaphor of God as a book implies that some aspect of the relationship is readable, even though it is not fully understandable, or knowable. *Nightwood* is our Book of Concealment whose secrets we have yet to uncover, and whose meaning we will never fully know. Is *Nightwood* merely a fiction, or is it autobiographical? Or is the distinction, as Derrida states, "undecidable" (*Memoires* 22)?

The undecidability of the judicial question of *Nightwood's* status as fiction or autobiography does not make a decision about its veracity less urgent. *Nightwood* bears witness to some traumatic event which raises the question of incest, whether one takes Herring's position that there is "little evidence of sexual involvement" (55) in the letters between Djuna and Zadel Barnes, her grandmother, or Anne B. Dalton's position that the letters reveal not only that "Zadel colonized Djuna to serve her sexual needs, but...that the other adults in the family had a matter-of-fact attitude towards this abuse" (121).[14] Real or imagined, the traumatic event is staged in the court of conscience, anticipating the critical debate. Like the letters, *Nightwood* testifies to incest without being able to prove it. Whether we accept Nora's fictional evidence or Barnes's autobiographical evidence, either figure as witness "calls forth" in Derrida's words, "the faith of the other in engaging himself [or herself] to say the truth" (*Demeure* 23). Derrida knows that no judge will accept a witness who ironically insinuates or declares that their testimony has the status of a literary fiction, but

> nonetheless, if the testimonial is in truth irreducible to the fictional, there is no testimony that does not imply structurally in itself the possibility of fiction, of the simulacrum, of dissimulation, of lying and perjury—that is to say also of literature, of the innocently or perverse literature which plays innocently by perverting all of these distinctions. (23)

To the extent that the event of incest will remain unproven and the whole truth of it unknown to us, including Barnes and her allegorical figure Nora, it remains an open secret. The only testimonial evidence of this crime of desire is the trace of the grandmother that remains in Nora's act of mourning.

According to a psychoanalytic reading, then, Nora's obsessive refusal to forget Robin testifies to incest by repeating her unconscious refusal to forget her grandmother, embracing the possibility of an unfinished, impossible mourning. She transfers her unconscious wish to keep the memory of her forbidden love of her grandmother onto her relationship with Robin.[15] For Barnes, keeping a lost object of desire, no matter how impossible to attain, turns an act of memory into an act of love. Their most intimate embraces invaded by "moments of insurmountable grief," Nora anticipates the burden of mourning Robin. She anticipates the pain of losing her that forgetting involves, the repetitive process of discharging the pain, bit by bit, with each recollection:

> To keep her (in Robin there was this tragic longing to be kept, knowing herself astray) Nora knew now that there was no way but death. In death Robin would belong to her. Death went with them, together and alone; and with the torment and catastrophe, thoughts of resurrection, the second duel. (52)

The only way Nora can "keep" Robin is to lose her to the living death of memory. The difficulty with Nora's prognosis of her mourning for Robin is that it shows no sign of giving up her mourning, regardless of the pain. This prognosis may just be a reflection of Nora's early entry into the mourning process, but her inability to accept her loss makes Nora's mourning resemble melancholy. Furthermore, Nora's sense of urgency with regard to her need to remember Robin at such an early point in the relationship may be influenced by the need to preserve the encrypted memory of her grandmother. Distinguishing the effort consciously to remember Robin from the effort unconsciously to remember her grandmother proves too much when she refers to her desire for Robin as incestuous.

The prohibition against incest, of course, does not apply to Nora's relationship with Robin as it would to her relationship with her grandmother, removing the obstacle that prevents the melancholic Nora from speaking the unutterable. The word "incest" may apply metaphorically to the lesbian nature of her love, but incest, which applies literally to her relationship with her grandmother, is chosen to condense both forms of taboo desire into one prohibition. In spite of this prohibition against her desire, the same prohibition that helped build the crypt to keep secret her desire for her grandmother, Nora still feels compelled to speak. She says to O'Connor, "I'm so miserable, Matthew, I don't know how to talk, and I've got to. I've got to talk to somebody. I can't live this way" (109). Her need to tell her desire for Robin exhibits another desire to remember by consciously repeating.[16] The therapeutic effects of narrativizing are confirmed by O'Connor, a mouthpiece for Barnes on many philosophical issues, when he explains to Nora that his motivation for telling his stories to people like her is "'to take the mortal agony out of their guts'" (113–14). The metaphorical condensation of the two "incestuous" desires in Nora's narrative indicates that she has overcome the prohibition against telling herself and others about her secret desire.

Barnes dramatizes the moment of undoing the effects of the prohibition against Nora's secret desire in some moving exchanges with O'Connor. After her second dream, Nora feels trapped by the need to remember Robin: "'Robin can go anywhere, do anything,' Nora continued, 'because she forgets, and I nowhere, because I remember'" (126). The inhibition felt by Nora brings her to accuse Robin of causing her grief, an accusation against which Robin would have no defence: "'How could she tell me when she had nothing to tell that wasn't evidence against herself?'" (126). O'Connor, significantly, focusses on the role of memory in Nora's judgement of Robin:

> My brother, whom I had not seen in four years, loved the most of all, died, and who was it but me my mother wanted to talk to? Not those who had seen him last, but me who had seen him best, as if my memory of him were himself; and because you forget Robin best, it's to you she turns. She comes trembling, and defiant, and belligerent, all right—that you may give her back to herself again as you have forgotten her—you are the only one strong enough to have listened to the prosecution, your life; and to have built back the amazing defense, your heart! (126)

Nora "forget[s] Robin best" because she loves her most and will consequently forgive her for the crimes of the heart. O'Connor intuits that Nora wants her love for Robin recognized rather than have him join in with her attack. O'Connor's psychological strategy of recognition allows Nora to avoid an unnecessary prolongation of her painful loss and has the additional benefit of offering her the conditions to accept and therefore release her feelings of guilt for the crime of repression, the buried desire for her grandmother.

The book ends before there is any evidence that O'Connor's advice has had any permanent effects. O'Connor's response to Nora, nevertheless, does not seem consistent with Abraham and Torok's assurance to analysts that the crypt will "vanish in the same movement as the rejection of the judicial realm" (161). However, O'Connor's legal metaphors are employed to encourage Nora to avoid judging Robin and to forgive her. The crypt, Abraham and Torok assert, "owes its existence to its being repudiated" ("Topography" 160)—the complete failure of memory, as opposed to normal repression—and none of O'Connor's words betoken any "judicial" challenge to Nora's "incestuous" desire for Robin or her grandmother. O'Connor has reproduced therapeutic effects analogous to psychoanalysis, for Abraham and Torok suggest that after prolonged presence on the analyst's couch the "heavy architecture" of the crypt will be shaken and anatomized, so it will appear bit by bit that, for lack of a lawsuit, the walls of denial have become obsolete. By means of the prohibition against not telling, the distinctive feature of the analytic situation, the unutterable will change its sign. It will turn into an actively and dynamically repressed desire *not to tell*, forging its paths, detours, and myriad ways of being symbolized. ("Topography" 160)

The "unutterable," secret desire for the grandmother will "change its sign" because the "repressed desire *not to tell*" will pass from the "preservative repression" (Abraham and Torok, "Mourning" 135) of the crypt to the dynamic repression of the unconscious. Once the repressed desire has passed from the artificial unconscious of the crypt to the unconscious proper by means of the prohibition against not telling—you cannot not tell—the repressed desire not to tell is translated by Nora into symbols, albeit hieroglyphic symbols, which tell us a secret, something that they do not tell.

Despite being reducible to the "image of a forgotten experience" or the "hieroglyphics of sleep and pain," Nora's grandmother and Robin remain to some degree incomprehensible and enigmatic figures to her. What *Nightwood* shows us, and Derrida reminds us to think about, is that we are given to memory and thus interiorization upon the death of the other "since the other, outside us, is now nothing." Derrida adds, "And with the dark light of this nothing, we learn that the other resists the closure of our interiorizing memory" (*Memoires* 34). In *Nightwood*, the other appears as other with what Derrida calls this "irrevocable absence." The other reveals to Nora, and us, our own limit, the possibility of our own death. Indeed, "We are only ourselves from the perspective of this knowledge" (34) of the possibility of mourning our own death. Derrida's point that "we lament being no more than 'memory,' 'in memory'"(33–34) serves as an apt reading of *Nightwood*. The "irrevocable absence" of the two lost objects of desire that Nora mourns constitutes an allegory for the reader. By interiorizing within ourselves this absence, the other as other, death "makes manifest the limits of a *me* or an *us* who are obliged to harbor something that is greater and other than them: something *outside of them within them*" (34). We too as readers harbour the absence of death, something outside us and also, paradoxically, within us that resists the closure of our interiorizing memory.

Nora's hieroglyphic dreams and the crypt of her grandmother are only two examples of an outside that resists us and our interpretive efforts to take the text within us, to anatomize her melancholy. Her work of mourning is not only Barnes's work of mourning, but the reader's too.

NOTES

1.   This essay was inspired by a directed reading course that I conducted with my student Shauna Reist. I am indebted to her enthusiasm for Barnes's *Nightwood*, which first brought the work to my attention.

2.   See also Mary Lynn Broe, *Silence and Power: A Reevaluation of Djuna Barnes* (Carbondale: Southern Illinois UP, 1991), 354; Louis F. Kannenstine, *The Art of Djuna Barnes: Duality and Damnation* (New York: New York UP, 1977) 37, 87.

3.   Jane Marcus's analysis of the "carnivalesque" elements in *Nightwood* in her article, "Laughing at Leviticus: *Nightwood* as Woman's Circus Epic" (in Broe, *Silence and Power* 221–50), provides a good starting point for the generic claim that the text is an anatomy. Marcus never calls *Nightwood* an anatomy, but her reference to Barnes as "the female Rabelais" (249) strongly indicates the presence of the tradition. Marcus borrows the term "carnivalesque" from Mikhail Bakhtin who develops the concept in his study of Menippean satire and applies it to the novel. See Bakhtin, *Rabelais and his World*, trans. Helen Iswolsky (Bloominton: Indiana UP, 1984).

4.   On Menippean satire or the anatomy, see also Eugene Kirk, *Menippean Satire: An Annotated Catalogue of Texts and Criticism* (New York: Garland, 1980). The riddling quality of the epigram produces the effect of discontinuity in narrative by shifting the emphasis from action to a fusion of "sensation and reflection," as Kannenstine (95) and Northrop Frye, *The Anatomy of Criticism: Four Essays* (Princeton: Princeton UP, 1957) 280, note. For Frye, the use of an object of sense experience to stimulate mental activity, particularly the close relation between the visual and the conceptual in the riddle, helps define the epigram and links it to hieroglyphic writing and the ideogram (280). The Baron, Felix Volkbein, delivers an epigram on epigram when he says, "An image is a stop the mind makes between uncertainties" (93). Felix, talking about his failed marriage with Robin, complains that he can visualize her, but he can form no clear conception of her. Robin, like Nora's grandmother, remains beyond comprehension, a riddle.

5.   Laurence Sterne, *The Life and Opinions of Tristram Shandy, Gentleman*, ed. Ian Watt (Boston: Houghton Mifflin, 1965) 198.

6.   As the "*philosophus gloriosus*" (311), O'Connor supplies us with the intellectual and verbal exuberance that typifies the figure. Recognized as the target of a Freudian parody (Marcus 221; Wilson 57), O'Connor is the confidant of the main character

Nora, and their long conversations give him ample opportunity to overwhelm his listeners with his theories of "the night" (69), or the unconscious, race, class, and gender identity, to name only a few of his favourite topics (see Harris 238; Marcus 221; Wilson 57). We are meant to laugh at the life and opinions of this transvestite gynecologist, but occasionally some of his many oracular utterances do show genuine insight into Nora's psychological struggles. It is proper to the irony of the anatomy genre that the reader be left to decide when the utterances are useful. Herring nicknames O'Connor the "bistro philosopher" (210). The most accurate description of his role in the text, to help Nora find a cure for her love melancholy, comes from O'Connor's own mouth when he says in one of his carnivalesque aphorisms: "You beat the liver out of a goose and you get pate; you pound the muscles of a man's *cardia* to get a philosopher" (75). O'Connor's role in *Nightwood*, more than that of any other character, demonstrates the anatomy genre's "special function of analysis, of breaking up the lumber of stereotypes, fossilized beliefs, superstitious terrors, crank theories, pedantic dogmatisms, oppressive fashions, and all other things that impede the free movemement (not necessarily, of course, the progress) of society" (Frye 233). It is not unusual, Frye informs us, for the *philosophus gloriosus* to expose the "inconvenient data" of the prevailing philosophical system, patriarchal gender roles in this case, by forming an alternative and equally plausible system (229). For instance, O'Connor's theory of the homosexual as the "third sex" (123), constructed out of alternative readings of children's fairy tales, has been given serious consideration by scholars like Andrea L. Harris in "The Third Sex" (248–53).

7.   All passages from "Mourning and Melancholia" quoted from *The Standard Edition of the Complete Psychological Works of Sigmund Freud*, translated by James Strachey, volume 11 (London: Hogarth, 1960), 243–58.

8.   See Perrault. See also the Grimm's version. The act of eating is alluded to as a metaphor for sexuality in Zipes 24.

9.   It is important to note here that the lesbian relationship in *Nightwood* is not limited to the mother-child relationship explored by Carolyn Allen, "The Erotics of Nora's Narrative in Djuna Barnes's *Nightwood*," *Signs: A Journal of Women in Culture and Society* 19.1 (1993): 177–200.

10. On the cryptonym, see Abraham and Torok, *The Wolfman's Magic Word* (19). Cryptonyms, sometimes in other languages, obstruct meaning through unusual lexical relationships like homonyms, synonyms, and "allosemes"—a list of a word's meanings or uses. Abraham and Torok have written on case histories in which a patient, such as Freud's famous "Wolf-man," generates emotionally charged words, or "word-things" which conceal a trauma that must be kept hidden not only from others, but from his or her own consciousness.

11. On this "artificial unconscious," see also Derrida, "Fors" 75.

12. Here I echo Derrida ("Fors" 72).

13. For mimetic rivalry, see Rene Girard, *Violence and the Sacred*, trans. Patrick Gregory (Baltimore: Johns Hopkins UP, 1977).

14. Victoria Smith's essay on *Nightwood* deals with similar themes such as the witness and his or her relation to a "narrative of loss" (194). She explicitly refers to Freud's theory of mourning and melancholy as having great explanatory power for Barnes's text, but she does not refer to Abraham and Torok, or to Derrida. She also calls the chapter "Bow Down" an "anatomy of loss" (196) but makes no observations about the anatomy genre. Smith's analysis of Felix Volkbein is indispensable. However, Smith makes no mention of the figure of the grandmother, a figure which would explain the "discourse of melancholia" (201) she tries to account for.

15. On transference as a "repetitive structuring principle" (137) between patient and analyst and the material of psychic life, see Felman 133–37.

16. As Peter Brooks states, "narrative always makes the implicit claim to be in a state of repetition" (713).

Colossal Departures

Figuring the Lost Father in Berryman's and Plath's Poetry

"—end of this
But an anger helps me"
    —JOHN BERRYMAN,
        on a handwritten draft of Dream Song 42, *dated 28/9 Dec. 1962*[1]

IN A TELEVISION INTERVIEW done for the BBC, a drunken John
Berryman spoke to A. Alvarez about his admiration for and fascination with
fellow American poet Sylvia Plath. Berryman especially singled out for praise
the famous poem "Daddy," quoting with relish the poem's final line: "Daddy,
daddy, you bastard, I'm through" (244). What particularly intrigued him,
Berryman noted, was that since Plath's father died when she was only eight,
the bitter poem is essentially "all fantasy; she's only dealing with a father
figure, or phantom, and it killed her."[2] While Berryman is perhaps naïve
about the awareness and maturity of any eight-year old, let alone a precocious child like Plath, it is both appropriate and ironic that Berryman should
focus on the early death of the poet's father and the subsequent mythologizing of this loss, for his own poetry enacts a similar ritual. John Allyn
Smith, father of the future poet, then named John Allyn Smith, Jr., died
when young John was eleven. Although some degree of mystery has always
shrouded Smith's death, it was ruled a suicide by gunshot. Berryman, his
last name quickly changed less than three months later, so as to match that
of his new stepfather, would be haunted all his life by this loss, and in his
poetic masterwork, *The Dream Songs*, would mythologize both the loss and
the figure of the father in larger-than-life terms very similar to those of

Sylvia Plath. Poems concerning the father are among the most memorable in each poet's body of work, and signal new directions for the elegy, both honouring and subverting many of the conventions and expectations associated with the genre. The element of raw and even violent anger triggered by the father's death, the range and honest expression of the disturbing inner emotions of the surviving child, mark new areas of language for the modern elegist.

In his landmark study, *The English Elegy: Studies in the Genre from Spenser to Yeats*, Peter M. Sacks views the "relationship between the language of elegy and the experience of loss as an event or action" (1). Sacks argues that the language of elegy is not a passive entity, a rhetoric already containing feelings associated with loss, but rather an active "work," both a product and a dramatic process, "a working through of experience" (1). Exploring Freud's phrase "the work of mourning," he analyzes the motivations and effects of elegiac verse, working almost exclusively with English and Irish elegies, with only a brief glance at the American elegy in his concluding chapter. A consistently Freudian approach throughout the study enables Sacks to highlight "a significant similarity between the process of mourning and the oedipal resolution" (8). Early on, Sacks lists the conventions most often associated with elegy, which include imagery involving weaving, vegetation gods, flowers, water, and light. Structurally and tonally, elegies commonly include series of questions, complaints, repetition or refrain, as well as feelings of guilt and attempts to distance oneself from the deceased. Finally, traditional elegies, especially the pastoral elegy, usually turn toward some form of consolation at the end of the poem.

As modern American elegists, Berryman and Plath use some but not all of the conventions listed by Sacks. Plath is more apt to employ some of the familiar imagery, such as water in "Full Fathom Five," or flowers in "Electra on Azalea Path." But instead of the consoling flowers associated with nature's cyclical renewal, Plath focuses on the faded plastic flowers atop her father's grave, an instance of subverting the expected function of the image. Berryman's Dream Songs concerning his absent father dispense with the familiar imagery of elegy, but like Plath's poems, they fluctuate between the sombre, sad tone of many canonical elegies, and the vitriolic level of anger that is unique to these two mid-century poets. As Jahan Ramazani notes in *Poetry of Mourning: The Modern Elegy from Hardy to Heaney*, while "self-destructive mourning had long played a role in elegy," a poet like Plath takes this tendency to new extremes in some of the violent fantasies in her elegies (264). The same is true of Berryman's father-elegies, even if those Songs also include the conventions of questions, repetition, and guilt. Guilt, and the ongoing struggle to distance oneself from the dead figure as a means of alleviating guilt, is common in each poet's work, and the oedipal conflict discussed by Sacks is at the heart of this endeavour. Both poets work to recreate, forge a reconciliation with, and finally overcome what Berryman at one point in his unpublished papers called "the blue father."[3] However, neither succeeds in ever achieving the consolation common in so many earlier elegies.

At the time of the BBC interview, Berryman was less than a decade away from taking his own life, and the recognition of a death attraction shared with Plath is possible.[4] Certainly the courtship with death is dramatically re-enacted throughout much of Plath's poetry and Berryman's Dream Songs. But even in these death-drive poems, the presence of the father is typically felt, and the poet's own death is alternately presented as a way of getting back to or back at the father, or in some instances, escaping his haunting presence. Contemplation of one's own death has been another frequent convention of elegy, but not in the intense, frustrated, or sometimes resigned tone found in the work of Berryman and Plath. Rather than musing generally on death and one's own mortality, what we find is an often desperate desire to join the father, the writers flirting with the possibility of ending their own lives.

Although consolation is never achieved, both poets do attempt to reconstruct, and thereby make at least partial peace with, the absent father. One of Plath's best-known early poems is "The Colossus," the title poem from her first volume (London 1960; America 1962). The poem begins with a frank, flat acknowledgement, and like so many poems by both Plath and Berryman, directly addresses the father:

I shall never get you put together entirely,
Pieced, glued, and properly jointed. (129)

The process of systematic re-piecing of the shattered iconic image, an effort of determination but recognized as sure to fall short, is presented in slightly different terms by Berryman in Dream Song 42. This poem returns, as the Dream Song sequence intermittently does, to the profound "departure" mentioned in Dream Song 1 ("All the world like a woolen lover / once did seem on Henry's side. / Then came a departure. / Thereafter nothing fell out as it might or ought.") By Song 42 Henry, the protagonist and speaker in Berryman's long poem, feels able to intimately address the father:

> I see you before me plain
> (I am skilled: I hear, I see)—
>
> Your honour was troubled: when you wondered—'No'.
> I hear. I think I hear. (46)

Here, as in Plath's poem, we observe a willing of the self to comprehend a father never quite known, and ultimately beyond knowing. Each poem wavers between a feeling of weary compromise with, if not acceptance of, the father's inscrutability, and a sense of Sisyphean incompletion. Henry tells the father he hears, but then qualifies himself: "I think I hear." Plath's speaker suggests that the colossus might possess some oracular wisdom, but admits:

> Thirty years now I have labored
> To dredge the silt from your throat.
> I am none the wiser. (129)

The simultaneous sense of intimacy and longing to bridge distance is reinforced by the use of apostrophe in each poem. Berryman's poem, which he once introduced at a reading as "addressed to the ghost of Odysseus," begins: "O journeyer, deaf in the mould." This figure provides a link between Henry and the father, in that by Dream Song 42 Henry is himself a tired traveller, well-embarked on what Berryman termed the "world tour" of his tortured narrator. Additionally, Henry is in a "cast" in this poem, having broken his ankle, the image of the cast referencing the father's "mould." The father is dead, and "Henry Pussy-cat" himself, we have already learned, seems able to die and come back to life as part of his cycle of endless suffering. The distance of the father is verified by his "deaf" state, which plays on "death," as "mould" suggests a "mould" or cast, and part of Berryman's characteristic irony as part of mourning is the notion that while Henry's auditor, the father, is "deaf," Henry is at last able to "hear" or understand why his father was driven to suicide.

But is Henry really addressing the father as much as he is talking to himself, working things through? After all, the deafness of the father does not interrupt the song of loss, abandonment, and hoped-for reconciliation. Part of the mythopoeic strategy here, as in Plath's verse, is to work toward an awareness of what Berryman terms in his earlier "The Ball Poem," "the epistemology of loss," an awareness not just of inevitable loss, but the process of finding a language to deal with loss. By mourning part of a lost self, by embracing the very act of mourning itself, each poet is able to transfer or displace the feeling of loss and abandonment from the father, so that often what is mourned is not the deceased but the self. The focus turns inward, toward the spiritually-paralyzed survivor, the poet-speaker. Near the end of "The Colossus" Plath's speaker says "My hours are married to shadow." Henry implores the father, or himself, to "consider me in my cast" (130).

Each poet presents death as a psychological drama, with the poet-speaker in the lead role. Loss is self-consciously staged, language foregrounded, in an attempt to impose aesthetic distance from the event of loss. Christina Britzolakis has observed how, "In Plath's poetry, the work of mourning appears as inseparable from its performance in language; it is inherently rhetorical and self-reflexive, a structure of exacerbated theatricalism" (7). In addition to staging the language of mourning, Plath will at times directly allude to drama, as she does by invoking the dramatic literature of antiquity mid-way through "The Colossus":

A blue sky out of the Oresteia
Arches above us. O father, all by yourself
You are pithy and historical as the Roman Forum. (129)

Nearly all of Plath's poems dealing with the loss of the father ("The Colossus," "Electra on Azalea Path," "On the Decline of Oracles," "Full Fathom Five") allude in some way to classical literature and myth. Others, such as "Daddy," choose to invoke recent political atrocities such as the Holocaust.[5]

But what is common among all these poems is Plath's attempt to render loss as archetypal. In commenting on Plath's poems about her father, particularly the late cluster known as the bee sequence, Helen Vendler has written: "While we may all need such myths to approach the enigma of family relations, Plath not only, with new insights, replaced one myth with another but also changed her style to fit the myth" (280). Late in her life, Plath herself expressed the need to feel that her sense of abandonment, at this stage by husband as well as father, was not parochial: "What the person out of Belsen—physical or psychological—wants is nobody saying the birdies still go tweet-tweet, but the full knowledge that somebody else has been there and knows the worst" (qtd. in Axelrod 313).

The mythologization in Berryman's poems of loss tends to work in the opposite direction, from the outside in. The analogy between the auditor of Song 42 and Odysseus is the exception rather than the rule, as most of the Dream Songs concerning the father present Henry in a dramatic situation, such as his father's grave site, and then telescope inward to explore his anguished emotions. Henry does not seem to feel that he needs the scaffolding of ancient family drama to analogize with his own situation; his own drama is striking enough. For example, Berryman struggled for most of his adult life to clarify a childhood memory of his despondent father swimming far out into the ocean, out of sight, with either himself or his younger brother, terrifying the mother. Late in his life Berryman wrote to his mother, again asking which son the father had taken with him. After receiving yet another of her contradictory responses, he finally determined that his father had only threatened to take one of the boys, and that his memory had transformed the threat into an actual event. Dream Song 145 presents the frightening scene:

> but he did not swim out with me or my brother
> as he threatened—
>
> a powerful swimmer, to take one of us along
> as company in the defeat sublime[.] (162)

Although this Dream Song does go on to compare the father's despair with that of a Texas murderer who shot thirteen people, what is more characteristic of Berryman's work is how the poem recasts autobiography on a grand, dramatic scale that parallels Plath's use of classical myths and texts. Henry, because he is in the midst of his own epic poem (there is a total of 385 Songs), needs to "cast" his own story on a large, sweeping canvas.[6] Of interesting note in this regard is the fact that among Berryman's unpublished papers is a folder containing ideas for a projected essay, "On Death," where he speculates that he "might use my own Maine experience" for a philosophical exploration of death. The experience he refers to is his first serious contemplation of the act of suicide, which eventually did wind up in a poem, "Henry's Understanding," included in Berryman's final volume, published the year of the poet's death:

> ...it occurred to me
> that *one* night, instead of warm pajamas,
> I'd take off all my clothes
> & cross the damp cold lawn & down the bluff
> into the terrible water & walk forever
> under it out toward the island. (162)

Plath's poems concerning the father's death also invoke the image of the sea, but not as both threat and seductress, as in Berryman's poems. Rather, for Plath, the sea is the mysterious, unfathomable depth where the dead father resides. In "A Life," he is a drowned sea-god who crawls "up out of the sea"; in "All the Dead Dears" he looms "under the fishpond surface." Plath's speaker in these poems is more the observer than Berryman's Henry, who acts as either a participant in dialogue with the father, or, as in "Henry's Understanding," a figure who by walking into the water reenacts, at least imaginatively, the father's death. Even in "The Colossus," which in its early lines presents the speaker engaged in attempting to reconstruct the figure of the absent father, ends with the image of the father being consigned to the sea, to re-emerge on his own, and not his daughter's, time. The poem closes:

> No longer do I listen for the scrape of a keel
> On the blank stones of the landing. (130)

This tone of resignation is present at the close of several father-elegies by each poet, including Dream Song 42, which presents Henry left to "pick up the tab" for his father's suicide. Again, Berryman turns the focus inward, intensifying the note of loss present in the address to the father's "ghost" in the poem's opening:

Think it across, in freezing wind: withstand
my blistered wish: flop, there, to his blind song
who pick up the tab. (46)

Despite emphasizing earlier in the poem a newfound ability to hear and see, Henry is once again cast into his familiar position of flinging a "blind" song into an indifferent wind. The indifference of the surrounding world, so different from the more sympathetic natural world presented in the conventional elegy, also assaults Plath's speaker in "The Colossus": "Nights, I squat in the cornucopia / Of your left ear, out of the wind" (129). Each of these poems ends by acknowledging an ultimate inability to connect with the lost father, despite the effort of elegiac catharsis through the act of writing.

Resignation, however, is not the tone struck in all of the father-poems by either poet. Resentment, bitterness, and anger frequently burst forth, two of the most direct instances being Plath's "Electra on Azalea Path" and Berryman's Dream Song 384, the penultimate poem in the sequence. Each poem is set at the graveside of the father, and this time it is Plath's speaker who directly addresses the dead, while Berryman's Henry, in an attempt to express and possibly dispel what he terms his "rage," ceases to address the father, and instead, literally assaults the grave.

I spit upon this dreadful banker's grave
. . . .
I'd like to scrabble till I got right down
away down under the grass

and ax the casket open ha to see
just how he's taking it.... (406)

As the final of several Dream Songs concerning the father's death, this poem confirms that resignation, acceptance, or even an "indifference" that Henry says he wishes for in vain, will never come. So, at last, Henry unleashes a violent, macabre fantasy in a desperate attempt to find a sufficient expression of mourning.

A similar scene of haunting the gravesite is found in Plath's "Electra on Azalea Path," where the speaker figures the father as a suicide, even though Plath's father, unlike Berryman's, did not take his own life. However, the naming of the cemetery path running by her father's grave, as well as Plath's notes on the poem, make it clear that the mythic father of the poem is her own:

...I found the stone: Otto E. Plath 1885–1940. Right beside the path,
where it would be walked over. Felt cheated. My temptation to dig him up.
To prove he existed and really was dead. How far gone would he be? No
trees, no peace, his headstone jammed up against the body on the other
side. Left shortly. It is good to have the place in mind. (*Collected Poems* 289)

The wish to violate the actual grave, astonishingly similar to Henry's fantasy in Song 384, is still not likely to bring "peace," the poet acknowledges. The poem itself emphasizes the stark, unadorned bleakness of the grave, a "charity ward" and "poorhouse, where the dead / Crowd foot to foot, head to head" (117). Again Plath uses the drama of a classical text, but even in casting herself as Electra, the spirit of vengefulness is absent. In a revealing admission of her own poetic strategy, she writes, "I borrow the stilts of an old tragedy," and what replaces revenge in this version of the story is an increasing sense of guilt. As the poem begins, the speaker asserts that she "had nothing to do with guilt" upon the death of the father, but by the end of the poem a guilt has developed that is so strong that the speaker blames herself for the father's death, and asks his forgiveness. The poem concludes with these lines:

I am the ghost of an infamous suicide,
My own blue razor rusting in my throat.
O pardon the one who knocks for pardon at
Your gate, father—your hound-bitch, daughter, friend.
It was my love that did us both to death. (117)

As in Berryman's Dream Song 42, it is once again the survivor who is left to pick up the tab, and the resulting guilt is so strong that the speaker presents herself as joining the father in death. Berryman sounds a similar note in Dream Song 235, his elegy for Ernest Hemingway, another suicide haunted by a father's suicide: "Mercy! my father; do not pull the trigger / or all my life I'll suffer from your anger / killing what you began" (254).

In this and other poems Berryman presents suicide by the father as a curse and a legacy, "a bad example, murder of oneself / the final death, in a paroxysm, of love" (254). Is the act an outburst of love, or a symptom of an insidious, pathological disease? Another poem written after Hemingway's suicide, Dream Song 34, conflates the deaths of Hemingway, his father, Henry's father, and the recounting by Berryman's mother of his father's death, a story which, from the poet's perspective, was contradictory from one telling to the next. Finally, amidst this swirl of associations, the poem concludes with Henry identifying with Hemingway's pre-suicide anguish:

> ... it's so I broke down here, in his mind
> whose sire as mine one same way—I refuse
> hoping the guy go home. (38)

Berryman's analogues for Henry's suffering are often other survivors of parental suicide, or even suicides themselves, including Plath in Dream Song 172. Beginning with the line "Your face broods from my table, Suicide," the poem generalizes Plath's death as emblematic of a long line of fellow writers who have preceded her, and Henry, in death.

> long falls your exit all repeatingly,
> a poor exemplum, one more suicide
> to stack upon the others
> till stricken Henry with his sisters & brothers
> suddenly gone pauses to wonder why he
> alone breasts the wronging tide. (191)

This attitude is a part of Henry's courtship with death, a "stricken" form of mourning akin to the feeling of abandonment upon the father's death.

Plath's earliest poem on what she termed "my father-sea god-muse" is "Full Fathom Five," and it is one of her most essential statements of loss. The poem's first line, sounding a note which will be echoed in nearly all the later poems on the lost father, emphasizes the father's inscrutability and literal inaccessibility: "Old man, you surface seldom" (92). Succeeding lines go on to associate the absent father with the vast sea and its ceaseless rhythms, the line of the tide troped as "wrinkling skeins / Knotted" (92). The familiar elegiac gesture of associating the rhetoric of loss with weaving or fabric is part of the suggestion here, in addition to the idea of the sea as a source, both life-giving and destroying. In the curved line of the surf's foam, figured as the father's hair, "survives / The old myth of origins / Unimaginable."

Plath continues to associate the father with the landscape in subsequent stanzas, first as frozen mountains of ice, deepening the sense of cold separation and danger. She presents herself as attempting to navigate a threatening sea course, one not easily measured, understood, or even contemplated: "All obscurity / Starts with a danger: / Your dangers are many" (92). Then, in a set of lines anticipating the difficulty in accepting the father's death expressed in "Electra on Azalea Path," she refers to that death as "rumors," which she can only "half-believe" (93). His powerful though infrequent resurfacing from the sea puts the rumours to rest, at least momentarily, but his visage is so stone-like as to defy the weather, as if he is beyond time and the elements. Ultimately, as the poem moves toward its powerful conclusion, the ghost-figure of the father asserts its absolute dominion: "You defy questions; / You defy other godhood." The speaker is fated to course the "kingdom's border" repeatedly, "Exiled to no good." This sense of the repeated but frustrated effort to access the father will become a theme in all the father-poems to come, especially "The Colossus" and "Electra on Azalea Path." In the final two lines of "Full Fathom Five," the speaker articulates the stifling feeling of oppression in the wake of the father's death, and the almost desperate desire to join him:

Father, this thick air is murderous.
I would breathe water. (93)

The ghost of the father as brutal oppressor reappears in the form of the "boot in the face" of "Daddy," the retreat and eventual self-accusation in the opening and closing lines of "Electra on Azalea Path," and the single-line stanza from "The Beekeeper's Daughter": "My heart under your foot, sister of a stone" (118). The same frightening image is employed by Berryman in Dream Song 241, which begins with the line, "Father being the loneliest word in the one language," and progresses to:

> Wicked & powerful, shy Henry lifted his head with an offering.
> Boots greeted him and it. (260)

No doubt this sense of being physically brutalized by the death of the father is what leads to the violent, vengeful outbursts of poems like "Daddy" and Dream Song 284. Although psychic and even physical suffering by the survivor, in the form of grief, has always been one of the conventions of elegiac mourning, the psychological violence perpetrated by the deceased, the dead as active oppressor, is an aspect of the modern elegy inaugurated by Berryman and Plath.

Much early criticism of Plath's work took its cue from Judith Kroll's claim that the apparently personal poetry is actually part of a larger "timeless mythic system" meant to present the parochial as impersonal, or at least universal (2). More recently, however, the attention given by Marjorie Perloff and others to Ted Hughes's drastic rearrangement of Plath's intended sequence of the *Ariel* poems clarifies the acutely personal nature of even the final poems, so compact and dense with their cool, precise imagery. Certainly Plath did mythologize the loss of her father in more traditionally mythic terms than did Berryman, but both poets construct a dramatically personal mythos of loss. Each casts the poet-speaker as central character in a recurring drama of struggle, a drama that serves to fuel creativity. Part of what Berryman meant in the handwritten note on a draft of Song 42 was that "an anger helps" by stimulating verse. For Henry, the loss of the father is the "departure" of Dream Song 1 that colours all subsequent events in the long verse-story of Henry's struggles, but it is also the impetus for the writing of 384 more Songs.[7] Other types of loss throughout the Songs, both specific and generic, are all framed in reference to this specific, personal loss. The same is true for Plath in the sense that it is the loss of the father to which she keeps returning in her work, a loss not worked through, but reworked, repeatedly. Earlier elegies in both the British and American tradition were largely written as attempts at closure, repeating the motif of the turn toward "pastures new" sounded at the end of Milton's "Lycidas." But for Berryman and Plath, poetic mourning becomes almost obsessive, a sort of wellspring for poetic creation, making it possible to read their elegies as sequences of poems centred around the same figure and theme. With Berryman, it is quite plausible to read that figure, the father, and that theme, loss of the father, as the overarching motif of the entire Dream Song series.

One of Henry's most poignant acts of mourning occurs in Dream Song 76, one of the rare Songs with a title: "Henry's Confession." The very notion of "confessing" to sorrow is in itself odd, suggesting again that some sort of blame for a father's loss be placed on the survivor. Rather than presenting grieving as a natural response to a loved one's death, "confession" implies wrongdoing, transgression. As the poem opens, Henry asks his nameless friend why things seem to have been going so smooth lately. The friend, whom Berryman once characterized as a "Job's comforter" figure, explains to Henry that part of his uncharacteristic tranquillity might be the result of laying off the booze, women, and long telephone conversations. Henry disagrees, and, using one of the more striking metaphors in all of the Dream Songs, pours out his sense of emptiness:

—If life is a handkerchief sandwich,

In a modesty of death I join my father
who dared so long agone leave me.
A bullet on a concrete stoop
close by a smothering sea
spreadeagled on an island, by my knee. (83)

Life as a "handkerchief sandwich" is Henry's characteristic summation of his utter aloneness. Of course the handkerchief connotes sadness and tears, as well as the attempt to muffle one's crying. At the same time, appearing in the form of a sandwich, the handkerchief of grief purports to "help" the griever by affording sustenance, in the form of food. But how can this be, when biting into this metaphorical sandwich once again leaves an empty, blank taste in the mouth?

In characterizing death as "a modesty," Henry cuts against his tendency to present the father's death as an act of defiance, or a conscious abandonment of others, as he does in several other Songs. The "modesty" of death suggests a more lonely sort of retreat, a quiet act of self-effacement as opposed to a loud gesture designed to frighten, or garner attention. This is the sort of death-gesture that Henry may wish to emulate, as, in his state of lonely depression, he decides to "join" his father. His friend, in an ironic gesture that reinforces the sense of Henry's suffering being so private as to be inaccessible, offers him a handkerchief for comfort. Of course this is the last thing that Henry needs, having tasted too often the emptiness of grief. Still, the friend attempts to dance Henry off the stage, as he does at several other points in the sequence of Songs, proposing a stroll by the "beautiful sea," the same sea that Henry has just described as "smothering," the symbolic representation of the vast void that overwhelmed his father, and threatens to overwhelm him. In a haunting, ambiguous final line, Henry responds to his friend's suggestion by saying: "I saw nobody coming, so I went instead." But where? Perhaps Henry alludes to going into death, or walking into the sea itself, or openly embracing grief, giving expression to his sorrow. It is significant that this is the penultimate Song in the initial volume of 77 *Dream Songs* published in 1964, closing Henry's story at present for the reader, until Henry's reappearance with an additional 308 Songs in 1968. In the next and final poem, Song 77, Henry is indeed getting ready to depart, perhaps joining his father in the void: "his head full / & his heart full, he's making ready to move on."

In gauging poetic expression of loss in mid-century American poetry, a reader encounters varied attempts to work within, and yet extend, the genre of elegy. While many of the conventions of the pastoral elegy tradition continue to surface, American elegies since 1950 tend to be shorter, more personal lyrics. Among poets coming to maturity during this period, Berryman and Plath are the most daring in their reworkings of the genre. Refiguring conventions of mourning into classical analogues, personal mythologies, macabre fantasies, stark expressions of jealousy, anger, and even hatred, they challenge what had previously been associated with the work of mourning. Bold and daring in their explorations of the innermost recesses of the private psyche, they present memorable characters, voices, and metaphors in treating the theme of loss, one of the major sources for expression in verse.

NOTES

1. John Berryman archive, University of Minnesota Libraries, Special Collections. My thanks to Kate Donahue for permission to quote from the archive.

2. The film is part of the Berryman archive at the University of Minnesota.

3. Berryman archive, University of Minnesota Libraries.

4. Of course Berryman, though anything but a casual reader, may, like so many, have been caught up by the dramatic details of Plath's final days and eventual suicide.

5. Plath's controversial use of Holocaust imagery in her poetry has been thoughtfully analyzed in several places, perhaps most notable in: Jacqueline Rose's *The Haunting of Sylvia Plath* (Cambridge: Harvard UP, 1991); Susan Gubar's "Prosopopoeia and Holocaust Poetry in English: The Case of Sylvia Plath," *Yale Journal of Criticism* 14.1 (2000): 191–215; Harriet L. Parmet's *The Terror of Our Days: Four American Poets Respond to the Holocaust* (Bethlehem [PA]: Lehigh UP, 2001); Robin Peel's *Writing Back: Sylvia Plath and Cold War Politics* (Madison [NJ]: Associated University Presses, 2002); and Amy Hungerford's *The Holocaust of Texts: Genocide, Literature, and Personification* (Chicago: U Chicago P, 2003).

6. For further discussion of what Berryman termed his "programmatic" for the overall themes and movements of *The Dream Songs*, see my essay "John Berryman's 'Programmatic' for *The Dream Songs* and an Instance of Revision," *Journal of Modern Literature* 23.3/4 (2000): 429–39.

7. Berryman's short fiction, limited to four short stories, is also crucial to an understanding of his vision of loss and regeneration. See my essay "John Berryman's Short Fiction: Elegy and Enlightenment," *Studies in Short Fiction* 30.3 (1993): 309–16.

Reading the Ethics of Mourning in the Poetry of Donald Hall

IN HIS THIRTEENTH BOOK OF POETRY, *Without* (1998), Donald Hall offers a series of poems that memorialize his marital life with the celebrated poet Jane Kenyon as she struggles with, and ultimately succumbs to, leukemia.[1] In addition to chronicling the nature and profundity of his grief, Hall's collection of poetry affords him a means for telling and retelling the stories of his final months with Kenyon. From such poems as "The Gallery," in which Hall reproduces the local headline announcing her death in April 1995—"POET JANE KENYON DIES / AT HER HOME IN WILMOT" (48)—to "Without," in which he laments the "hours days weeks months weeks days hours" that pass swiftly by "without punctuation" in his grief and isolation (46), the obviously cathartic aspects of this process provide Hall with an avenue for narrating his grief and contextualizing the breach in his life engendered by Kenyon's glaring and painful absence. Using recent insights in family systems psychotherapy and ethical criticism, we will explore the manner in which Hall employs *Without* as an explicit forum for both embracing and transcending the barriers of time and death. As we witness Hall's struggle to transform his grief into a narrative of mourning that might hold together the reality of his loss within the context of art, the power of narrative therapy—one of the principal means of treatment in contemporary family systems psychotherapy, as well as a valuable and illuminating form of literary critique—emerges as the principal means of coping for Hall. Because Hall devotes particular energy in his verse to not only narrating but also recontextualizing his grief and anger over Kenyon's untimely—and indeed, very public—loss, we will construct an ethics of mourning in this essay in order to confront the important, and often unexamined, work of narrative therapy in literary works of art and its significant role in the grieving process for both the writer and his audience.

In *Narrative Means to Therapeutic Ends* (1990), Michael White and David Epston augment the tenets of the family systems paradigm to account for the ways in which narrative experiences provide readers with a means for interpersonal development and growth. As White and Epston note, "In order to perceive change in one's life—to experience one's life as progressing—and in order to perceive oneself changing one's life, a person requires mechanisms that assist her to plot the events of her life within the context of coherent sequences across time—through the past, present, and future" (35). These mechanisms—works of narrative therapy—offer cogent methodologies that assist clients (or readers and writers) in simultaneously identifying with and separating from the dilemmas that plague their lived experiences. Therapists such as White and Epston argue that the externalization of interpersonal problems through narrative therapy enables these readers and writers to address their various issues via the liberating auspices of the imagination. Such stories encourage them "to explore possibilities for establishing the conditions that might facilitate performance and circulation of their preferred stories and knowledges" (76). In short, the telling and retelling of story furnishes readers and writers with the capacity for transforming their lives through the therapeutic interpretation of their textual experiences.[2]

An ethics of mourning challenges us to account for the ways in which we go about the business of mourning, a largely uncharted territory in contemporary ethical criticism's growing body of scholarship.[3] As a composer of elegies throughout his long and distinguished career, Hall possesses a special knowledge of the manner in which we communicate and memorialize loss. Yet as Alice Attie notes, contemporary poets such as Hall often seize the emotional brutality of death, and, in sharp contrast with their eighteenth- and nineteenth-century precursors, eschew the clichés of mourning and commemoration in favour of the more explicit embrace of their personal desolation. "The modern elegy," Attie observes, "often attempts to be painfully close to the loss it mourns. The absence of traditional consoling clichés becomes, in itself, an interrogation both of the arrogance of attempting to speak at all and of the compromise involved in hiding behind the consoling fictions" (110). In a perceptive essay on the loss of his father and his own deferral of mourning, Geoffrey Galt Harpham describes our various clichés for grieving, including the time-honoured phrases for discussing the ways in which we "got on with it," "took care of business," and "handled the situation" (541). While such homilies equip us with a means for communicating our dignity and resolve in the face of human loss, they scarcely provide us with healing methodologies for confronting— and ultimately transcending—the mourning of our loved ones. "Where do tears go when they don't flow out?" Harpham astutely asks. "Do they just circulate around in you? Do you sweat them out?" (544).

As a form of narrative therapy, an ethics of mourning reflects the struggle each human faces with the death of an other: the reality of our own mortality, the finality that we discover in our loved ones' deaths. As a poet, Hall addresses this inevitability by looking backward, by elegizing not only the person that he mourns but also the events and places that shaped his experiences of that person. An ethics of mourning begins and ends with a recognition that while every moment passes from us in an infinite procession that denies our desire to return to a place or person in the past, we may still find some solace in the balm that language affords as a means to build a bridge across time's expanse in order to testify to the strength of love, even within the desolation of loss. As an act of literary interpretation, an ethics of mourning cultivates empathy in the reader. Without the ability to assume the role of the characters who grieve within the confines of the story or poem, the reader will not be transformed. As an ethical paradigm, the act of mourning encourages the reader to take part in the grieving that the writer records, to experience the death of a person whom we have never known, except through the artifice of language. Similar to the suspension of disbelief, an ethics of mourning draws us into the circle of grief so we may shed tears that are at once our own and not our own. Within this act of textual grieving, an ethics of mourning implores us to recognize how our own lives—and their inescapable endings—are tied inextricably to the lives and deaths of others.

In *Without*, Hall's postulation of an ethics of mourning allows him to utilize his elegies as forums for encountering, in all of its brute narrative force, the pain of Kenyon's suffering and absence. By concentrating on the particularities of Kenyon's existence and their relationship in his verse, Hall's ethics of mourning functions as a means for progressing from the sorrowful explication of her death to the healing power of her memory. The act of grieving leaves us "without force," Jacques Derrida writes in his essay

"By Force of Mourning," or that "state of being drained, without any force, where death, where the death of a friend, leaves us, when we also have to work at mourning" (174). Rather than merely console himself with hazy recollections of a healthy Kenyon, however, Hall forces himself to "work" on his grieving in *Without*, and, in so doing, compels himself to examine the depths of his mourning for Kenyon through his careful depiction of the bittersweet nuances of their final days together, as well as the awful emptiness of the "hours days weeks months weeks days hours" that transpired after her death. Hall's ethics of mourning in *Without* functions as a form of narrative therapy that not only allows him to immerse himself in the pain of Kenyon's passing, but also to celebrate the simple majesty—the "ordinary pleasures" and "contentment recollected," he writes in "Weeds and Peonies" (81)—of her former existence.

Hall uses poetry throughout his career as a medium for understanding our impending mortality, a space in which at times he can rage against the uncontrollable forces of life and death. Yet Hall's poetry is not one of futility; while he may not be able to control the forces that inevitably and ultimately end our lives, he does, at other times, suggest a kind of peace that might be discovered by coming to a deeper understanding and acceptance of the act of dying. Hall's writing activities establish an ethics of mourning that demands that our stories of grief be told and retold. A collection such as *Without* offers a model of the manner in which we may face the looming absence that invariably follows the death of a loved one. Hall's poems demonstrate that the survivors of the deceased can only reshape their own lives by telling stories of their shared past, as well as stories of a future they must face without the one they have lost.

By naming our experiences, we begin not only to understand them but to transform them into stories of coping and of healing. In *The One Day* (1988), a book-length poem whose working title was, tellingly, *Building the House of Dying* and for which he received the National Book Critics Circle Award, Hall confronts the pain endemic to grief and mourning. In his writing of that book, Hall contends that the process of mourning itself functions as an imaginative act:[4]

The bed is a world of pain and the repeated deaths
of preparation for death. The awake nightmare

comforts itself by painting the mourner's portrait:

> As I imagine myself on grief's rack at graveside
> I picture and pity myself. When pathology supplies
> the jargon of reassurance, I have buried your body
> a thousand times. (60)

Only in understanding the death of another do we begin to comprehend our own mortality, and only through such an understanding can we begin to enter into the ethical act of grieving the loss of another. In *Tales and Transformations: Stories in Families and Family Therapy* (1994), Janine Roberts relates the experience of Katie, an eight-year-old girl who confronts death for the first time; subsequently, Katie names her initiation into the knowledge of life and death in a rather straightforward, laconic manner, calling the moment, "When I First Really Learned About Death" (46–47). Katie's experience demonstrates powerfully the efficacy of placing our pain or fear into language. By using language to describe our struggle with the knowledge of death, we wrest the power of grief away from the physical absence of the one we loved, and in so doing we become empowered to reconstruct our present reality in such a way that it may account for our loss without obliterating the continued healing presence of memory.

In the title poem of *The Old Life* (1996), Hall's own initial encounter with death mirrors Katie's experience as she names her fear and grief. At the age of nine, after the death of his great-aunt Jennie, Hall lay awake,

> repeating a sentence over and over
>   in my head: It was as if
> I had read it in a book: "When
>   he was only nine
> years old, 'Death became a reality.'" (32)

This reality haunts much of Hall's work. Hall appears to be nearly prescient, moreover, about the deaths that will come. In The *Museum of Clear Ideas* (1993), he writes of Henry King, a man who has lost a young wife and whom Hall implores to "teach us / to grieve with gratitude" as we explore "grief's borders, boundaries of mourning / and lamentation, wild cries and unending tears, / when the unexpected and unacceptable / death happens" (78).

Although he wrote these lines many years before Kenyon's death, Hall already recognizes in the stories of others the grief that borders all existence, that intrudes into the very centre of every life at some point. Long before the personal struggle that serves as the impetus for *Without*, Hall establishes a central tenet for an ethics of mourning: empathy must preside over our grief, helping us to comprehend how our own lives end in certain irrevocable ways with the death of another.

In *The Evolving Self: Problem and Process in Human Development* (1982), Robert Kegan describes the human condition as one that demands "making meaning" out of those events that we face daily. In confronting death and the ensuing loss, however, Kegan asserts that our ability to make meaning may be compromised in some fashion by the apparent finality of the event. The crisis prompted by the devastating loss of a loved one, for example, may actually create a powerful disassociation in the person who grieves such a loss. "One is unable to re-cognize, or re-know, oneself and one's world," Kegan explains. "One experiences, even literally, being beside oneself" (265). Hall demonstrates this kind of disassociation through the rhetorical structures he chooses to use in composing *Without*. Hall's volume consists of a variety of shorter poems interspersed with the extended narrative poem, *Her Long Illness*, which serves as the unifying structure for much of the collection. Hall shifts from the first to the third person throughout the volume, speaking of himself exclusively in the third person in *Her Long Illness* and adopting the first person in the majority of the other poems. In this manner, Hall the poet and Hall the grieving husband who "acts" within the margins of the poem effect a kind of narrative separation. Hall achieves distance by using the third person, and that distance enables him to examine his own complex and, at times, contradictory reaction to the trauma of Kenyon's battle with leukemia. In the text of the poem, Hall stands beside himself—the husband who has lost his wife and who now writes the story of that loss, alongside the husband who still cares for his dying wife and who struggles in the midst of her efforts to live. Hall gains emotional strength via this dual perspective in order to work through the grief that consumes him, the despair that threatens to rend him from his future life.

In the course of *Her Long Illness*, Hall meticulously describes the progress of the disease, its treatment, and the toll that it takes on both Kenyon and himself. With the precision of a documentary filmmaker, he stands behind the camera of his poetic lens and allows it to record objectively what plays out within the purview of the frame. The "I" that speaks elsewhere in the volume, often confessing the most intimate of details, becomes subordinate to the "he" who "drank coffee and read / the *Globe*," who "paced" and "worked on / poems...rubbed her back / and read aloud" while "chemotherapy dripped / through the catheter into her heart" (1). Such a means of seeing— at least within the world of the poem—bestows Hall with a range beyond his own limited vision in the physical world beyond the text. Like a novelist, he enters the lives of his characters, taking on their joy and their pain, their love and their sorrow. Through the act of writing, he becomes an omniscient observer, a witness once removed from the crisis that in the past threatened to engulf him. Now, through the therapeutic practice of creating a narrative—a process that demands precision, the culling of exact detail from the morass of potential events left in the wake of grief—he enters into a kind of covenant with his sorrow.[5]

Such narrative techniques allow Hall both to punctuate the helplessness he felt as Kenyon's body wasted away under the onslaught of chemotherapy and to assault the irony of the chilling technology used to combat the disease:

As they killed her bone
marrow again, she lay on a gurney
alone in a leaden
room between machines that resembled
pot-bellied stoves
which spewed out Total Body Irradiation
for eleven half-hour
sessions measured over four days.
It was as if she capped
the Chernobyl pile with her body. (20)

With a detachment that renders his story more poignant, the controlled, even tone of Hall's voice indicates the remembered agony of the event, while suggesting the accuracy of his observations. Behind the factual, dispassionate prose he uses to report the medicines that Kenyon must consume— "He counted out meds / and programmed pumps to deliver / hydration, TPN, and ganciclovir" (24)—we witness the barely controlled grief that encircles his life, that pushes him toward desperation. Twice in the course of the volume Hall confesses that he considers suicide: first, while caring for Kenyon in Seattle—"Waiting for the light / to cross the avenue, briefly he imagined / throwing himself in front / of that bus" (23)—and later, in a letter to his dead wife,

> I daydreamed burning the house:
> kerosene in pie plates
> with a candle lit in the middle.
> I locked myself in your study
> with Gus, Ada, and the rifle
> my father gave me at twelve.
> I killed our cat and our dog.
> I swallowed a bottle of pills,
> knowing that if I woke on fire
> I had the gun. (78)

Hall's ethics of mourning demands that he candidly recount his trial of grieving. He must not—and, indeed, cannot—polish the memory of Kenyon's slow deterioration with the glossy oil of sentimentality, nor can he manipulate the rhetoric of superficial courage or unfeeling stoicism in order to present himself as untouched by the hand of extinction. Hall's ethics of mourning obliges him, moreover, to reveal the very aspects of death that he has been taught to conceal by a culture that has banished the act of dying out of our homes and into the fluorescent glare of hospital rooms and the hushed quiet of funeral parlours.[6] Hall refuses to hide his grief from others, just as Kenyon refuses to die in a hospital. Instead, as he recounts in "Last Days," Hall brings Kenyon home and stays by her side until he "watched her chest go still. / With his thumb he closed her round brown eyes" (45).

Distressing and unsettling, the revelation that Hall considered suicide, even momentarily, or that he smelled the "sharp, almost sweet / smell" which "began to rise from her open mouth" (45) just before Kenyon's death, underscores the importance of narrative therapy as a tool for examining oneself and later shaping one's identity. In this case, Hall actually remembered lines from Kenyon's poem, "Gettysburg: July 1, 1863," as

Kenyon expired, and later used her very words to shape this experience in his own work. As Hall explains in a letter, "I smelled the smell that she spoke of. She had not only been with her father at the moment when he died, but she was also a hospice worker. When I smelled that smell, I remembered her poem" (Letter to Todd Davis). By structuring our experience, the narratives of others coalesce with our own narratives, giving them shape and form. "The recognition that humans use narrative structure as a way to organize the events of their lives and to provide a scheme for their own self-identity," Donald E. Polkinghorne explains in *Narrative Knowing and the Human Sciences* (1988), "is of importance for the practice of psychotherapy and for personal change" (178). *Without* appears to serve both as a testament to the validity of narrative therapy and as a way for Hall to engage in positive personal change as he experiences the act of mourning and its considerable ethical import. An elegy for Kenyon, *Without* functions as a vehicle for Hall to express not only his grief but his love for the person with whom he has shared his life for twenty-two years. In a particularly moving passage from "A Long Illness," Hall relates the "celebration" of their twenty-second wedding anniversary:

> He gave her a ring
>   of pink tourmaline
> with nine small diamonds around it.
>   She put it on her finger
> and immediately named it Please Don't Die.
>   They kissed and Jane
> whispered, "Timor mortis conturbat me." (9)

In many instances, Robert Coles contends, "Death is our problem; for the one in the hospital bed, death has already come and gone, regardless of the presence of a pulse, a heartbeat, and a normal electroencephalogram" (167). Yet in Kenyon and Hall's case, the fear of death confounds both the dying and the living. As Kenyon herself remarks later in Hall's "Last Days," "Dying is simple. What's worst is...*the separation*" (42). Her words make explicit reference to the ending of Hall's previous collection, *The Old Life* (1996), in which, having been given the news that Kenyon has contracted leukemia, Hall makes "a slip / of the tongue: 'My life has leukemia'" (123).

After more than two decades with Kenyon, Hall can imagine no other life beyond the boundaries of his experiences with her at Eagle Pond Farm. The rhythms of his workday are filled with the presence of his spouse. With separation as an impending reality, dread overtakes Hall and forces him to regress: "Inside him, / some four-year-old / understood that if he was good— thoughtful, / considerate, beyond / reproach, *perfect*—she would not leave him" (13). Hall's "life" truly has leukemia, and it threatens his existence as poet and as husband. As with many poets of his generation, the borders in Hall's life between his personal and professional existence seem porous at best; no clear line signifies the boundary where one ends and the other begins. Instead, Hall writes about his life in his poetry and lives much of his life while he writes.[7] The world of his text—where Kenyon appears so often and where Hall and his neighbours and relatives muster the strength to make do for another day—becomes mortally threatened by the debilitating effects of leukemia and the loss that it portends.

In one sense, then, the ethics of mourning that Hall maps in the composition of *Without* determines the shape of the poetry itself. The threat of extinction that confronts Hall with the news that Kenyon's leukemia has become terminal forces him to face what Therese A. Rando, in *Grieving: How to Go on Living When Someone You Love Dies*, describes as the imminent loss of "the hopes, dreams, wishes, fantasies, unfulfilled expectations, feelings, and needs you had for and with that person" (17). Because Hall spends no time creating other narratives of his life that do not include Kenyon—both poets in fact believed that Kenyon would outlive Hall by many years due to the marked difference in their ages and Hall's narrow survival of a serious bout with colon cancer that later metastasized to the liver—he seems bewildered by the prospect of her absence in both his physical and textual world. Yet in the composition of *Without*, which clearly maintains Kenyon as its focus, Hall undergoes a breakthrough of sorts as he experiences the process of mourning. Three-quarters of the way through the volume and after he records Kenyon's death, Hall begins to compose letter-poems that at once look backward to the memory of his time with Kenyon and forward to the days that mark life's unceasing momentum into the future.

Yet Hall's letter-poems are not indicative of their author's easy recovery; in fact, these poems might best be compared to other kinds of "survivor" narratives. In such texts, the one who returns to the world after enduring the torment of death's presence—whether that be in the midst of war or natural disaster or some other life-threatening occurrence—not only confronts the void left by the deceased's glaring absence but also the memories of the death experience itself. Because Hall works within a theological and ethical structure that asserts the unique, individual nature of each person, his burden as survivor becomes compounded and he cannot merely mourn Kenyon's death and facilely construct a new life. As Alan Soble explains in *The Structure of Love* (1990), the "love for the person [the deceased] conceptually involves irreplaceability.... The beloved is *phenomenologically* irreplaceable" (290). In this sense, the life that Hall occupies remains essentially the same: he lives in the same house, continues to engage in the same form of work, socializes with the same friends and family. But in the midst of this sameness lies the bitter, irrevocable change—the looming absence of his irreplaceable spouse. In *The Therapy of Desire: Theory and Practice in Hellenistic Ethics* (1994), Martha C. Nussbaum underscores the gravity of such a loss. "We might think of a stretch of daily life with a big empty space in it, the space that the loved person used to fill by his presence," Nussbaum explains. "In fact, the representation of this evaluative proposition, properly done, might require a whole series of picturings, as she would notice the person's absence in every corner of her existence, notice the breaking of a thousand delicate and barely perceptible threads. Another sort of picturing would also be possible: she could see that wonderful beloved face, and see it both as enormously beloved and as irretrievably cut off from her.... Whether pictorially displayed or not," Nussbaum adds, "it represents the dead person as of enormous importance, as unlike anything or anyone else in the world" (375).

Read in terms of Nussbaum's observations about the enormous power that the dead exert upon the living, Hall's recourse to the letter-poems seems remarkably apropos. Although Kenyon has been physically and irretrievably removed from Hall's life, she still exists in his mind as a figure of "enormous importance." To deny her place in the workings of his everyday world by attempting to move precipitously beyond their shared memories would in itself be unethical; to discount the significance of the accretion of shared experience would be a lie of enormous consequence. "The breaking of a thousand delicate and barely perceptible threads," which Nussbaum proffers as an image of mourning, while apt, might be better transformed, in Hall's circumstance, into the image of frayed and dangling nerves, shorn by the impact of the death of the person with whom he shared his life. Nothing could prepare him for the loss of so significant a part of his being. In their marriage, Hall and Kenyon truly cleaved to one another; their love— a shared joy in the physical pleasures of their bodies, as well as a recognition of the ways in which their minds met and transformed each other—binds them with an irreplaceable intimacy.

In "Letter with No Address," Hall offers frank testimony about the distressing reality of his situation: Kenyon has no address; Hall has no way to reach her. As he writes in this initial letter, "You know now / whether the soul survives death. / Or you don't. When you were dying / you said you didn't fear / punishment. We never dared / to speak of Paradise" (50). Yet whether Kenyon now knows "Paradise" or nothing at all, Hall remains a survivor in "hell," as he phrases his situation in "Letter after a Year," playing "in repertory the same / script without you, without love" (77). But an ethics of mourning, while acknowledging the "hell" in which the mourner lives, attempts to fashion healing methodologies for contending with grief. In *How We Grieve* (1996), Thomas Attig refers to this phenomenon as the process of "relearning the world." In short, Hall must come to terms with the void in his life left by Kenyon's departure. Attig explains that the death of a loved one is a "choiceless event.... As survivors, we control little of death's timing or character," he continues. "Most of us, with a choice, would will that the dead live" (32). Yet Hall, as with others who mourn, never enjoys such a choice. Kenyon cannot live again, nor can Hall stop communicating with her in his verse.

In what would appear to be an impossible predicament, Hall uses the tools of his literary trade to transcend the physical barriers of the grave in order to speak with Kenyon. For Hall, the letter-poems serve as a form of narrative therapy. He writes with no illusion that his words may somehow miraculously find their way to her, but rather, with the knowledge that he must express himself in this way or be damned to a life of repressed rage, to an abiding sense of pain that could threaten his very sanity. The letter-poems yield Hall with individual moments of catharsis. He begins his series of epistolary poems by sharing his "news," by telling Jane about the weather, about births and deaths in the village where they lived, about visits with friends, about his enduring grief over her absence.

Buttercups circle the planks
of the old wellhead
this May while your silken
gardener's body withers or moulds
in the Proctor graveyard.
I drive and talk to you crying
and come back to this house
to talk to your photographs. (49)

Hall concludes "Letter with No Address" with a reverie, imagining that while he drives home from his visit at the graveyard, Kenyon has returned, "bags of groceries upright / in the back of the Saab, / its trunk lid delicately raised / as if proposing an encounter, / dog-fashion, with the Honda" (52). Although the erotic humour of Hall's lines cannot be overlooked, the ultimate loss of the possibility for such an encounter, "dog-fashion" or otherwise, presides over the passage. Such a moment of displacement—clearly Kenyon cannot rise from the grave to join her husband in the present—reflects the spatial and temporal "relearning" to which Attig refers. "Within the lived space of human care we experience things, places, and persons as near or remote, not more or less distant by some objective measure," Attig observes. "Within the lived time of human care and concern we experience past, present, and future as inseparable and interpenetrating phases of personal life history" (118). Not surprisingly, then, as we progress with Hall through *Without's* therapeutic pages, we witness his various encounters with profound obstacles in his attempt to "relearn" his world. At many instances in the volume, Hall rages against the reality of Kenyon's death and longs for "everything to end," or as he explains in "Midwinter Letter," "I lean forward from emptiness / eager for more emptiness" (74).

At the same time that we witness Hall's rage and despair, we become privy also to the initial epiphanies of healing that will ensure his survival.[8] In these moments of recovery, the function of memory plays an essential role in the composition of his verse. While "recovery" may fallaciously suggest that one may fully advance beyond or recover completely from the loss of another, it more usefully implies a return to equilibrium; rather than imply that we should eschew our memories of the dead, recovery in this sense connotes a movement into a new relationship with them. In short, the presence of the deceased never really leaves us. An ethics of mourning instead allows us to recognize the continued proximity of the deceased in memory and the manner in which this relationship impacts our conceptions of the world in the here and now. As Hall struggles to regain his equilibrium—a balance between his grief that with each day recedes into his past and the everyday activity of his life in the present that is, at least in part, guided by the memory of Kenyon—he learns to objectify his sorrow. In "Postcard: January 22nd," Kenyon's death metamorphoses into a child he bears: "I feed her, / bathe her, rock her, and change her diapers. / She lifts her small skull, trembling / and tentative. She smiles, spits up, shits / in a toilet, learns to read and multiply. / I watch her grow, prosper, thrive. / She is the darling of her mother's old age" (73). By writing a postcard to his dead wife, he recognizes the privileged position that he has afforded his grief. The nature of the act of writing permits him to perceive from a new perspective what his life has become, and Hall understands that if he hopes to avoid being consumed by the presence of Kenyon's death, he will have to allow this child born from death's ashes, "darling of her mother's old age," to grow up and leave the house.

Hall's interactions with the living world ultimately provide him with a means for regaining his equilibrium and with the capacity for sending his grief out into the world.[9] The emotional and geographical proximity of his son Andrew, as well as his grandchildren, buoy his spiritual state; in many respects, they act as his saving grace. To sustain an active and healthy relationship with his son, his grandchildren, or his friends, Hall must invest at least a portion of his energy in the present. When all three of Andrew's children sit on Hall's lap while he reads them stories, or, perhaps, when he cooks a meatloaf for their dinner, their presence allows him to recognize the interpersonal value inherent in living in the present, a significant factor in any ethics of mourning. While at times Hall still cannot bear the company of others—in "Letter at Christmas" he recounts spending Thanksgiving at Andrew's home, where for "three hours we played, / teased, laughed together. / Suddenly I had to drive home" (63)—the vitality of his visits with family and friends resonates within him. The very fact that he relates such events to Kenyon via the letter-poems speaks volumes about the significance of such moments. In "Midwinter Letter," a visit from his daughter Philippa and her children transforms the poet's soul, as well as his sense of purpose:

> Philippa brought
> the children from Concord
> to wade in Eagle pond. Allison
> showed me a wild strawberry plant.
> Abigail snatched at minnows
> and laughed. For an hour
> I watched them play.... (57)

By bringing "play" back into their grandfather's life, Allison and Abigail nurture Hall towards what Rando, in *Grief, Dying, and Death*, refers to as the "reestablishment phase," a time when "emotional energy is reinvested in new persons, things, and ideas" (35).

Striving to "reinvest" his life in others, Hall confesses to Kenyon in "Midwinter Letter" that he often reads his "letters aloud / to our friends" (75). As a form of narrative therapy, it becomes important for Hall not only to write to himself (and to Kenyon) but also to share the act of healing with others. By reading these letter-poems to friends, Hall releases himself from the strict intimacy of grief that he maintains with his deceased wife. He invites those friends and family members who are close to him, who already share his life and in the past shared Kenyon's as well, to enter fully into his being by visiting him in his grief. In this act, he opens the door to the living without closing the door to the dead, establishing human community as a reference for meaning in both his present and his past lives. In "Weeds and Peonies," the last poem in *Without*, Hall reveals that his progress has been slow, that his grief remains fresh. In the poem, he walks among Kenyon's peonies in the garden where she spent so much of her time. As Kenyon often did, Hall carries "one magnanimous blossom indoors" to float in a glass bowl. This action demonstrates the tenderness of memory and the importance of past ritual, as well as the force of "grief's repeated particles" which "suffuse the air— / like the dog yipping through the entire night, / or the cat stretching awake, then curling / as if to dream of her mother's milky nipples" (81). Hall concludes the poem by recalling Kenyon's daily hikes up Mount Kearsarge and his loving words of caution to her as she started her journey each day. He employs the image of the peonies who "lean their vast heads westward / as if they might topple" to speak to the fragility and precariousness of our condition, as surely an ethics of mourning ought to do.

As poets, Kenyon and Hall shared an enduring belief in the transcendence of language. Taken from her poem, "Afternoon at MacDowell," the epitaph on Kenyon's headstone—a grave that Hall will one day occupy with his wife—underscores art's healing powers and its capacity for celebrating the mysterious interpersonal fabric of human relationships: "I believe in the miracles of art but what / prodigy will keep you safe beside me," it reads. Through his poetry, Hall miraculously survives the death of his wife by writing her into existence each day, by making life from death in his verse. Yet at the same time, Hall's ethics of mourning provides him with a means for sharing his recovery with others. By publishing *Without* and giving poetry readings across the United States—indeed, throughout the world— Hall succeeds in sharing his grief with the multiplicity of other "friends" who also registered Kenyon's loss. It is through this enduring narrative process—an extended form of narrative therapy in itself—that Hall finally constructs an ethics of mourning that allows him both to revel in Kenyon's memory and to enjoy a healthy sense of personal renewal. In *Without*, Hall not only memorializes Kenyon's life, but saves his own as well.

NOTES

1. We are especially grateful to Donald Hall for his insights and his generous correspondence during the composition of this essay.
2. For additional discussion regarding literature as a means of narrative therapy, as well as a vehicle for the interdisciplinary study of family systems psychotherapy, see Barbara A. Kaufman's "Training Tales in Family Therapy: Exploring *The Alexandria Quartet*," *Journal of Marital and Family Therapy* 21.1 (1995): 67–75. Kaufman argues that "inclusion of novels in didactic contexts encourages trainees to search their own experiences, thereby maximizing the opportunity for positive therapeutic interaction and highlighting the variety of treatment approaches in the field" (70). See also Janine Roberts's *Tales and Transformations: Stories in Families and Family Therapy* (New York: Norton, 1994), which features an appendix that enumerates a host of existing "family systems novels." It is important to note, however, that in many forms of narrative therapy, including that of which White and Epston speak, narratives are told to reshape the experience, to help the person by recasting stories and

thus breaking away from old patterns of behaviour. This is not the case for Hall in *Without*, a long narrative poem that does not recast events but instead narrates those events as a form of release. By serving as an emotional release—similar to the story of a survivor of some irremediable event—Hall's story of Kenyon's death serves as a means of expiation, an act that over time will not so much recast the narrative, allowing for behavioural change, but instead release the power of grief through dissipation.

3.   For another example of the ways in which ethical criticism accounts for the moral import inherent in the act of mourning, see Kenneth Reinhard's fine interpretation of Henry James's *The Wings of the Dove*: "Death is both that which we 'cannot possibly not know,'" Reinhard writes, "and that which we 'never can directly know,' since it marks the end of our knowledge" (138).

4.   Thomas Attig insists that grieving, if one is to move beyond it, must be an active process. While he does not suggest, as we have in this essay, that grieving is necessarily an imaginative act, he does contend that "it is vital that we reject ideas of grieving as passive and embrace ideas of it as active. By definition, bereavement *happens to us*.... [But] grieving as coping requires that we respond actively, invest energy, and address tasks" (32–33).

5.   Both Hall and Kenyon write about their move to Hall's ancestral home in New Hampshire as a turning point in their marital and writing lives, and in Bill Moyers's award-winning documentary, *Donald Hall and Jane Kenyon: A Life Together* (1994), we observe them as they speak about the creation of their shared life in poetry and in the natural world beyond poetry as something that coalesced out of a keen sense of place. For more discussion regarding Hall's connection to Eagle Pond Farm, see *Here at Eagle Pond Farm* (1990) and *String Too Short to Be Saved* (1981).

6.   In his essay, "Graveyard People," collected in *Principal Products of Portugal* (1995), Hall addresses the manner in which America has attempted to gloss over death through the ways that we mourn and bury our dead. Speaking about his visits with Jane to graveyards in New Hampshire, he remarks, "Reading the names and dates of the old stones, as we root around in boneyards, we note the omnipresence of death for our ancestors—so many dead children, so many wives dead and husbands remarried and new dead infants of new brides. Is it by a reaction, now, that we avoid any confrontation with death?" Rather sadly, Hall concludes that "contemporary memorial institutions—like Forest Lawn—attest to avoidance only" (65).

7.   While clearly choosing the "right" details are essential to the success of a narrative or a poem for a publishing author, Polkinghorne explains the importance of such choices in terms of narrative therapy. "The reflective awareness of one's personal narrative provides the realization that past events are not meaningful in themselves but are given significance by the configuration of one's narrative," Polkinghorne notes. "This realization," he continues, "can release people from the control of past interpretations they have attached to events and open up the possibility of renewal and freedom for change" (182–83).

8.   In one sense, Hall serves as his own therapist. By writing poetry about his loss and the "epiphanies" that lead him back toward the land of the living, he fulfills what Robert Coles considers to be poetry's vital role: "Poets try to sharpen the sight, to nurture language carefully in the hope of calling upon it for an understanding of what is happening.... Poets give us images and metaphors and offer the epiphanies doctors and patients alike crave, even if it is in the silent form of a slant of late afternoon light" (101). Importantly, Hall does not rely solely on his own verse in his quest for transcendence. Instead, he turns to other poets for healing. In "Art for Life for Art," collected in *Principal Products of Portugal*, Hall reveals that the "mathematics of poetry's formal resolution does not preclude moral thought, or satisfaction in honest naming, or the consolation of shared feeling. When someone dear to me dies, I go back to the seventeenth-century poets for consolation" (79). In yet another essay from the same collection, "The Unsayable Said," Hall intimates that poetry may be used as a form of narrative therapy: "When I grieve I go to poems that grieve.... In the act of reading, we exercise or practice emotion, griefs and joys, erotic transport and the anguish of loss—as if poems were academies of feeling, as if in reading poems we practiced emotion and understandings of emotion" (86).

9.   During the course of this essay, we often use the word "begin" to refer to Hall's position in the coping process for two reasons: first, *Without* only chronicles Hall's initial year of grieving, never speaking to his present state of mind, and, second, "relearning" one's world remains at all times a process in which we are involved, not one that we "complete" or "finish." An ethics of mourning demands that we resist the narrative desire for absolute resolution, for a "complete" recovery, because it simply does not exist. Instead, we acknowledge that we share the burden of our loved ones' deaths until we also die; in this way, we participate in an enduring process of human interrelationship. As Rando explains, "The loss is not forgotten, but merely put in a special place which, while allowing it to be remembered, also frees the mourner to go on to new attachments without being pathologically tied to the old ones" (*Grief* 35).

"If Only I Were Isis"

Remembrance, Ritual, and Writing in Lola Lemire Tostevin's Cartouches

> We have learned that, if death cannot still the voice of genius, the reason is that genius triumphs over death not by reiterating its original language, but by constraining us to listen to a language constantly modified, sometimes forgotten—as it were an echo answering each passing century with its own voice—and what the masterpiece keeps up is not a monologue, however authoritative, but a *dialogue* indefeasible by Time.
>
> —ANDRÉ MALRAUX, *The Voices of Silence*

LOLA LEMIRE TOSTEVIN'S 1995 BOOK *Cartouches* is a complex and accomplished work that operates in and across a number of dimensions. With *Cartouches* Tostevin presents not just a many-faceted meditation on death, an act of remembrance, perhaps, but she also elaborates a ritual for herself and for the reader. This enacted ritual is a movement towards renewal and consolation. At the same time, part of the ritual is a postmodernist reflection on the process. Tostevin's writing and our reading take place multi-dimensionally: she is the mourner who remembers her father as she remembers her self. She is the creator of the rituals of mourning, the mediator between cosmic planes. As readers, we participate in this charging of language by making the necessary connections, and thus also in the resurgence of life for which Tostevin's writing itself is the sacred site.

The volume includes poems and journal entries in French and English. Dedicated to the memory of her recently-deceased father, Achilles Lemire, *Cartouches* mourns his death. The book tells the story of the poet's pilgrimage to Egypt, where she learns about the ancient deities and the sacred Egyptian traditions concerning death. Embedded in this journey is a quest for a renewed self-identity in the aftermath of her father's death. The book comprises two movements, as the term is used with a musical symphony—or a Requiem. The first is characterized by profound ceremonial solemnity; the later by informality and intimacy. The movements direct the mourning ritual from its being a public event towards becoming a personal experience.

The overall trajectory of the book may be suggested by two quotations. At the start of the poet's visit, in Cairo, she writes that "In a country where you can't read the signs, you can't always measure the extent to which you are lost."[1] After her experiences in Egypt, she is empowered to write,

> In the depth of dreaming
> a perfect moment blooms
> against words closing in:
> a trace more luminous than light
> as you imagine yourself
> no longer here or there, but everywhere.

The last line epitomizes the most extraordinary feature of *Cartouches* in referring to the universal conception of sacred space, lucidly formulated in *The Sacred and the Profane: The Nature of Religion* by Mircea Eliade:

> where the sacred manifests itself in space, *the real unveils itself*, the world comes into existence. But the irruption of the sacred does not only project a fixed point into the formless fluidity of profane space, a center into chaos; it also effects a break in plane, that is, it opens communication between the cosmic planes (between earth and heaven) and makes possible ontological passage from one mode of being to another. (63)

Ancient Egypt's monuments and artifacts are well-known evidence of a culture's preoccupation with the sacralization of the dead, and so, considering Tostevin's circumstances, Egypt was a fitting place to go to.

Openings

> *Cartouche*: a French word also used in English, meaning a scroll or
> tablet designed to take an inscription; called "shenou" by the Egyptians;
> the elongated oval shape signified everything that was encircled by
> the sun; the writing combines signs representing sounds and signs
> representing ideas. Cartouches often contained royal names. The
> cartouche, therefore, shows that the regent whose name is written
> inside it is monarch of all that the sun surveys. (Watterson 18)

Tostevin begins her enactment of remembering in language immediately
with the book's title, *Cartouches*, and with the book's epigraphs. In her
acknowledgement, Tostevin mentions the "master-name who gave me the
definition of a cartouche that best describes the nature of this book
[*Cartouches*]: 'I not only have a cartouche, I am it. This is my cartouche, I'm
the one who's stolen it. This is my body, the body of my name.'"

The cover illustration of *Cartouches*, drawn by Zoya Niechoda, features a
picture of an Egyptian cartouche whose symbols, "Lion Dove Lion Vulture,"
in one version of the hieroglyphic alphabet, spell "Lola." In a journal entry,

Tostevin writes: "All this I am and want to be: at the same time lion, dove and vulture." And, in the poem which follows this journal entry,

> a cartouche
> puts into play
> the bodies
> of my name
> a lion
> a dove
> a lion
> a vulture·
> oh mummified me

The cover illustration juxtaposes the poet's name in Egyptian signs in the vertical cartouche with her names in the Latin alphabet in the horizontal cartouche.[2] So the cover story, emblematic of the book's contents, could be read as "Lion Dove Lion Vulture, all this I am and want to be: at the same time, Lola Lemire Tostevin." (This name can also be pronounced both in French and English.) Franco-Ontarian poet travels to Egypt, brings home cartouche as souvenir. Her name, her very being, even, inscribed in gold. A remembrance. A memory. Tostevin explains that a cartouche "was worn on the body so the wearer wouldn't forget her name, wouldn't forget who she was." She remembers, then. Remembers herself through language as she remembers her father. Re-members.

Early in *Cartouches* the poet recalls when she was a child and her father reassembled one of her damaged dolls, which she had placed in a box. This deed parallels the ancient Egyptian story of Isis' putting back together the body of her brother and husband, Osiris, who, after she flaps her wings over him, returns to life and thereby becomes the god of resurrection. Tostevin hatches the design for a trip to Egypt after her father dies, addressing him:

> Now this. If only I were Isis.
> I would transform myself into a swallow
> and fan you with my wings. I would
> retrieve her recipes that can bewitch the heavens.
> If only. I would go to Egypt and retrieve

the box from the base of the tamarisk tree.
The iron box that contains other boxes like memory.
The bronze box and the box of ebony and ivory.
The box of silver and one of gold which holds
a book whose words disappear into thin air except
for the trace of a lingering story.

Here, early in the book (in the eighth poem of the "Small Amulets" section),
we witness the poet's focussing of her quest onto language, the "trace of a
lingering story." *Cartouches* is saturated with language. As Tostevin remarked
once in a book review, "knowledge of the self is inseparable from the practice of language ("Smart" 171). In *Cartouches*, this knowledge and this practice
combine to return life to her father.

Compared to her 1994 novel *Frog Moon* and her 1982 poetry collection,
Color of Her Speech, Tostevin's concern in *Cartouches* is less directly related to
how the French and English languages interface around and in her. In
Cartouches the poet's sensitivity to languages as whole cultures, and to how
and what they signify becomes a dynamic basis for interacting with the
languages of Egypt. As with all of her previous work, though, the English/
French concern in *Cartouches* is similarly an important feature of the book's
relentless intertextuality. "Cartouche" of course is both a French and an
English word, and *Cartouches* features a French and an English epigraph. The
first, from Anne Hébert's "Les Mains," a poem in her collection *Le Tombeau
des rois*, is

Les signes du monde
Sont gravés à même ses doigts. (24)

(The English translation, given in the original bilingual edition, is

The signs of the world
Are graven on her very fingers. [25])

This poem describes a woman—or is it a goddess? A mother?—"assise au
bord des saisons"/ "sitting at the edge of the seasons." This figure graces
our lives, but there is a catch:

From her for us
No place of welcome and of love

Without that pitiless offering
Of hands decked with sorrows
Open to the sun. (25)

Isis, the prototype of the good wife and mother for ancient Egyptians (and for many Christianized European worshippers of "Black Virgins," possibly until the present), is also, along with her sister Nephtys, the singer of the lament for their brother Osiris, which became the official Egyptian funerary dirge (Sykes 106–07, 151). Like the woman in Hébert's "Les Mains," Isis bears both darkness and light.

The connection between Tostevin's poetic interest in Egypt and her choice of this first epigraph is more explicit in Hébert's title poem, "Le Tombeau des rois"/ "The Tomb of the Kings" —the title Tostevin uses to identify her quote from Hébert. "The Tomb of the Kings" describes a visit by Hébert to Egypt, in particular to a royal tomb. During this visit, the poet becomes imaginatively enmeshed in the sacrifices depicted on the tomb's walls:

Ranged in a single row:
The smoke of incense, the cake of dried rice
And my trembling flesh:
Ritual and submissive offering. (89)

The poem ends with the wondering poet's question, "What glimmer of dawn strays here?" Hébert's "Le Tombeau des rois" sketches the general, much more complex, movement of *Cartouches* from death to resurrection, the profane to the sacred.

The English epigraph of *Cartouches* is from the eighth section, Book I of the "Pallinode" of H.D.'s *Helen in Egypt*:

are you Hecate? are you a witch?
a vulture? a hieroglyph? (15)

Tostevin has slightly altered the original of these lines: in *Helen in Egypt* there are commas, not question-marks, in the second line; and Achilles' imperious questioning of Helen ends with a third line, "the sign or the name of a goddess?" (16). (In H.D.'s vigorously anti-war long poem, the real Helen is in Egypt, a place of peace for her. The Greeks and Trojans had fought their war over an illusion created by the Egyptian god Amen. The arrow that seemed to kill Achilles was actually "Love's arrow" [9], and Helen believes that she was the one who removed it [8]. The dialogue between these two figures, and "H.D.'s" commentaries make up the text of *Helen in Egypt*.) Reflecting later on Achilles' questions, Helen realizes that

...with his anger,
that ember, I became
what his accusation made me,
Isis, forever with that Child,
the Hawk Horus. (23)

The introduction to this section of *Helen in Egypt* observes that Helen "herself is the writing" (22), so that Achilles' accusing her of being a hiero-glyph is accurate, and is directly relevant to Tostevin's understanding of cartouche, mentioned previously, that "I not only have a cartouche, I am it." Helen is also identified with Isis in her aspect of mother of Horus, the falcon-headed god of the sun, of light, of day—of all goodness (Sykes 96). At the same time, she is Hecate, the Terrible Mother, and a witch. Recall Tostevin's "oh mummified me" after the transcription into English of her own cartouche signs, the last of which is the vulture.

These words from *Helen in Egypt* are obviously germane to Tostevin's project in *Cartouches* as well:

Helen achieves the difficult task of translating a symbol in time into timeless-time or hieroglyph or ancient Egyptian time. She knows the script, she says, but we judge that this is intuitive or emotional knowl-edge, rather than intellectual.... She says she is 'instructed,' she is enchanted, rather. For from the depth of her racial inheritance, she invokes (as the perceptive visitor to Egypt must always do) the symbol or the 'letter' that represents or recalls the protective mothergoddess. This is no death-symbol but a life-symbol, it is Isis or her Greek counterpart, Thetis, the mother of Achilles. (13)

Such invoking of the Isis hieroglyph is a part of the ritual through which *Cartouches* leads the reader. (H.D.'s mother's name was Helen; Tostevin's father's name was Achilles.) We remember Tostevin's father's reassembling her doll, and the poet's "Now this. If only I were Isis." In summary, for *Cartouche's* epigraph Tostevin abbreviates the stanza from *Helen in Egypt* because at the start of *Cartouches* she does not see herself as "the sign or the name of a goddess." Tostevin is not Helen, nor is she Isis—yet. But as a poet she begins to enter the mysteries of resurrection which H.D.'s Helen and the Egyptians' Isis disclose.

The critic and poet Rachel Blau Duplessis writes about *Helen in Egypt* in terms that could equally apply to the Tostevin of *Cartouches*:

Helen's major activity is decoding and remembering: decoding the Amen-script in a temple very like Karnak...; decoding two hieroglyphs. One is the 'bird' of Isis, the other is nenuphar or water lily, which in this poem alludes to the Great Mother with child, around which all other petals are arranged in a 'subtle genealogy'.... (110)

Tostevin uses this lily image in an address to Isis:

A thousand pillars from the Moon
Gate to Sun Gate where you came
to anchor a thousand-petalled
lily in the Hall of Morning.
And now all that is left are
clumps of papyrus springing
from the head of the dead.

Perhaps the grandeur of ancient Egypt has diminished, but still the process of sacred rebirth is evident.

Heart

Immediately following *Cartouches'* two epigraphs are two poems that explain the heart sign and initiate the reader into the ritual that the book creates and animates. Tostevin notes that

> In ancient Egypt the heart, the AB,
> is represented by an inkwell in the shape of a heart.

The reference here is to *The Egyptian Book of the Dead*, a collection of spells and illustrations, called vignettes, for use by people who had died and needed to gain entry to the afterlife of bliss in the Field of Reeds, the Egyptian heaven. The spells and vignettes were written and painted onto papyrus, then enclosed with the mummy in its tomb. From these ancient texts we have learned much about ancient Egyptian funerary customs. A key part of the rite of passage was weighing the dead person's heart, the centre of life, to ascertain its purity; it was not supposed to outweigh the feather of Maat, which stood for truth, justice, morality and balance. When the deceased passed this test, the heart was stored in a jar to foil those who would like to steal a pure heart. Its place in the spiritual body was sometimes taken by a scarab-shaped amulet engraved with a spell which had the power to replace the heart in the afterlife—"Hieroglyphs in lieu of a heart," in Tostevin's words. Not surprisingly, the next section of *Cartouches* is entitled "Small Amulets."

Each of the nine poems in "Small Amulets" is headed by the ideogram for the heart. Tostevin says in *Cartouches* that the AB, the heart, "is represented by an inkwell in the shape of a heart." The concatenation of ink with the heart's blood thus underlies Tostevin's act of writing the "Small Amulets" for her father. The words of these poems become part of another dimension:

> Spirit of the letter.... A prayer
> recited over the amulet of the heart
> prevents the heart from being carried off
> by those who plunder hearts.

The first of the "Small Amulets" reveals how Achilles Lemire's death has caused each word and line that Tostevin writes to be invocations of her father's name. In the second, Achilles answers the prayer, and appears, in order to comment on his daughter's writing:

> 'You exaggerate
> everything,' he'd shrug, reading this.
> His way of saying that the need
> to recollect is just another metaphor.

The poet responds,

> But exaggeration is the summit
> of every living image, I want to tell him.
> At least those we try to hang on to.
> So, father, let these small poems speak.
> Let them speak volumes.

The poignancy created here by the father's presence and the poet's intense desire to "hang on" to it, accentuates the power of her words, and draws the reader into the poet's effort to have her father hear her words and thus rejoin the living.

The third of the "Small Amulets" describes how her father's illness has reconfigured her family in ways strongly reminiscent of the multiple relationships among the ancient Egyptian deities:

> ...Bodies levitate beyond
> their usual boundaries. My father is my son,
> my son, my father. I am my mother's mother.
> My daughter is the grandmother I never knew.

In the next poem, the poet illustrates how this levitating sometimes took place while her father was alive. "If anything," she writes, far from being an abusive father, "he is the one who is intimidated by me." She then remembers a conversation they had during which she saw him as

> The nine-year-old waterboy working in lumber camps,
> the fresh face of a child.

"Oh, father," she asks, "Are you afraid?" The question exists both in the past and in the present. Once again he is invoked. The rest of the poems in "Small Amulets" continue the conversation. In the seventh Tostevin reflects, in her father's presence again, on how others might take this writing:

I know. This order of language is not easy
to accede to. Sentiment, they'll say.
Yet these words also lie in the realm
of my other, father, and you are not just
another arbitrary sign. These poems
are of a body that links us, inescapable,
given.

The poet's intentions on a theoretical level seem clear: to expand upon the characteristically feminist project of writing the body. In this instance, she claims for critically frowned-upon sentimentality another dimension that validates her words beyond the aesthetic.

Another way that Tostevin pushes beyond the limits of feminist thinking in *Cartouches* is at first less apparent than this stretching of the notion of writing the body, but it is plainly noticeable to readers of her prose works prior to the publication of *Cartouches*. These words addressed to her father, just quoted, introduce the topic: "you are not just / another arbitrary sign." For years Tostevin has been distinctly uneasy with the dominant feminist and psychoanalytic theories regarding the figure of the Father, and she has written extensively on the subject.

Generally, Tostevin is sceptical about all ideologies which limit people. "Let's hope," she wrote in *Sp/Elles* in 1986 concerning the ongoing development of feminist theory,

that it will be in the spirit of a poetics whose purpose is not only to perceive but to transgress and subvert in order to open new possibilities. Let's hope that it does not advocate absolute knowledge which only serves to repress in order to accede to idealization; and that theory is not replaced by another ideology which defines itself in terms of opposition or enemy resembling more a construct and less a human being with a capacity for change. (96)

In "Paternal Body as Outlaw," a brief article on bpNichol from the same year, Tostevin specifically addresses this "capacity for change" in the context of male/female patterns. She observes that "Since many women are now rethinking the maternal at the level of language and writing, it's conceivable that the same can be done by male writers, but only in terms of maternal but also in terms of the paternal" (78). She quotes Nichol as having stated that "the hierarchy's a difficult place to stand," and comments that the late 1960s, when Nichol said this, was "a period preoccupied with confronting the old within the new. The engendering of new life within old fictions" (78). Her description of Nichol's writing demonstrates that

> his language is felt through all the senses, both writer's and reader's, so that the relation between inside/outside, between enveloping and being enveloped, moves inside and outside language. If we were to compare Nichol's writing to the sexual paradigm, it would be less phallic and more oral, moving towards what the French call *écriture féminine*. (79)

In 1990, when she interviewed Anne Hébert for *Brick*, she mentioned to Hébert the traditional formulation of patriarchal oppressiveness, at that time having been recently applied to Hébert's work by Patricia Smart in her book on Québec women writers, *Writing in the Father's House*. Did Hébert feel a need to rebel against her father?

> 'No, not at all,' Hébert replied. 'On the contrary, I was always encouraged by my father. He was responsible for much of my education.' ("Remembered Conversation" 23)

Tostevin's lines in *Cartouches* suggest that her regard for her father in this personal respect is similar to that of Hébert for her father:

> It seems incongruous these day to write
> about a father who never abused his daughter,
> our ties unmediated by concept or mastery.

Another important strand of Tostevin's thinking about the Father more strongly emphasizes alternatives to some of the feminist thought which strikes Tostevin as dualistic and exclusive. She is very clear about this point in a letter to Smaro Kamboureli, "Contamination: A Relation of Differences," published in *Tessera* in 1988, two years before the Hébert interview: "We must focus on an ideology of difference, not as binary opposition, but as multiplicity of differences which defy definition" (23). On the issue of the Father, she writes to Kamboureli that

> It's high time we stopped being threatened by the term 'Father.' Sexual discrimination was caused primarily because half the population was threatened by the term 'Mother,' and I don't think simply reversing it will achieve much. (17)

She goes on to provide more detail in her remarks on Julia Kristeva's idea that the Father is a third element generated by the Mother/Child combination:

> I'm not totally comfortable having it defined as 'Father' but neither can I see why, given the Mother/Child combination, we can't have the third element as Father. I don't believe this paternalizes 'woman' per se, but the child, and there shouldn't be anything wrong with that as long as we continue to 'maternalize' the child as well. We wouldn't be so threatened by this third term if the boundaries weren't so sharply delineated and divisive and if we didn't accord so much authority to the term of the Father. I have no doubt that Kristeva sees the Word, linear language, theory, as belonging to the third term (Symbolic), but I think perhaps the reason she doesn't mind assigning the third term to the Father is that she doesn't give it any more authority than that of the Mother (Semiotic). (24)

Tostevin does not leave her critique here, though; she posits further alternatives to the "divisive boundaries" model. In addition to her critique just outlined, these positive formulations are the underpinnings of her approach to the Father/her father in *Cartouches*.

Tostevin discovered in Walter Benjamin's writing a key idea which parallels a model that she developed, a more practical approach for her work. In

"Reading after the (Writing) Fact," a reflection on her book 'sophie, she says that she chose a painted allegory for the cover because she was

> fascinated by [Benjamin's] concept of the allegorical as originary fragment as opposed to the classical notion of the symbolic, which, according to Julia Kristeva, implies a language and culture fixed within grammatical and social constraints that are bound by paternal law. Benjamin's reflections celebrate the basic characteristic of allegory as ambiguous, capable of yielding multiple meanings, a richness of extravagance, a *jouissance*, to use one of Kristeva's favourite terms.... The voice of allegory is, in its very notion of multiplicity, a polyphonic voice. (62–63)

Tostevin alters Benjamin's aural metaphor to one of touch, and broadens it in another article on 'sophie where she formulates the idea of "Contamination: A Relation of Differences." This article focuses on her inclusion of French and English in 'sophie, but clearly the principle of contamination is more widely applicable:

> Because I don't believe in a pure space of language anymore than I believe in a 'pure race,' I find the concept of contamination as a literary device rather appealing. Contamination means differences have been brought together so they make contact. It is from this point of view that 'sophie (and to a great extent all my work) was conceived. (13)

If "the Father"—the Symbolic order—is substituted for "pure space of language" in this quotation, then the connection between that theoretical issue and her father in *Cartouches* becomes clear. Nothing, whether theoretical or physical or linguistic, exists in isolation. By developing the ramifications of this insight, the intensification of the mourning which occurs in *Cartouches* is truly startling.

As already noted, in the eighth poem of "Small Amulets"—"If only I were Isis"—Tostevin focuses on the power of language. The Egyptian imagery of the next and final poem of the section coalesces, bringing the reader full circle to the heart amulet, to a sense at once of closure for the first movement of the book, and of anticipation:

So with these words, father, I make you a pillow
to cradle your head toward the horizon.

With these words I give you a cake to eat
on the eastern side of the Lake of Flowers.

With these words I give you a heart
of lapis lazuli—a stone heart, maybe,
but nonetheless, everlasting.

Silence

Between the "Small Amulets" section and the succeeding poems is an italicized poem in French and an epigraph for the second, untitled, section of
Cartouches, emphasizing that her book is moving into a new register. The
italicized French poem is a signal of transition, reminiscent of the moments
of passage in such myths as those of Odysseus' and Dante's visits to the
underworld:

La mort m'enjôle, m'humecte
la nuque, pendant que j'erre,
étrangère, dans cet espace
sans temps où le silence
s'engouffre, fait place
à son flot
(Death entices me, dampens
the nape of my neck, while I wander,
a stranger, in this place
out of time where silence
overwhelms itself, wave
after wave)[3]

The mention of "silence" is especially noteworthy since, as Tostevin says
in the last of the "Small Amulets," "With these words I give you a heart." In
the silence of the death-haunted desert, however, she begins her project.
The epigraph, a quotation from the American postmodernist poet Clark
Coolidge, underscores what he believes to be the ancient Egyptians' outstanding

achievement: "they gained a clarity of the mystery." Although as a site for interaction with the dead, Egypt does indeed seem ideal, it involves a serious drawback. Barbara Watterson points out that "it is only from written records that we know ancient Egyptian; we cannot be sure how ancient Egyptian was spoken" (45). This verbal silence is part of the overwhelming silence Tostevin feels as she commences (again) with her *Cartouches*. The need for voice inspires—and is also a metaphor of—Tostevin's quest to reincorporate her father into (her) life. According to the statements Tostevin makes in her article "Reading after the Writing Fact," this "need" is, however, neither the traditionally defined location of art "in the archaic definition of desire, the experience of some originary loss," nor in the more recent definition of "desire as impulse, a beat that liberates writing from its metaphysical, historical and psychoanalytical treatment" (66). Instead, Tostevin claims, "I know that for myself it's no longer possible to write from a concept of absence, of loss" (66):

> Other than the joy that writing gives me, I don't know what I want to achieve when writing, what trace, what configurations I can fashion as I travel my trajectory.... I don't know where I'm heading as I continually toss myself into the air, but as one of my favorite writers and mentor, bpNichol taught me, I trust the words to take me to what place I don't know.... (66)

She goes on in this article to quote a poem from 'sophie about Billie Holiday, invoking the experimental, free spirit of jazz as a parallel to her way of writing. Reconsidered in these terms, the silence which Tostevin experiences after her father's death, in Egypt, is not absence at all. The silence is the melody of the dead for which Tostevin improvises words. She writes in 'sophie:

> I write because I can't sing   I am the book exiled
> from my voice in search of a melody   but like the woman
> who is blind because her eyes are filled with seeing
> and like the woman who is deaf because her ears are
> filled with hearing I am mute because my voice is filled
> with words and unlike music I can only be understood
> and not heard[.] (10)

Ritual

Following the opening movement of *Cartouches*, the second part of the book consists of journal entries and poems, a form similar to that of *Helen in Egypt*, but without H.D.'s structure of *personae*. After the solemnity of the opening movements' invocations of Tostevin's deceased father, the journal entries sometimes seem offhand, even chatty. "Personal" might be the best word, different from "ceremonial." "We've rented a room near Midan Tahrir, the main square in the heart of modern Cairo," she writes, for instance. This change in tone is not maintained consistently, but it recurs amidst entries and poems of varying levels of solemnity. (The change is strictly in tone; *Cartouches'* artistic seriousness is omnipresent. It is the "heart" of the city where she rented a room, after all.) The impression which these variations of tone reinforces—along with the brevity of the individual pieces, their disjunctions as poetry and prose, and their achronological order—is of fragmentation. In parallel with Isis' reassembling of Osiris, Achilles Lemire's reassembling of his daughter's doll, and Tostevin's reassembling of her/the father, the reader is called upon to reassemble the poems and journal entries, to make them cohere as a whole.

This personal tone has other purposes in *Cartouches* as well. In *Figuring Grief*, her study of the fiction-elegies of Mavis Gallant and Alice Munro, Karen E. Smythe also says much about poetic elegy which illuminates elegiac aspects of *Cartouches*. Directly relevant to these matters of personal tone and reassembling the fragmented text is Smythe's argument that

> an emphasis on the art of mourning as well as on the mourner— the artist and survivor— has always been a significant component of elegy.... Poetic continuity is achieved in the very writing of the elegy; in this sense, self-consciousness functions as a trope of consolation. (6–7)

So, for example, in *Cartouches* Tostevin narrates the story of her trip to Egypt, often foregrounding her own actions, putting herself in the picture. One journal entry begins,

> I am sitting on the veranda of the old Cataract Hotel in Aswan, recording my daily journal entry, jotting down ideas for poems, recalling other writers' lines on Egypt.

As well as the self-consciousness evident here, the trajectory of this piece is noteworthy. The entry concludes with the poet's watching the sun set,

> the moon already high in the sky. Thoth, god of the written word, was conceived to replace this setting sun. The moon is to day what speech is to writing.

The trajectory of the following piece reverses this "self-to-ancient-Egypt" movement of the focus:

> Thoth has as many faces as there are names....

> Beheader of men, women, children, he determines the manner in which all are written—fixes their thoughts into his. Seed, egg, great cackler, he is hidden father of all things. A wild card. Records the weight of heavy hearts, tips the scales to restore balance.

> Today he is daughter. Wears on his ibis head my cusped moon.

These two examples show Tostevin's use of "contamination," in these cases to bring together in a live relationship figures from ancient Egypt and herself. Tostevin also contaminates ancient Egyptian cultural artifacts and monuments with modern ones, and vice versa:

> Crouched inside
> the museum door the jackal
> Anubis guards the dead
> with the sweeping curve
> of gilded ears while Elvis
> blares somewhere from
> a transistor radio.

> Transmuted, hieroglyphs
> live on within our own

small daily alphabets.
Anubis, you ain't nothing
but a hound dog.

Elsewhere, while gazing at the Sphinx, Tostevin hears Fred Astaire singing "Heaven, I'm in heaven, and my heart beats so that I can hardly speak." These (and many other in *Cartouches*) humorous coincidences are interesting partly because of their mutual shedding of light. Such contaminations, though, are especially pertinent to the elegiac project of *Cartouches* and its seeking of consolation. As noted before, Tostevin was well aware of the possibilities for "The engendering of new life within old fictions," or in "reinventing the past from a present point of view," as she puts it in her interview with Christopher Dewdney (1).[4]

Language

Tostevin's mourning ritual in *Cartouches* is multifaceted and multidimensional, but it starts and finishes with her faith in the power of writing. In this way, the consolation generated by *Cartouches* is based on a celebration of all kinds of language. Again citing Kristeva, Tostevin explicitly declares her belief in language's powers in a review of Miriam Mandel's *collected poems*:

> Almost ten years ago, Julia Kristeva wrote: 'we have not yet grasped the importance of a change of venue that involves thinking about the subject on the basis of literary practice rather than on the basis of neurosis or psychosis' (*Desire in Language*, p. 97). Since then, many women have come to realize that the poetic function can transform the dependence of the subject into a test of freedom in relation to language and reality. If poetic language communicates meaning, nevertheless meaning does not exhaust the poetic function. Poetic language cannot be reduced to phenomenological perspectives; it exceeds these perspectives and strives toward a space or language where social codes, laws and traditional concepts of the subject are exploded so that they can be revised, renewed. (52)

No wonder then, that one of the main intertexts of *Cartouches* is *The Egyptian Book of the Dead*. As Tostevin notes in a journal entry after buying a copy in the Cairo Museum, she is

> searching for spells that can unlock the jaw, open the mouth, and keep the heart from being plundered, again and again. Let's not fool ourselves. Language serves those who can use it best and these rituals were meant for the living, each hieroglyph a bated breath.

When Tostevin meets Isis in her temple at Philae, it is a moment of mutual self-recognition for them:

> Surrounded by doves and pigeons and other low-flying prey,
> Isis leans back on her lions—one named Yesterday, the other,
> Tomorrow—while, above, an eagle whirls its black-armed swastika.

> In your effort to recapture Yesterday, Isis, you fashion words into perfect bodies. Dictate for posterity your embalmer's craft: how to preserve flesh in unguents and spices; how to knit together bones....

> So, Isis, you are a poet. You transform ghosts into letters and images. Convert winter or summer, a lake, a few stars, into a fabric of echoes, until the entire world begins to rhyme and rhyme becomes the only reason for living.

In the end, Achilles Lemire, the poet's father, is resurrected through the powers of language. Of the truth of this assertion a reader is convinced after reading *Cartouches*. The experience of reading Tostevin's book generates this transformation. To explore *Cartouches* further confirms the reader's impression: the world Tostevin creates does rhyme. And rhyme.

NOTES

1.   The pages of *Cartouches* are unnumbered.

2. Rather than a "dove," the second sign is a quail chick, the phonetic symbol for "u" or "w." During our telephone conversation, Tostevin declared that her calling the sign a dove was a "creative manoeuvre" on her part: there was no way she'd say "chick"—and she thought nobody would look it up.

3. My translation, for the reader's convenience.

4. Linda Hutcheon regards this reinvention as quintessentially postmodern (4), as is also the writer's expressed self-consciousness.

Land of Their Graves

Maternity, Mourning and Nation in Janet Frame, Sara Suleri, and Arundhati Roy

Dear, dear England! why was I forced by a stern necessity to leave you? What heinous crime had I committed that I, who adored you, should be torn from your sacred bosom, to pine out my joyless existence in a foreign clime? Oh, that I might be permitted to return and die upon your wave-encircled shores, and rest my weary head and heart beneath your daisy-covered sod at last! Ah, these are vain outbursts of feeling— melancholy relapses of the spring home-sickness! Canada! thou art a noble, free, and rising country—the great fostering mother of the orphans of civilisation. The offspring of Britain, thou must be great, and I will and do love thee, land of my adoption, and of my children's birth; and, oh, dearer still to a mother's heart—land of their graves! (73)

THE WORDS "restrained" and "cheerful" rarely spring to mind when reading Susanna Moodie's *Roughing It in the Bush*, and this passage is typical— she has not been called "moody Moodie" by thousands of Canadian university students for nothing. Despite the rather turgid tone which begins this excerpt, however, there is genuine pathos in the final line and in Moodie's equation between the death of her children and an identification with Canada. This is only the end of an extended trope, which begins with the comparison of England with a mother and Moodie herself with an orphaned child: she is "torn from" England's "sacred bosom" and left to a "joyless existence in a foreign clime." This representation of England as parent and colonies or colonials as children is a cliché in the literature of empire; what is unique is Moodie's association between mourning and nation: it is the literal death of her own children in Canada that allows the figurative separation from her mother nation (England) and the attachment to a new nation as a mother in her own right. Mourning quickly becomes ritualized, moving from an expression of personal grief to an expression of cultural values. Mourning can be thought of, in short, as discourse. I will argue here that the association between mourning, maternity and nationality is a recurring theme in the writing of women in postcolonial nations, and that this particular representational matrix may shed some new light on how nationality may be understood.[1]

As Peter Metcalfe and Richard Huntington write in *Celebrations of Death*, cultural attitudes toward death have much to reveal about attitudes toward life:

> the study of death is a positive endeavor because, regardless of whether custom calls for festive or restrained behavior, the issue of death throws into relief the most important cultural values by which people live their lives and evaluate their experiences. Life becomes transparent against the background of death, and fundamental social and cultural issues are revealed. (2)

Ralph Houlbrooke argues that as funeral rites were simplified in England between 1500 and 1930, largely as a result of the Protestant Reformation, the service itself focussed as much on the living as the dead: "By removing the intercessory elements from the funeral service, the reformers made it first and foremost a vehicle of instruction for the living, not a means of assisting the dead" (34). Indeed, all funerary ritual manifestly serves the living as it relegates the dead to the imaginary: representation is always the purview of the living, even when the order it constructs contains the dead. A number of theorists of funerary ritual have made this argument: that is, that in a post-Enlightenment world of increasingly secular values, funerals and other rituals surrounding death centre more on the living than the dead and also more on the body or its remains than the soul. In "Mortuary Practices, Society and Ideology," Michael Parker Pearson argues that shifts in attitudes in the Victorian period have "reduced the power of the dead as symbols manipulated by the living," and further that "we are losing a language of death cele-bration" (111). Pearson suggests that this loss coincides with the rise of a modern, scientific world view:

> Burial ritual is susceptible to ideological manipulation within the construction of social strategies. An analysis of mortuary practices in modern and Victorian England leads to an interpretation both in terms of the way the dead are seen by the living and in terms of the social relationships between competing groups. Since the Victorian era when burial ritual was a forum for the display of wealth and status, the dead have come to be seen more and more as unwanted matter to be disposed of quickly, without extravagance. This development, involving changes in the use of cremation and in the physical traces of the burial, is part of the increased use of hygiene, science, and medicine in agencies of social control. (99)

Not only has mortuary ritual come to focus more on the living and the physical remains of the dead with the rise of modernity, it has also become more overtly discursive as it has become more secular, according to various commentators. For instance, Michel Foucault suggests in "Different Spaces" that

> [the] cemetery, which was lodged in the sacred space of the church, took on an altogether different look in modern civilizations; and, curiously, it was during the time when civilization became, as we say very roughly, "atheist," that Western culture inaugurated what is called the cult of the dead.
>
> Basically, it was quite natural that at a time when people really believed in the resurrection of bodies and the immortality of the soul they did not attribute a cardinal importance to mortal remains. On the contrary, from the moment that one is no longer quite sure of having a soul, that the body will return to life, it may be necessary to devote much more attention to those mortal remains, which are finally the only trace of our existence in the midst of the world and in the midst of words. (180–81)

Ralph Houlbrooke argues similarly that during the Reformation, "The rise of literacy prompted a long-term shift from pictorial representation to the epitaph, which could say more, and say it more eloquently, that all but the very best and most expensive engraving or sculpture" (39). As Pearson succinctly puts it, "material culture can...be seen as a form of non-verbal communication through the representation of ideas" (100). Communication is no guarantee of clarity, however, even ritualized communication. As Pearson argues, "the context of death is one of ritual action and communication as opposed to everyday communication," but "what is clear about ritual is how to do it but its meaning may be clear, complicated, ambiguous, or forgotten" (100). In a sense, all writing about death might be regarded as epitaph or memorial; such writing is likely to contain the signs of ritual but also of ambiguity and forgetting.

The shifts in the meaning of mortuary ritual—from a spiritual commemoration of the dead to a secular assertion of life and materiality—coincides with the rise of concepts of nation. As the authors of *Key Concepts in Postcolonial Studies* point out, "the idea of nation is now so firmly fixed in the general imagination, and the form of state it signifies so widely accepted, that it is hard to realize how recent its invention has been" (149). Though there have long been political and ethnic groupings of people, the concept of the modern nation-state is generally recognized to have developed into its current form in the nineteenth century. E.J. Hobsbawm writes of the "period when the 'principle of nationality' changed its map in the most dramatic way, namely the period from 1830 to 1880," adding that "for Walter Bagehot 'nation-making' was the essential content of nineteenth century evolution" (23). Indeed, Hobsbawm states bluntly that "The basic characteristic of the modern nation and everything connected with it is its modernity" (14). However, as Adrian Hastings points out in *The Construction of Nationhood*, lofty theoretical constructions of nation are not always identical to daily and practical experiences of nationality:

'Nationalism' means two things: a theory and a practice. As a political theory—that each 'nation' should have its own 'state'—it derives from the nineteenth century. However, that general principle motivates few nationalists. In practice, nationalism is strong only in particularist terms. (3–4)

The paradox of death is that it is perhaps the epitome of particularity at the same time that it is universal; representations of death often contain this paradox. Likewise, representations of nation often negotiate tensions between particulars and universals—one might think of Canada's "multicultural" policies versus the American notion of "the melting pot," two nationalisms over which much ink has been spilled. Historically, death and nation have been associated precisely in the context of an elaborate negotiation of particulars and universals, perhaps the clearest example being the commemoration of individual soldiers killed in wars:

> A major class of memorials commemorating the dead are the war memorials— the Cenotaph in London and cenotaphs scattered all over Britain. The war dead are commemorated as 'warriors' who died fighting for their country and the ideals of freedom and equality which it enshrines. Nationalism as an ideological means of control is thus legitimated through remembrance of the war dead of Britain (as opposed to the dead of all countries involved in the World Wars). The fact that the soldier buried in Westminster Abbey is named the "Unknown Warrior" further advances the cause of nationalism since he is related solely to his country, transcending all kinship, regional and class connections. (Pearson 111)

As I have already pointed out, however, the construction of nation which evolves from the paradigm of death in battle is evidently masculine; in fact, I would argue that the transcendence of kinship enacted through the "Unknown Warrior" is a marker of the masculinity of this death and the male construction of nationality to which it contributes. But there is more than one way of constructing the mythology of death or a nation, for, as Adrian Hastings writes, "The nation-state has always been itself to a very large extent an unrealized myth; it only too manifestly does not fit the complex reality of human society very helpfully in many places" (7).

Just as the "Unknown Warrior" dies in a masculine performance of nationality, I would like to argue here that there are deaths which perform nationality in distinctly female forms. Furthermore, these deaths do not "[transcend] all kinship" of "regional...connections," but work instead to reinforce precisely these connections. Kinship and region are equally points of reference in discourses of particularity and are also implicated in both the representations of death and nationality; as women are often associated with domesticity and family—indeed, they are imagined to be the heart of the home and the family—it seems unsurprising that one can discern in postcolonial women's writing a discursive thread that weaves together maternity, death and nation. And, as I will show with an analysis of the work of New Zealand writer Janet Frame, Pakistani writer Sara Suleri, and Indian writer Arundhati Roy, this particular discursive thread transcends specific nationalisms through the transcultural experiences of maternity and mortality.

Postcolonial writing almost compulsively explores ideas of nation, sometimes in theoretical or abstract terms, but what I want to examine here is a more intimate, material, indeed, bodily construction of nation through the lives and deaths of mothers, sisters and children. This is not the nation of grand ideals and the "unknown Warrior," but the village that Foucault imagines in the cemetery in "Different Spaces": "it was in the nineteenth century that each person began to have the right to his little box for his little personal decomposition.... Cemeteries...no longer constituted the sacred and immortal wind of the city, but the 'other city' where each family possessed its dark dwelling" (181). Unlike Foucault, however, I would not diminish the "personal decomposition," because for women, the work of nation-building occurs not only in the imagination but literally in the body. For example, as John Belshaw writes, settler societies were "founded on the premise of fertility. Settlers would come, often as families, with an eye to building bigger families that would constitute new communities, towns, villages, and cities" (n.p.). All nations, not just those created partly through settlement, emerge from the bellies of women, because nations are made first and foremost of people, children. Why, then, is postcolonial women's writing not marked by a simple equation between nation and birth? Because, of course, children die, and they die with alarming frequency in emerging nations where political uncertainties make life itself uncertain. As Belshaw points out, the "bucolic frontier mythology belied the very real and crucial presence of death alongside renewal"(n.p.). Thus, in postcolonial women's writing, nations are made largely through maternity and mourning.

I would like to discuss three particularly cogent examples of texts which elaborate this representational nexus of maternity, mourning and nation:

Janet Frame's An Autobiography (1991), Sara Suleri's memoir Meatless Days (1989), and Arundhati Roy's novel The God of Small Things. I will begin this analysis in psychoanalytic terms by returning to the Susanna Moodie citation with which I began. First, Moodie expresses grief at having been "torn from [the] sacred bosom" of England, which she conceives as "the great fostering mother or the orphans of civilisation." In this analogy, she compares her sense of British nationality with the sense of plenitude the infant experiences at the breast ("bosom") of the mother. Object-relations psychoanalyst Melanie Klein writes extensively and compellingly about the attachment between mother and child which is initiated at the breast; here, I will focus on her 1936 article "Weaning." Among other things, Klein understands the breast to represent both satiation and separation. There are three points which Klein makes in "Weaning" which are important to consider here. First, she suggests that the breast nurtures the child literally and symbolically, becoming a sign of fulfillment: "the [infant] child receives his main satisfaction through his mouth, which becomes the main channel through which the child takes in not only his food, but also, in his phantasy, the world outside him" (291). Second, Klein recognizes that, from the moment of birth, the infant is always already weaned: "in so far as the baby never has uninterrupted possession of the breast, and over and over again is in the state of lacking it, one could say that, in a sense, he is in a constant state of being weaned or at least in a state leading up to weaning" (295). Finally, Klein argues that "the feelings of having lost the breast lead to the fear of having lost the loved mother entirely," a fear which is "interwoven with feelings of guilt at having destroyed her (eaten her up)" (295). These latter two points, emphasizing infantile experiences of separation and loss, link maternity to our first subjective grappling with death, among other things.

One way in which a woman may reconcile her own feelings of infantile loss and guilt is through the experience of nursing a child of her own: "If she can enjoy it thoroughly, her pleasure will be unconsciously realized by the child, and this reciprocal happiness will lead to a full emotional understanding between mother and child" (300). Clearly the breast/mother is symbolic in Klein's work, but equally clearly she is material, or "real." This same ambivalence about literal and figurative maternity is embedded in Moodie's references to mothers: the allusion to the "fostering mother of the orphans of civilisation" is obviously figurative, but the reference to "a mother's heart" brings the trope down to earth, literally, to "the land of [children's] graves" (73). Thus, the significance of "nation" in this passage undergoes a semiotic shift through the figure of the mother, from the abstract and external "bosom" of mother England to the adopted, internal and material "heart" of the mother in Canada. The narrative perspective shifts also, from that of abandoned child, to adopted child, to mother of children. The vehicle for both shifts in signification is death. Interestingly, in the work of Janet Frame, Sara Suleri and Arundhati Roy, written a century later, one finds precisely the same representational conjunction of death and maternity in nations constructed in a postcolonial context.

From the earliest moments in *An Autobiography*, Janet Frame associates maternity, death and nation in a description of her own birth:

I was delivered by Dr. Emily Seideberg McKinnon at St. Helens hospital, Dunedin, where I was known as 'the baby who was always hungry'. I had a twin, which did not develop beyond a few weeks. Twins were hereditary in Mother's family, and she would often quote the poem by (I think) her grandmother, whose two sets of twins died in infancy: 'Four little locks of gold'. Mother's memory of my birth always had two repeated references—her boast that I was delivered by the first woman medical graduate in New Zealand and her pride in the abundance of milk that enabled her to feed myself and other babies. (10)

Frame situates her birth in two explicitly female historical contexts: the matriarchal history of her own family, and the national history of the "first woman medical graduate in New Zealand." Notably, embedded in the narrative of her own birth into a female-marked New Zealand is the simultaneous death of a twin and reference to the deaths of four other children; infant mortality is thus equated, as much as infant birth, with the birth of a nation. There is also a reference to nursing and mother's milk here, as in the Susanna Moodie citation, implying that the mother's body nurtures and mourns in equal measure.

Two of the most significant events in Frame's life are the deaths of her sisters, Myrtle and Isabel, both by drowning. In the case of the first drowning, it is the mother who predicts the death of her daughter when she receives developed photos in which Myrtle looks transparent; in the same moment the mother conflates the geography of New Zealand and a national epidemic of "infantile paralysis"(83) with predictions of the death of her daughter:

> When the photographs of Rakaia were developed, Mother gave a gasp of horror when she saw that in one of the photographs Myrtle appeared to be transparent: all except Myrtle had taken flesh and blood photographs. It made her feel afraid, Mother said, everything coming at once, the death of Grandma Godfrey, the beautiful Rakaia River, snow-fed, flashing green and blue, the Southern Alps with their autumn snow, the epidemic that filled the country with sadness and dread, and the sight of the victims who'd escaped severe paralysis, walking about with their leg irons to support them; all combined to bring to the surface the buried fear that Myrtle might die at any time. (84)

The final line of this passage is interesting in that it refers to the burial not of Myrtle's body but rather of the mother's fear for both her own child and all the children of New Zealand: the grave itself is represented here as the locus of a mother's understanding of her role both as the mother of children who emerge from her own body and as a symbolic "Mother New Zealand," like the "Mother England" in Moodie's work, or the "Mother India" we shall encounter in Roy's work; that is, the mother here makes an unconscious analogy between her relationship with her children and the relationship between the landscape of New Zealand and her children, her vulnerable child-citizens. After Myrtle is buried, the ritual markers of mortuary are quickly eroded, and the grave sinks into the earth of nation: "And soon the rain rained on the flowers, and the ink on the cards was smudged, and the coloured ribbons frayed and rotted, and the grave itself sunk until it was level with the earth" (86–87).

When, some ten years after the death of Myrtle, a second sister, Isabel, also drowns, Frame again links the death to a sense of nation: "This new death came as an epilogue to the old stories and a prologue to the new, in our own land where the 'great sea' and the rivers would speak for us and we would 'speak for ourselves'" (208). This passage immediately follows references to the work of T.S. Eliot, Virginia Woolf, Thomas Hardy and the Brontë sisters, and so Frame clearly equates the emergent voice of a postcolonial national literature with the death of her sister. As I suggested earlier, modern constructions of death tend to foreground the discursive qualities of mortuary ritual and mortality itself; child mortality becomes implicated in a female-centred representation of nation where the mother is not a generalized or archetypal "mother Earth" but rather is an historically situated "mother nation/state," actively engaged in nation-making through reproduction. As Charles Sugnet points out in an article about Zimbabwean writer Tsitsi Dangarembga's novel *Nervous Conditions*, when a writer (most often a woman, undoubtedly) "refus[es] the usual terms of heroic, masculine, national narrative" and "center[s] on a particular, dynamic woman" (as does *Nervous Conditions*), then the text "is in no danger of producing a univocal Woman, who can be allegorized to serve the national purpose." Sugnet's further comments about *Nervous Conditions* apply equally to all of the texts included in this study:

> ...because the narrator is the writer of her own account and therefore in some senses a maker of history and a producer of knowledge, the novel connects the "old deep places" of childhood, homestead, and inner self with history, change, and agency, rather than isolating them in some eternal essence of Woman/Landscape/Nation. (42)

This is an important point to make: because the particular construction of nation which I am delineating here is so firmly grounded in the grave and in the bodies of mothers and their children, it is not the monolithic, homogenous or jingoistic sort of representation one usually associates with constructions of nation. Indeed, it is made abundantly clear in these texts that the cost of the construction of national mythologies for mothers in postcolonial contexts is horrendous: Frame writes that after the drowning of her second daughter, "Mother's burden was unthinkable" (208) and further on that "Mother was bewildered, her eyes were frightened and her hair beneath the 'picture hat' of straw had turned from brown-grey to white" (209). It is as though through the deaths of her children, Frame's mother has merged with the landscape of New Zealand itself, taking into her body "the beautiful Rakaia River, snow fed" and "the Southern Alps with their autumn snow" (84).

It is this latter point—that the discourse of nation is firmly rooted in women's bodies in postcolonial women's writing—that becomes most evident in Sara Suleri's *Meatless Days*. In her memoir of the restless and violent history of Pakistan's independence, it is a mother, Suleri's sister, Ifat, who dies. Through the story of Ifat's brutal murder, Suleri's narrative weaves together the history of an emergent nation with conceptions of maternity and death. At the time of her first pregnancy and delivery, Ifat tells Suleri that "Men live in homes, and women live in bodies." Suleri continues,

> For she was preoccupied with the creature living inside her: I could watch her make a dwelling of her demeanor, a startling place in which to live. My heart was wrenched to see her lying there later, with her infant boy next to her side, red and wrinkled as an infant is after living so long in water! Ifat's eyes smiled at me from her bed, as she lay with her beauty and her discourse and now a baby, too. (143)

The homes of men, including their homelands, Suleri suggests, are abstract, constructed entirely outside of their bodies; women know intimately that our first homes are within the bodies of women, and these are the homes which precede nations and from which nations may emerge. In a later conversation, Ifat makes this association between home and women's bodies explicit:

> "Oh, home is where your mother is, one; it is when you are mother, two; and in between it's almost as though your spirit must retract..."—she was concentrating now, in the earnest way she concentrated as a child—"your spirit must become a tiny, concentrated little thing, so that your body feels like a spacious place in which to live—is that right, Sara?" she asked me, suddenly tentative. "Perhaps," I said, "perhaps. But when I look at you, Ifat, I am in home's element!" (147)

Not only does Ifat equate home with maternity in this passage, but the mother (Ifat) becomes a child herself in her concentration, and her spirit, "a tiny, concentrated little thing," becomes necessarily childish in the construction of "a spacious place in which to live," a place like a nation, but a place which is "your body" above all else. Very clearly, nation is not regarded as an external, rhetorical formula which is taken into the constitution of individual subjectivity; rather, the nation is born from the necessarily female subject. Men may live in a nation, but only women can produce a nation— "Men live in homes, women live in bodies." As Michelle Boulous Walker writes of Melanie Klein's work in *Philosophy and the Maternal Body: Reading Silence*, "While Freud manages mostly to avoid the question of the mother and Lacan erases her almost entirely behind the linguistic operation of metaphor, Klein insists that we think through the mother's body" (141). Walker adds that "we can understand this complex process of object relations in Klein's work only in relation to the *real* mother" [Walker's italics] (141). The rhetoric of nation can never come close to the immediate authenticity of the maternal bodies of nation, Suleri suggests, because words feed only our minds, while mothers feed our bodies and our minds:

> I am content with writing's way of claiming disappointment as its habit of arrival, a gesture far more modulated than the pitch of rapture. In any case—although I did not know it then—to fall asleep on Ifat's bed was milk enough, to sleep in crumbling rest beside her body. Sometimes like water she runs through the sentences of sleep, a medium something other than itself, refracting, innocent of the algae it can bear and capable of much transmogrification. Her water laps around me almost in reproach: "You were distracted, when I requested your attention. You were not looking. I was milk." (186)

In this passage, it is Suleri who becomes a child, while the memory of her sister becomes the "milk" which nourishes Suleri's narrative.

Furthermore, Moodie, Frame and Suleri all link this representational network of maternity, death and nation with another representational network of water and nostalgia or memory. Moodie longs for England's "wave-encircled shores," Frame recalls "the beautiful Rakaia River," and Suleri imagines that the memories of her sister are like "water" which "laps around" her. In a psychoanalytic context, water may be linked to the womb and the amniotic fluid from which human life is born; the equation between water and memory in these passages further connects prenatal status with prelinguistic formulations of subjectivity. Finally, in each case, the prelinguistic fluids of subjective ambiguity are also tied to place — to water that encircles or circulates through both the subject and the place where she locates her life, and, by extension, her nation. In Arundhati Roy's novel, *The God of Small Things*, the connections between water and maternity are clearly implicated in the birth of India and Pakistan, a birth of two nations which is initiated ironically by the separation and loss of Partition which, in the novel, is symbolized as the death of a child.

The novel centres on children and their mothers. The mother, Ammu, and her children, Estha and Rahel, are the family at the core of the text. Estha and Rahel are twins who are separated from each other and then from their mother over the course of the novel; on one level, these separations may be linked to the separation of India and Pakistan from Empire (Ammu/Mother England) and then from each other (the twins/India and Pakistan). Partition is often characterized by Indian writers as a violent and tragic separation; when Shashi Tharoor describes Partition in his book *India: From Midnight to the Millennium*, he describes this event through a metaphor which we have seen to pervade postcolonial women's writing, the metaphor of birth:

> If the structures of British rule tended toward the creation of a united
> India for the convenience of the rulers, its animating spirit was aimed
> at fostering division to achieve the same ends. This seeming paradox
> (but in fact entirely logical construct) of imperial policy culminated
> in the tragic Partition of India upon independence—so that August
> 15, 1947, was a birth that was also an abortion. (15)

In his speech of August 14, 1947, made on the eve of Independence, Jawaharlal Nehru also describes Independence as birth, but with a greater sense of the mourning and loss always already embedded in any birth: "Before the birth of freedom we have endured all the pains of labour and our hearts are heavy with the memory of this sorrow" (1). In *The God of Small Things*, the narrative of the twins is linked to memory, and on one level their memories represent the memories of a nation: "In those early amorphous years when memory had only just begun, when life was full of Beginnings and no Ends, and Everything was Forever, Estahappen and Rahel thought of themselves together as Me, and separately, individually, as We or Us" (4).

However, as time passes and the twins become alienated from each other, Estha ceases to speak and withdraws into himself, his silence taking the shape of a foetus within a "Spider Woman":

> He retreated into further stillness. As though his body had the power to snatch its senses inwards (knotted, egg-shaped), away from the surface of his skin, into some deeper more inaccessible recess. The silence gathered its skirts and slid, like Spider Woman, up the slippery bathroom wall. (89)

Estha's silence is triggered by several significant events in the novel, but probably the most dramatic is the death of Sophie Mol, a cousin of the twins who has an Indian father and English mother, marking her as the hybrid child of a postcolonial world. The children play frequently at an abandoned house on an estate across the river from their home, referred to both as "History House" and "Heart of Darkness"; it is during a passage across the storm-swollen river that Sophie Mol drowns, her death ironically signalling the end of the marriage of Britain and India, represented by her parents, or the death of empire on the banks of history and the "heart of darkness." After her death, the missing twins are sought by the police, "a pair of two-egg twins, hounded by history" (248). Again, death, nation (history) and maternity are linked in this text, for the children's destination of "History House" is also the destination of their mother, who meets her lover, an untouchable, there, in the "heart of darkness," initiating a series of events which lead to her separation from her children.

The "heart of darkness" itself, a metaphor at the centre of so much of postcolonial literature and theory, may be equated with the body of the mother, as a metaphor of the centre of the "dark continent" (as Freud so notoriously called women) from where the rivers of life and history flow. As Roy writes of "History House"/"Heart of Darkness," "Rotting beams supported on once-white pillars had buckled at the center, leaving a yawning, gaping hole. A History Hole. A History-shaped Hole in the Universe" (291).

David Spurr has argued that the "heart of darkness" is "a modern trope which treats the colonized landscape as emblematic of the void which surrounds, or lies at the heart of, the human condition" (94). "The great emptiness," Spurr continues, "signified by the blank space on the map becomes the site of a narrative colonization in Conrad's story, but also the site of the subject's terrifying encounter with his own nothingness" (94–95). Spurr's point about modernity here recalls the beginning of this paper, specifically the argument that mortuary ritual and representation has become more secular and thus more centred on materiality and the body in an epistemological shift which is essentially modernist. Or, as Ralph Houlbrooke puts it, "Some refer to the 'denial' of death in the twentieth century when what they really have in mind is its evasion or concealment" (15). Likewise, the "heart of darkness" is not denied but rather concealed, much as the history of women in the building of nations is understood to have existed but has also been hidden or silenced. As Charles Sugnet says, in practical terms, "nationalism and national liberation movements continue to be criticized for their failure to serve women's needs" (33). In a more philosophical context, Michelle Boulous Walker argues that imagining women in spatial terms—as the interiority of the "heart of darkness," for example—both delimits and silences women: "this spatial alternative is too simplistic as woman simultaneously inhabits philosophy's (empty) interiority while remaining exterior to the practices that would confer subjectivity and voice upon her" (20). And this, in the end, is why it matters that women inevitably must understand nation differently than men, as their physical relation to nation-making is different from that of men: it matters because this alternative place where nation is made not of women (the land being seeded) but rather by women, through their own bodies, is a potential site for the empowerment of women. As Rose Wietz argues in The Politics of Women's Bodies, throughout history, ideas about women's bodies have centrally affected the strictures within which women live. Only by looking at the embodied experiences of women, as well as how those experiences are socially constructed, can we fully understand women's lives, women's position in society, and the possibilities for resistance against that position. (10)

Perhaps if men and women themselves were to come to believe in the truth of "the embodied experiences of women," including maternal mourning, to understand, for example, that nations are born from the blood and water and babies that emerge from between the thighs of women, then perhaps (but this is too naïve to hope for, don't you think?), perhaps then people would be much more reluctant to sacrifice those children (borne within their mothers' bodies, born from their mothers' bodies, and fed by their mothers' bodies) to those brutal and grotesque myths of nation which are abstracted entirely from the flesh.

NOTE

1.   There are obvious associations between masculinity, death and emergent nationalisms, particularly in narratives of war and conquest. What I am interested in exploring here, however, is a specifically female construction of nationality that is represented through links between mothers, children and death.

Using Up Words
in Paul Monette's AIDS Elegy

IN THIS ESSAY, I argue that AIDS elegy succeeds not just in aesthetic, literary, and metaphorical terms, but in terms of cultural productivity. The idea of an active poetics, a politically and socially *effective* literary body, is manifested through AIDS elegy in bodies of work and persons. AIDS elegy collects data as if substantial weight will force change. It pares away affect and the unnecessary (although often through experiencing and exhausting them first) and remains robust and full of information for an ongoing community of mourners. It is because of the active engagement between AIDS elegy's work and the future reality of a community of sufferers that I insist on separating this mode of elegy from classical pastoral elegy, which tends to reflect and console in the present. The mourning community in *Lycidas*, by contrast, is not one that fears mass drownings in the wake of Lycidas's death. Even in Tennyson's *In Memoriam*, which seems to be battling theology and scientific development as it mourns Hallam, it is talking in these moments about the personal faith of the poet and not the life of the dead one *or others like him*.

I begin by opening up some issues—to which I return later—about writing and representation both in *Love Alone* and artistic creation as a whole. This incorporates setting *Love Alone* and earlier elegy side-by-side for initial comparison. In part two, I discuss in more depth the role of AIDS elegy in the real-world cultural setting of AIDS (in America), and how Monette begins to push past his anger (and his depiction of the AIDS "war") toward a reconciliation with heterosexual mourners. This consolation, I argue, is again different from the traditional apotheosis; it is the creation of healing for the future and for others as well as the poet, whether or not Monette really cares to be part of that wider process. The real effectiveness of language, communication, and writing is interrogated later in section two where I discuss Monette's replacement of concepts with objects. I hope here to illustrate how AIDS elegy pulls itself away from a less severe pastoral mode. Part three continues the discussion of the power of words and of the ways in which *Love Alone* both uses and breaks out of convention. I close with an extended discussion of the final elegy in *Love Alone* and suggest that in the end Monette recalls traditional closure, but—while writing some of the best poetry in the collection—achieves uniqueness by leaving language for a reliance on the permanence of a single image.

Considering the book as text, as a play of signifiers in an expanding field, we see that *Love Alone*'s engagement with AIDS speaks—or rather shouts— across a gap in communication. As a reinvention of the classical elegiac genre, with the shadow of AIDS cast upon it, *Love Alone* takes language from the heterosexual shelves, appropriates it, re-presents it, and exposes it under the banner of AIDS specifically to be opened up and reflected back onto the world at large. It is part of Monette's achievement in the open-ended mode of his free verse in this collection of elegies that he emphasizes the role of what Lee Edelman has termed "homographesis," exposing the difference and *différance* in gay inscription. "Like writing," writes Edelman,

> homographesis would name a double operation: one serving the ideological purposes of a conservative social order intent on codifying identities in its labor of disciplinary inscription, and the other resistant to that categorization, intent on *de*-scribing the identities that order has so oppressively inscribed. That these two operations, pointing as they do in opposite directions, should inhabit a single signifier, must make for a degree of confusion, but the confusion that results when difference collapses into identity and identity unfolds into différance is...central to the problematic of homographesis. (10, italics original)

If we consider the book as a cultural work or object with assigned meaning regardless of how the text works, we see on the one hand that the acts of printing a book with a "Stonewall Inn Editions" cover and of stating that the book should be filed under "AIDS" rather than "poetry" (Monette xi) work to publicize the voices of gay men in the world at large. On the other hand, they allow confirmation by an extreme heterosexual system of difference that sees as inevitable the gap of silence—Baruch Blumberg's term is "fear gap" (87)—between homosexuals and heterosexuals.

These acts of text and work, however, are also accommodations of power: the words, phrases, acknowledgements, are all burdens of the heterosexual order's inscription. By being carried across the "gap" they are appropriated not as confirmations of that order's original view of the other, but are homographically rebuilt, redefined, and resemiotized. The words still echo the other order, but the identity that has been formed by an ignorant "difference" now "unfolds into différance" as the new queer regimen of signifying units slowly but surely homes in on its own referential identities—or rather keeps shifting away from its opposing heterosexually assumed identities. Such creation of newness is something akin to gay life, as defined by Jeffrey Weeks:

Lesbians and gays have a sense of their own creativity because they are, day by day, involved in self making, constructing their own meanings, networks, rituals, traditions, calling on the inherited traces of the past, but responding all the time to the challenges and possibilities of the present. (134)

It is arguable whether this notion can be claimed as a perquisite of gay and lesbian experience; processes of self-fashioning have been in place for white, powerful, heterosexual males for centuries. For the present, however, there is a symbiosis, strongly identified by Monette, between being gay and confronting AIDS, and this dynamic dyadic is explored in improvisatory and exploratory language and acts of selfhood. Each experience promotes understanding of the other and insists on vocalizing that learning. The resulting texts are lessons on sexual life and the frailty of life for self-styled "mainstream" readers as well as homosexuals.[1]

The methods for this improvisational creativity are stark and forwardlooking. If the literary text is infused with its cultural and literary past, it also feeds the cultural and communicative future. In spite of the almost violent wielding of his textual tools, Monette manages to bridge this gap between radical AIDS "warrior" and the resisting reader because of what I will show to be the inevitable continuum of the text through all cultural forms. The notion that everything is text, inside and outside of the literary work, is hardly new in a poststructuralist age, but studies of Monette's prose and poetry have struggled to let go of affect as the central driving force of the work, even as they claim to be centralizing politics. Monette's inability to escape generic and expressive convention in his work means that he at once reappropriates any heterosexism in language to an opposing cause and also speaks back to (or at) the heterosexist majority in ways they might resist, but are forced to understand.[2]

It is because of this premise that *Love Alone* behaves as one text among many—whether literary, political, religious, or artistic, or all of these—that I would place *Love Alone* within Barthes's paradox of pop art:

> [In pop art] on the one hand, the mass culture of the period is present in it as a revolutionary force which contests art; and on the other art is present in it as a very old force which irresistibly returns in the economy of societies. There are two voices, as in a fugue—one says: 'This is not Art'; the other says, at the same time: 'I am Art.' (198)

Monette's *Love Alone: Eighteen Elegies for Rog* contest the notions of traditional pastoral elegy and its infusions of nature by importing the mundane and mass-produced; yet we realize that benignity in elegiac trauma is traditional. His lexical disturbance and typographical non-conformity vocalize the departure from the norms of literary response to death; yet by imposing radical alterations the text takes its place in a genre that relies on a rhetoric of special effects such as narrative interruption and direct speech. Elegies have always had to do the impossible and they do it through forcing language where it has hitherto feared to tread. That Popean allusion placed back in context of course indicates recklessness, and there is indeed a reckless intelligence throughout *Love Alone*, at once rejecting and incorporating the caring elements of the world, from people to flowers. I argue here that Monette's elegies are "pop art" in this sense of the contrapuntal fugue, screaming "I am *not* the same, not usual," while letting in signifiers that indicate "I *am* another small example of the familiar in history." Pop art foregrounds difference from classical art, but it foregrounds sameness and repetition in its own aesthetic. It relies on certain aspects (though not wholes) of universal experience (e.g., mass-produced consumer goods), but it is always fighting against the frustration of deconstruction, of never being able to make its point in a place of semiotic stability ("originality" becomes a contested term).

It is an apt if unfortunate fact that "AIDS" is an acronym, a powerful indication of the inscrutability of satisfying closural language for the state of a diseased nation and world; the letters highlight deferral of the cure, or even the ability to communicate effectively in the AIDS arena. Monette's elegies are similarly caught in these tensions between independence and incorporation, and between textual and personal definition and loss. They inevitably draw on traditional elements in spite of the text's radically disturbed surface, multiple social situations, and stark politics breaking through the poetry—in fact, *because* of it. If we think of great elegies such as Milton's *Lycidas*, Tennyson's *In Memoriam*, or even Yeats's *In Memory of Major Robert Gregory*, they all foreground textual instability, changes of voice, and political commentary as necessary features of elegy.[3] Kinereth Meyer, discussing "the mythology of modern death" (Coleridge's term), argues that it "represents not a radical shift away from the elegiac tradition, but rather a further intensification of its basic concerns" (Meyer 25). Celeste Schenck also speaks to the "pop art" paradox with which I began. Modern elegy, she reminds us, either speaks in "elevated registers" of poetry's restorative power or reacts cynically to the prospect of poetic recovery. This latter form,

> usually resorting to parody and inversion, deliberate rupture of ceremonial patterns, results in works that are generically mutant— *élégies manquées* which register, in their disruption of inherited form, the impossibility of conventional transcendence. These anti-elegies, often reproducing elegiac conventions more faithfully than poems of the first type, should be viewed in their own right as survivals of a sustaining literary mode; these peculiarly modern poems, by their acts of criticism, testify to the resilience of elegy as a form both *in* which and *against* which to couch literary ambitions, thoughts of mortality, death, love, potency, and poetry. (108)[4]

For all the weight of traditional precedent and usefulness of paradigms, *Love Alone* shows us a discrete mode within the genre of elegy. Its immersion in the inescapably altering infusion of AIDS produces difference, because the improvisation of the text reveals new identity not in the tricky manner of the anonymous swain of *Lycidas*, but in two unique ways. First, the constant searching for, and learning about, the right objects, drugs, cleaners, and tokens of affection to employ ensures ongoing revelation and re-evaluation of the self; second, the white, middle-class American gay male autobiographer's position in "a no-man's land somewhere between the male and the 'other'" (Newtown 52) requires constant self-assessment and recognition of one's place in a culture that categorizes around the trope of the "norm."

The combination of these differences yields elegiac success, which is enabled through new experience, contact with psychological and material impetuses unimaginable before the rise of AIDS, and therefore excluded from elegy before the 1980s. Jahan Ramazani speaks eloquently of the work of the NAMES project Quilt in his major work on elegy, but it is telling that his discussion, published the year before Monette's own death, remains only in a coda to a large book. While AIDS elegy, like modern elegy before it and concurrent with it, returns to tradition as well as defying it, its job and sense of effectiveness separate it from much of elegiac writing. AIDS elegy attaches itself at places with war memorial and employs war metaphors as well as those of apocalyptic plague extensively (which I examine below). David Jarraway has reminded us in his essay "From Spectacular to Speculative: The Shifting Rhetoric in Recent Gay AIDS Memoirs" that the use of the tropes of plague and terror to talk about AIDS has run its course; here, however, we still have to speak about Monette's work on its own metaphorical terms of the 1980s, while trying not to perpetuate the rhetoric. The notion of fighting and of dying for a cause that few can understand connects the modes, both expressing frustration for their cause being either ignored or perpetrated and perpetuated by authoritarian figures who are not directly, and in the present, affected by such death. For all its contiguity with traditional pastoral elegy, then, its premise—the reason for and explanation of loss—is so distinct from tradition that the major studies on elegy by Ramazani, Sacks, Shaw, and Potts, among others, can only speak gener(ic)ally to poems like those in *Love Alone*.[5]

This is not to say that extended study of the genre is not useful to a reading of *Love Alone*; simply that we must reread the earlier work for an emergent, more relevant mode within elegy. As a very brief example, we can expand Schenck's trace of the adaptation and "literalization" of classic elegiac motifs after *Lycidas*. She turns to Crane's *Cape Hatteras* as an example of elegiac myth-making or story-telling. Crane is talking to Whitman, speaking to the dead, asking "if infinity / Be still the same" as when Whitman had walked in Long Island. Crane meditates on Whitman's stomping ground, "Not this our empire yet." Schenck writes, "clearly Crane intends to inherit that 'empire' of recognition" (100), but does not focus on Crane's apparent desire to incorporate this homosocial region of his precursor. The empire is not yet gained (through mythologizing or real action) for gay men. Traditional, and possibly oppressive, elegiac practices, such as flower-collecting or flower-strewing, must be altered and appropriated for use in the modern, ravaged world. The spinning windmill toy on little Brian's grave (in the poem "The Losing Side," discussed below, Moncttc 37), for example, is a plastic flower, made of the modern material that saves and sustains lives in hospital, blown and turned by the pathetic winds that care about the dead. In the process of replacing natural beauty with artificial interruption, AIDS elegy can force us to feel the alienation of persons from a place or community (e.g., Whitman's Paumanok) while it is unable to avoid alluding to (the work of) that excluding community, thus reproducing elements that are "startlingly conventional" (Schenck 101).

———

WE WILL HAVE TO KEEP making our way into AIDS elegy through its predecessors. James Miller adapts the notion of the classical elegy's resurrection of the dead one, or *anastasis*, to write, "In AIDS elegies anastasis comes as a blessed moment of recovery when the dead rise from the mass graves dug for them by the fatalistic discourse of public health and join forces with the living against the World, the Flesh, and the Virus" (266). Added to this trinity should be the "Word." For what is used as weapon and counter-weapon in all situations of "battle" involving the AIDS debate is the "word." In the beginning was the Word, and it was a word of creation; next came the words of naming; then the words of seduction, of sin, of expulsion; and then those of resurrection and new life. It is the end of this lexical chain that elegy represents, and it tends to strive to connect the final links into a circle. The end of the elegy is not the end of the battle. We are in the upturn of the AIDS crisis, and the product that is the printed (the "finished" book) can be a weapon. Monette's agnostic clinging on to a non-traditional belief in some greater power that is not the conventional God suggests that every book on AIDS or written under the shadow of AIDS is a challenge to the Bible itself, a challenge to the order that returns time and again to the joke about Adam and Steve, and to the word of destruction against Sodom and Gemorrah. Even at this extreme, however, we should temper the interpretation by remembering that Milton's attack on the "corrupted Clergy then in their height" was a challenge to orthodoxy;[6] and Tennyson's biggest dilemma is keeping his faith as his intellect shows him natural evolution. Radical disturbance to reigning ideology has long been a child of the creation called elegy.[7] In the end, Monette's anger is only doing what comes naturally: it is ironically an orthodoxy to be heterodox in elegy.

Anastasis, in Miller's interpretation, cannot actually happen in AIDS elegy. A stable resolution through language cannot be achieved to close the mode, a fact that may have much to do with the inability yet to name the cause of death. Elegy needs this information to place the deceased successfully in a tangible and permanent state of rest (albeit often through mythologizing the real situation). Edelman notes that the U.S. Government definition of AIDS in 1991 ran to fourteen pages (93–94). Whereas Lycidas "suffer[ed] death by submersion in water" (OED, "drown"), Rog died through an indefinable complex of fourteen pages of viral infections, cancer attacks, and weakening conditions, none of them finally blamable alone. To locate the precise mode of death, the location of death, and to suppose the repose of the dead, is essential if the traditional elegy is to be able to end. But then Monette's elegy does not end. There is (literally) no full stop. There is a metamorphosis, a move from word to song and image, but the constantly mimetic work takes us on a journey "toward death" that does not end by falling down, but by a sudden and final upturn, a small ramp that throws us lightly into the air, as a "song." From there, to imagine the place of Rog is as much our guess as Monette's.

Extremities often highlight contrasts, and thus the indefinability of Rog's disease highlights the particular centrality of Paul's grief. Both men are fighting for their own and their brothers' causes. Monette is particularly interested in depicting their roles as fellow warriors. Sheryl Stevenson proposes that we read past Susan Sontag's and Susan Jeffords's concerns with the dangers of over-militarization and "remasculinization" of cultural texts and discuss why those in a position to lose out by metaphorical over-load in fact appropriate such modes (241–43).[8] Monette consistently uses war as representation of the struggle of persons with AIDS ("PWAs"; compare, of course, military tags such as POWs). Through such language, he can assert the heroism of AIDS sufferers, notes Stevenson (243–44). The idea of war enables deeper assessment of an individual's role, too. The concept of "winning" in this war is quite different from that of destroying your human enemy: to win is to survive. To have survived is, of course, different from being in the process of surviving, which is another, partial victory. And it is survival against a number of enemies. The fight becomes at once selfish and magnanimous, utterly like elegy itself. Persons with AIDS must take any opportunity to sustain life for themselves and learn how to cope (and to record their findings) for the sake of others. Those others, Monette proph-esies harshly, will be "those / who are not yet touched" by the disease. Those people "will beg us to teach them how to / bear it we who are losing our reason" ("Manifesto," Monette 42).

> The war fought in AIDS poetry thus occurs on multiple fronts; the enemy is defined and then redefined. Observing the many casualties of AIDS, one poet notes that the "war has no name / so it's everywhere and not" (Young 8), suggesting that not recognizing this war allows it to be denied, in spite of its omnipresence. (Stevenson 246)[9]

The elegist must contend with the "AIDS" label, which—it bears repeating—is not a name but an acronym. It substitutes for a name we do not yet have, one that defines the indefinable disease(s). It is also appropriate to note that "acro-" means the tip or the uttermost, for the name gives us just the tip of the iceberg, the suggestion of what lies beneath and keeps it hidden from those who cannot, or will not investigate its shape, force, and future move-ments.

At some point, the impossibility of comprehending the disease or the scale of its devastation, and the impossibility of communicating with all necessary parties and getting them to listen leads to irony and sardonic humour. The poetry understands its own weaknesses and the limits of its metaphors. Stevenson efficiently brings out this problem in her reading of the poem, "The Losing Side" (Monette 37–39). In this poem, Paul is at

Rog's graveside when he meets Eve, a woman visiting her son Brian's grave, who died when he was two years old. "By continuing to develop military metaphors" in such inappropriate circumstances, Stevenson writes, "this passage makes a point by their inaccuracy, showing that the struggles of life have even fewer rules than those of warfare" (247). By acknowledging that "somehow we got to be men together" (Monette 39), Monette is building a bridge between the AIDS dead and those killed by multiple other causes. Monette is perhaps also setting the example for his resistant readers by outlining communicative success between homosexual and heterosexual mourners. Such recognition on the poet's part pulls us away from familiar suspicions of narcissism and self-victimization in elegy. Here the contiguous methodologies of mourning (Monette's and Eve's) and the manner of ending (Rog's and Brian's) come as close to touching as may be possible. At this point, however, with spoken and written metaphor finally inadequate, the words are replaced by an object, a thing to evoke new representations—a toy windmill:

> Eve is five graves over or Brian is at least
> d. 18 June two years old Eve elbow-rubs
> the bronze plaque changes her flowers before
> the least brown edge and sticks a pinwheel in
> the ground above think what a brave toy it is
> to flutter here on the hill catching the vague
> random air like an amnesiac trying to
> hum a few bars of the wind.
> ("The Losing Side," Monette 37)

Rather than recover Rog as a man, the windmill causes Eve to lament that Brian could not live to be a man and Monette to be reminded of the years as a boy that he did not know Rog. At all points the elegy forces displacement. The object not only stands for the promise, "I'll remember everything," and does away with the Sisyphean task of using language to attempt to get to any sufficient signification; it stands also for all those things that were not allowed to be, for the time and experience death takes away from all mourners.

The loss of metaphorical power, the inability to get to the essence of the disease, and the beginnings of cross-community communication all lead to the necessity for naming the dead. This traditional elegiac moment takes on vital importance, whether we consider the dead as victims of war who must be remembered for the fight or, more harshly perhaps, as exhibits, evidence in the case against denial. Both these purposes are folded into the elegiac text that is the NAMES project AIDS Quilt.[10] The Quilt sections are often submitted with letters and include pictures and names of those who made each piece. Unlike the inscriptions on the Vietnam Memorial wall, the names on the Quilt are looked for and found in a context that does not isolate the community of the dead, but rather one that infuses the words and image—the presence—of the living. This may be the closest any attempt at mourning or epitaph has come to properly representing the dead within the full context of their own death—that context being one that includes the living, the surviving. Here, despite the indefinability of the disease, AIDS deaths find a delimited place.

The Quilt is a politically active place of discourse and representation, for it is mobile, can be set up on any large, flat surface, and cannot be avoided by anyone who wants to be in the same place for other reasons. This is why the Quilt seems so "at home" on the Mall in Washington, DC. It lays itself like a veneer of dissension over the established order's centre of rhetoric and silence (an especially important act in the late 1980s and unfortunately also in the current regime of barely disguised inhumanity). Of course, the text in the Quilt is a silent one, for it is a text of death; but it also presents a discourse for the dead in an act of substitution. The Quilt represents highly performative statements and appropriately emphasizes the duality of AIDS death: the single category of "disease" under which all those remembered are classified as having died, yet the individuality and infinite variations (instability) of the disease and persons, as expressed in the starkly different sections, threaded together. In her discussion of the role of AIDS elegy as creating "a common geography of the mind," Kimberly Rae Connor differentiates between the "textual" presence of Monette's work and the "actual presence in the NAMES Project" Quilt (48). But all the aspects of the Quilt's "actuality" are aspects of textual—or at least discursive—experience. For just a couple of examples, we might take the Quilt sections with their definite borders sewn together, individual yet inextricable, and compare these with the separate elegies in *Love Alone*, independent yet collected, detailing various aspects of character and decline yet connected under the umbrella of AIDS. Or the practicality of the Quilt, laid out on the ground with its passages between sections into which the reader inserts him- or herself to examine the text sections from alternate angles, and *Love Alone* with its constant breaks and interstices, references to the mundane and recognizable that pull the reader in to examine from new angles the profundity of the subject (person and topic) being addressed or discussed.

In his great Quilt-like collection of names and things and textures, Monette is not afraid to pull in other voices from the past and the twentieth century to aid his cause; his rather trite but perhaps revealing allusions, such as hospital "Room 1010" (Orwell's "room 101"?) as the worst of all worlds, locate the state of elegy in the modern world; poetry is not the force at hand here—AIDS is the force; the word, the material object, and the noise constitute the response. The AIDS elegy must (re)cite the past and revivify it in the deadly present. When Monette goes on to write,

> war is not all
> death it turns out war is what little
> thing you hold on to refugeed and far from home,
> ("Here," Monette 3)

we can understand that war reveals the *différance* of the practicum of life— after "everything extraneous" has burned away, after war takes away all things in death, what is left is the result of war, thus strangely war = life. The fight against AIDS, similarly, can be seen as a celebration of life, of what defies the disease. This battle is a war of words, but ones, as we have seen, with doubtful efficacy. Monette falls to naming things a few lines later, "Glad Bags One-A-Days KINGSIZE," as he almost disposes words, words that denote pacifying but ineffective objects. Words are perceptual building blocks to create something real: they resurrect things from the past, place them in the unprecedented context of the present, and build bridges into the future. Monette is always repairing what went wrong with Rog and setting us up for the inevitability of the future. He enacts the cleaning and re-presenting of Rog by the rejection of the actual cleaning items, "the junk that keeps men spotless" ("Here," Monette 3); he washes Rog's hair in "No Goodbyes" (Monette 4), reminiscent of *Lycidas*, where "With nectar pure his oozy locks he laves." But of course, this ending in *Lycidas* is the evoking of the—rhetorically, at least—*effective* resurrection of the dead one; Monette is listing the "junk" that does not work. Here soap is no cleanser. The word is a new signifier. We no longer have sweet scent and pleasure signified, but the bare referent of a useless block—every noun challenges us to reassess the place of the referent we thought we knew, taking it on for the post-modern world, and more precisely for the AIDS-ridden world where the notion of "value" is constantly refigured.

To take this further, we can see that the retention of youth and health that classical elegy insists on doing for its dead is so much more literal and challenging in an age of plastic surgery, deodorant, and vaccination, where appeals in the lexical tradition can seem paltry in comparison with the power of the scalpel. Roberta McGrath writes in her essay, "Dangerous Liaisons":

> the mode of desire is not, in the late-twentieth century, an ascetic mode of desire but an excessive mode, a "culture of pleasure" where the body itself anointed with perfumes, decorated with jewels, swathed in silks and cashmeres, accessorised to the hilt becomes a prize investment; purchases become magic fetishes which give not only sexual pleasure but can ward off disease. They offer a safe decontaminated arena of desire and pleasure. (145)

It is all the more shocking for America, then, that it is faced with AIDS, such a forceful enemy to modern human power in the developed world. Peter Cohen begins his book, *Love and Anger*, with the following observation:

> For middle- and upper-middle-class gay men in the United States, AIDS has constituted two kinds of crises: most obviously a health crisis, but simultaneously a crisis of consumption. Accustomed to having market access to whatever commodities they wanted, middle-class gay men found themselves faced with an epidemic for which no cure could be purchased because none existed. (9)

Paul knows that all the surgical tools and "elixir" ("Black Xmas," Monette 18) in the world cannot cure Rog: "my groping docs might just as well use leeches / for all they can touch my invisible disease" is his response to medicine ("Current Status 1/22/87," Monette 35). At each point we are forced to reconsider the potential use(lessness) of any product, person, or action in the midst of the postmodern viral world. "Virus," McGrath states, "has become a key term of late-twentieth-century life, ascribed alike to both human bodies and bodies of knowledge" (143). But it is not a new metaphorical concept: early modern authorities understood the "infection" possible by subversive example in the public places of recreation. That the attainment of knowledge and the interference and transmission of that knowledge via today's media (paper, celluloid, electronic) has been called viral, lends postmodern elegy a certain air of irony. To begin the elegy is necessarily to be infected with predecessors of centuries. To write the elegy is to investigate the virus (the success of the elegy is to [have] live[d] with the virus), to have created antibodies against its outdated, disastrous elements, and to create with the hosts of words in the elegy a life strong enough to be recreated or mutate in the minds of the readers and accepted as relevant for the postmodern world. The way to achieve this is to keep adding to the language of the elegy all the time, to reconstruct where the new AIDS elegy has necessarily deconstructed in order to reinscribe itself. The additions involve the very naming of postmodernity: Kleenex, One-a-Day;[11] naming flowers and grave markers; names added to the cause (Brother John in "Brother of the Mount of Olives" [Monette 60–65], and castigation by naming the enemy, Lady Hay, in "Manifesto" [Monette 40–42]). These are new threads in the *textum*, the shroud, the new synthetic fabric of mourning.

Once again, the comparison—or rather imbrication—of elegiac text and the Quilt comes to mind, as both events supplement text with recourse to three-dimensional objects of memory. The direction that *Love Alone* is heading, out of pure text and into material representation (*material* in both cultural senses of being politically aware and of producing material substantiality), is the same as the ongoing process of the Quilt. This shared activity of text and textile goes some way to answering an objection of writers like Timothy Murphy who ask whether "elegiac writing isn't sometimes a poor substitute for informed and effective political discourse" (307), as though AIDS elegy can somehow not be political discourse.

Since the language of material addition has been turned to reveal the backside of its pre-AIDS signification, and since we are in a world where money does not play its "culture of pleasure" part in buying a pretty cure, Paul puts his Visa credit card to use, not to buy "magic fetishes" to "ward off disease," but to purchase a pair of rings to commemorate Rog's life through an affirmation of his death:

> I NEED A
> MOURNING RING longing you see for an age of
> widows in veils thick as bedsheets...
> ...
> and there it was the very thing black jade
> banded in gold three fifty good god no
> I'll lose it on the plane besides it's just
> for the picturesque like keeping a stuffed cat
> ...
>   of course
> I knew right along it wouldn't touch the pain
> it was just a game but one hungers so
> for ritual that's portable you can't walk out
> ...
> back in LA I decided to keep a perfect
> circle and bury the jet in the grass above
> your folded arms so many along the way
> ...
> at least you had no agony at the end the ring's
> all hidden and suddenly I'm moaning out loud
> this very specific moan the echo of you.
> ("Three Rings," Monette 29–31)

Monette vigorously rejects affectation where necessary, and these rings are no "cure." They alter the norms of dominant fashions of desire and dissociate themselves from protection of the body of Rog to the extent that they celebrate Platonic unity. We could question Monette's character, choosing to bury the cheap ring with Rog and excusing the lack of decoration on Rog's grave. But this aside, the rings he buys are fitting rejoinders to any doubt about his relationship with Rog, and are not purifiers, but articles of acceptance. Moreover, and most important for my reading here, this appears to alter the traditional gestures of gathering flowers and remembering youth. The classical sense of rings as "sovereign," or healing, is re-inscribed with the notion of the ring as a symbolic confirmation of the impossibility of somatic recovery: "it's just / for the picturesque," as we have just read, "like keeping a stuffed cat" (Monette 30).

That latter statement pinpoints Monette's position on the edge of comedy and satirical anger; the stuffed cat is the memorial turned macabre, at once understandable and stupid. The flowers that are the absolute metaphor for the elegies sung to Lycidas or for the dead president are rejected by Monette: "pain is not a flower pain is a root / and its work is underground," he insists ("Gardenias," Monette 8). Pain, death, love, and sex all come together in AIDS elegy and in this image. Schenck notes that Hart Crane too "was very much aware of the peculiar eroticism—at once bridal and fune-real—of the pastoral floral bouquet" (104). AIDS elegy cumulatively copes with its forebears and their desires for life and death. It may be that "in pastoral initiation poems from Theocritus to Milton, a man is treated to arcane lore and welcomed to mature poetic stature by a member of the same sex" (Schenck 103), but the homosocial initiation is now fearful as well as epiphanic. Whitman and Crane could not write of such tension, thus my earlier point that while we must work through earlier elegy, studies of that elegy will not lead us to a final understanding of AIDS elegy. It must be dealt with in its own right, for it is work about men who are connected not just by love, but by physical contact that has left an indelible mark. Monette here opens up to us his journey of exploration wherein AIDS is a discourse inscribed upon the body. From within, from "underground," from the "root," AIDS attacks. It puts out its petals, its lesions, but the bloom of course will die; there is always something unseen, something we are blinded against, some-thing yet to come and envelop us.

That "something yet to come," Monette warns, is the spread of the disease. While the heterosexual order was denying the extent of AIDS, it was also frightened by the invisibility of homosexuality and its ability to infiltrate their ranks silently. AIDS thus created a visibility that could be equated with homosexuality. AIDS, while heightening awareness, has also enabled a new widening of the "fear gap" and an emphasis on a simplistic homo/hetero binary society. But there is a second wave of invisibility called the future. So it is that Monette can look outside one morning and see that "half the city's Capri and half Buchenwald." So it is that he can make his "Belsen" prediction in a poem to which I alluded earlier:

> I had a self myself
> once but he died when do we leave the mirror
> and lie down in front of the tanks let them
> put two million of us away see how quick
> it looks like Belsen...
>   ...for those who are not yet
> touched for soon the thing will ravish their women
> their jock sons lie in rows in the empty infield
> the scream in the streets will rise to a siren din
> and they will beg us to teach them how to
> bear it we who are losing our reason.
> ("Manifesto," Monette 41–42)

This is a vision of death "underground," of genocide unseen or unheeded, and according to this moment in the elegies it involves a selflessness, a giving up of identity (with the tensions that such a concept entails in the postmodern world) for the name of the community. It is a claim of expertise, a greatness that has been thrust upon the gay western community. In the end, Monette tells us, it is the (homosexual) survivors to whom the "ravaged" world will come for help. The old order will need the experience of what Monette and his fellow mourners have witnessed.[12] In the end the resurrection of the writer and not the dead one is the more powerful effect. This resurrected writer is the one who has witnessed, denied under the duress of loss, and returned via his own words to be witness of the past for future generations. As Woods says in his forward-looking essay, "Lamentation is itself an acknowledgment that the one who sheds tears *has a future*" (163, italics original). But Monette's moment of life is more vital than usual. Milton (or the swain) is not drowning as he sings for Lycidas. Monette on the other hand writes from "within" the cause of Rog's death, since he was himself diagnosed with AIDS shortly after Rog. The concept of a "witness" is as transitory as words themselves.

FOR ALL THE RADICAL EXPRESSIONISTIC strokes in *Love Alone*, Monette is reinscribing dominant cultural forms on several levels. Finding useful words, we are seeing, is highly important. But phrasing, use of epigraphs, form of the whole poem, managing of a collection, and the drawing on apparent convention (and the necessary shifts that occur therein), are all instrumental in the multivalent form of communication in which Monette is engaged. Joseph Cady condones what he calls "immersive" writing about AIDS, writing that does not apologize for its style and content and does not overtly cater (or worse, pander) to the resistant reader. He writes,

> the quality that makes *Love Alone* the fullest and finest example so far of immersive AIDS writing is each poem's seemingly chaotic form, in which Monette consciously disrupts all traditional notions of focus, sequence, tone, and structure. (247)

The "seemingly" is important here. He goes on to quote the poem "Three Rings" at length, and to say that "Here, as in all of *Love Alone*, Monette matches his harrowing content with a harrowing style by upsetting every conventional expectation of order an audience might bring to a text" (249). This is a difficult assumption to make about an audience who has read through the poetic disruptions of the Modernist aesthetic or "minority" literatures; it is even doubtful in the light of the conventional texts with which I have been comparing *Love Alone*. Deborah Landau would support Cady's feelings about Monette's text. She talks of Monette's poem, "Ed Dying" as having "an aggressively antilyrical style" (204).[13] She then goes on to say that this is exemplified by Monette's own proclamation that "I don't mean them [the *Love Alone* elegies] to be impregnable, though I admit I want them to allow no escape, like a hospital room, or indeed a mortal illness" ("Preface," Monette xii). This does not seem to be evidence for antilyricism, however. The lyric is often strictured, stanzaically and metrically confined; it forces the reader to remain within a small, formally-furnished room. If we want to divorce this poetry from traditional lyric, perhaps we should be thinking psychologically as well as physically or spatially. Within the room of the formal lyric, the enclosed structure can guide and comfort us in its containment. The enclosures of Monette's poems, however, frustrate our desire to break out, keeping us in maddening ratruns of missed opportunity and fading memory. The tightness of the room does not hold us together so much as force our minds to race while denying the body its rest.

In a way, *Love Alone* is ultimately structured. There could be no better holding pen, no stronger form, than a "stanza" (a room) that allows entry (for these poems certainly are not impregnable) but no exit until all the walls, the ceiling, and the floor have been examined or "scoured" (Monette 11), by which time the way out is revealed to be into another similar but shifted room (the next poem, the next Quilt panel) on this inevitable journey through death. Inscription is in itself a material form. Monette comes to realize this need for writing when, with Rog, he sees a marble block with Greek lettering. "'I hope somebody's recorded all this,' I said, realizing with a dull thrill of helplessness that this *was* the record, right here on this stone" ("Preface," Monette xii). Records of records of records can be made, but what we turn to in the end is always a substitute for the thing being recorded. There is no ultimate veracity in the mode of inscription; there is only hope for a transcendent signified. Since the "battle" of AIDS elegy is not simply to recover a single person (who will not return from the dead), but rather to recall all those dying from the disease, there is purpose to documenting experience. Textual intervention, then, the activity of making noise, avoiding deadly silence, will at some point be seen to have played a role in the cure that will come and the lives that will be saved.

This is why we can be more confident that AIDS elegy enacts a role quite different from other modes within the genre; and this is why we can be more positive about the real-world, cultural effectiveness of AIDS elegy. Responding to ActUp's silence = death slogan, Jason Tougaw writes,

> Silence = Death appears to offer a tidy formula for the decimation of a catastrophic plague. The implication is that if we speak, write, and act, we can defeat the epidemic. However, the discourses instigated by the trope as a call to arms almost always defy the apparent simplicity of a metaphor that takes the form of an equation. AIDS memoirs are constructed by the slogan at every turn, but as narratives they complicate and even repudiate its claims. (237)

The equation does not seem to attempt to claim all-encapsulating meaning, however, or a direct line to a "magic bullet." Rather, it aims toward Acting Up, Unleashing Power—a force to set textual precedent for those who do have the ability and skill to find a cure. Neither is this premise so radical or new. While not referring directly to AIDS, Karen Mills-Courts points out that silence = death as the inversion of language = life can be traced back to Plato's reading of textual work (22–23). To keep talking—as Stephen Hawking and Pink Floyd reminded us—is to know that one is in the semi-victorious state of surviving in the face of the multiple medical, physical, and political hindrances we have already talked of.

Writing, then, is not artistic or creative cultural cure, but a tool with which to effect a constant awareness of the dead and the living and also a process of building an identity (or a pair of identities) that eventually moves beyond text.[14] We may see the activity of composition as substitutional or vitally actual. Mills-Courts details the conflict between two opinions on the role of writing as a process of truth-telling. Derrida's insistence, as Mills-Courts remarks, on the deferring signification of the word means that "words only seem to stand in truth's place"; "Heidegger, on the other hand, insists that truth 'is,' and that it 'happens in being composed'" (20). The conflict comes into focus when applied to AIDS elegy. Of course words are standing in place of medical truth, for we do not yet know the answers we seek. Words have also not provided Monette with required precision to get at "truths" of his emotional state, hence the substitution of rings, pinwheel, and finally a photograph (which I discuss below). However, if there is any purpose and solidity in human communication at all, then no under-standing of what it means to face AIDS (whether it be an ultimate "truth" or only our poor compensation for it) is indeed happening in these acts of composition. The tension of searching for truths in an activity that may deny truth's discovery in its very process is apt for AIDS elegy. In the begin-ning, we realize, after rereading our own commitment to text, was not the word. My discussion of the "Word" to open part II needs this complemen-tary consideration. The sign that the utterance forms is always infinitely removed from the referent, the primacy of which can never be appropriated by language. But this does not spell doom. Once we can dream that

the world be a
fragment like an ode on marble erasing
in the rain sleep be our blue drink of life
wide as a camera turned on the morning sky
("Dreaming of You," Monette 59)

we can understand that elegiac inscriptions have always been temporary in
the sense that they will be washed away by the rain, and permanent in the
sense that they will continue to be (re)written and to recall the memory of
the world. This understanding of the history of elegy as a repetition ("Yet
once more"(1), writes Milton in *Lycidas*, instead of "For the first time..."),
and as a *recording* of something original (not as something *itself* original)
allows Monette the freedom to appropriate and wield both the tropological
excursions of classical elegy and late-twentieth century phenomenology as
political and social—as well as personal—weapons. However, even carved
rock erodes in the rain and weathers in the wind. Monette turns to a photograph in the end as the antithesis to this fading, as something that *develops*
while he waits silently without words, something that absorbs light and
colour to become and revivify, something that stops *motion* from leaving us
with an empty text as Milton's swain seems to, but instead *stops* motion to
leave us with the image of Rog and Paul that is the culmination and fruition
of the textual work.

Monette makes the point in his Preface to *Love Alone* that these poems are
for those who have experienced AIDS at first hand (xi). The enclosure that
these poems construct might, after all, be comforting, even at its most
violent and angry and desperate. The poems are consoling in their dedication, attention to detail, ritual, and ceremony; and most of all they comprise
a piece of work that suspends one's life for the time that it is being read. For
that time, the reader must spend it entirely with Rog alive, or with Monette
alive. Like the desperate search for the "magic bullet," like the useless
doctors running around, Monette's writing is a desperate will to the power
of life in the word, understanding all the while the inevitable deferral of
truth, answers, and comprehension.[15]

By the time we accompany Rog and Paul through the abbey in the Tuscan
hills in the final poem, "Brother of the Mount of Olives" (Monette 60–65),

Monette has chiasmically dragged himself across the chaotic gulf between the "godly" (upper?) heterosexual order and the "underworld" of homo-eroticism. James Miller writes:

> Heaven has literally gone underground here. And if an underground heaven sounds like a paradox, something the Devil would think up to keep the Sodomites and the Sodoma-worshippers on their toes in the burning sands, don't be perplexed: it only exists in the anticlerical brink of AIDS fury reached by Monette with the spiritual counterpart of the "Spartacus Guide." (294)

But there is more to it than this. Why do I say this is a "chiasmic" journey? Because at first this poem tropes on the return journey (Hell to Heaven) by portraying a move from the light Hills of Tuscany down into the dark abbey, and then, as the narrative develops, we realize the move is one, paradoxically, of enlightenment—conservative Catholic Hills to the subversive Brother John-guided underground. Yes, it is a heaven underground, but far from existing only in the "AIDS fury reached by Monette," this is the moment when we are finally confronted with solid structures of recovery, truths deep within the political arena of orthodox religion. We have a poem that places itself consciously in a location of upturned phenomenology. We follow Paul and Rog through a sequence of pragmatic, ideologically confrontational re-inscriptions: speech versus books; temporary speech versus xeroxable papers/writing; speech versus painting; the look versus the touch; literature versus photography:

> and we patter round the cloister in his wake
> duck through a door up a stone stairs and peer
> through a grill wrought like a curtain of ivy
> into the library its great vellum folios
> solid as tombstones nobody copying out
> or illuminating today unless perhaps
> all of that has died and there's a Xerox
> glowing green in the abbot's study John
> pokes you to look at the door carvings it seems
> he is not a bookish man but who has time

to read any more we must descend and see
the frescoes fifty years without the world
pray work pray work and yet such drunken gaiety.
("Brother of the Mount of Olives," Monette 61–62)

Recalling the arguable objection against elegy's ineffectiveness, we can see that if elegy must *do* something, become something *else* to be effective, then here is where Monette's strongest effort to perform a new, metamorphic apotheosis occurs. As though words have been exhausted, used up, and worn out by their rough ride through the improvisation and tough poetic terrain of *Love Alone*, Monette's AIDS elegies bail out of the structures of textuality that have been the vehicle up to now and turn to the care of tropologies and iconographies, of visual representation and semiotic ambivalences. James Miller's sharp "Monette's underground heaven is as exclusionary as any dreamed up by the Cistercians in Dante's day or the Calvinists in Milton's" (295) may be true, but that is not Monette's concern; the Calvinists can have their heaven, the Cistercians theirs, and Paul and Rog and John and all the Sodoma-lovers theirs. In this sense it could be argued that Monette finally alienates the "denying" reader (Cady 246, 250), or the heterosexual reader, but that is not quite right. For all his rage, Monette cannot entirely leave the orthodoxy of his genre. The deconstruction of his lexical vehicle of life (which has taken the reader through the elegies) at just the point of death (the underground journey), and the subsequent return to the surface (the rebirth) in blasts of light-filled images, is precisely the process of classical elegy. It is itself troped upon in this instant, however, by a reinvested history of homoeroticism as telescoped into the fresco of naked Jesus, and the figure of the silent monk, Brother John, as they drive away:

gasping anew at the cloister's painted wall
clutching my hand before the bare-clad Jesus
bound at the pillar by the painter so-called
Sodoma the parted lips the love-glazed eyes
JUST WHAT KIND OF MEN ARE WE TALKING ABOUT
are we the heirs of them or they our secret
fathers and how many of our kind lie beneath
the cypress alley crowning the hill beyond

...
    we wave him off
and leap in the car we're late for Rome flap
open the map
...
in the breeze a hooded monk is walking
head bent over his book of hours in passing
I see that it's John wave and grin rividerci.
("Brother of the Mount of Olives," Monette 62, 63, 64)

Monette takes on the familiar inversion of Silence = Death to Sound = Life
and makes it vital in the final elegy. Like Wilfred Owen, with whom he tenta-
tively aligns himself in the Preface, Monette has proved that poetics are
never divorced from politics (whether personal or public), and thus personal
observation literally speaks to public or institutional dogma. Brother John
chats away to Paul and Rog in Italian, yet the communicative achievement
is not in the comprehension of the tongue ("no matter we spoke no Italian")
but in the gesture that speech is being performed at all:

...the real thing monks in Benedictine white
pressing olives and gliding about in hooded
silence Benedict having commanded *shh*
along with his gaunt motto *ora et labora*
pray work but our particular brother John
couldn't stop chattering not from the moment
he met us grinning at the cloister door
seventy years olive-cheeked bald and guileless
no matter we spoke no Italian he led us
gesturing left and right at peeling frescoes
...
as the old monk takes my arm I'm certain now
that he likes touching us that we are a world
inside him whether he knows or not not that
I felt molested I can take care of myself
but a blind and ancient hunger not unspeakable
unsayable you think he knew about us Rog

how could he not pick up the intersect
the way we laughed the glint in our eyes as we
played our Italian for four hands.
("Brother of the Mount of Olives," Monette 60, 62)

It is not just a matter of this "sound" meaning "life," however, but a matter
of the dominant cultural sound (the modern vernacular of the Roman
Church) being dispensed with. If silence within a dominant language =
death, then the silence that follows the exhaustion and expiration of that
lame language = *new* life.

The memory detailed in this poem comes to Monette while looking
through words on a page (Rog's letters) and relating his experiences through
words on a page. Monette comes across the vital hidden message: an undeveloped film, communication to be deciphered. The film reveals a whole
narrative. Monette gets the film developed, then sits

... on the curb poring over
prints of Christmas '83 till I hit paydirt
three shots of the hermit abbey on the moors
southeast of Siena our final crisscross
of the Tuscan hills before the sack of Rome
unplanned it was just that we couldn't bear
to leave the region quite the Green Guide barely
gave it a nod *minor Renaissance pile*
but the real thing monks in Benedictine white.
("Brother of the Mount of Olives," Monette 60)

The revelation in the Abbey is an expanded version of Monette's enlightenment after coming across the roll of film. Monette finds that the bordered,
enclosed space of the photographic frame is a room that captivates him in
the way he wants us to be captivated in his sequence of elegies ("I want them
to allow no escape"). The shift that this discovery entails—from text to
iconic image—brings the inevitable ending of elegy, which is a double awareness: first, the transcendent achievement of memory and honour done to
the dead and comfort of the self, with the coming together of the two
subjects—"we were the song" (Monette 65), writes Monette in the very last

line; and second, the devastating inadequacy of the textual and tokenistic process of elegy—"it doesn't get easier Rog" (Monette 64). Seen in this light, "Brother of the Mount of Olives" confirms something we have known all along: the secondary nature of words, the insufficiency of language, and the failure of elegiac language, whether heterosexually prescribed (and proscriptive) or homoerotically described and re-inscribed in Edelman's homographic shift.

This final poem may well be the finest in the book. That Monette ends his sequence of elegies with the story of an underground "religious" journey—an Orphic or Virgilian descent—with a guide, a comprehension of some sense of the self in the context of a beloved other, and a conflict of pain and success, is an exquisite stroke of closural deftness. In reading "we were the song," we see Paul and Rog leaving Tuscany, rather like Milton's uncouth swain twitching his mantle blue and walking away—or rather, it would be like the swain if Monette had discarded the language without giving us the photograph. Elegy is always autobiographical lament, and all poetry is essentially the epitaph of the writer. An elegy is that peculiar text that re-presents the dead person, positing (not entirely truthfully) him as the primary subject of the poem; at the same time elegy publishes the name of the author, and eternalizes it.[16] Through a reading of Eve's self-recognition moment in *Paradise Lost* and then the mirrored representation of heterosexuals and homosexuals by homosexual writers, Edelman cleverly points out the narcissism inherent in Monette's own work, which plays against Monette's own apparent bashing of narcissists in the poem, "Manifesto" (Edelman 101–11). Indeed, that Monette is writing about himself as much as Rog is clear throughout *Love Alone*, and that he is in danger at many points of re-inscribing not a new aesthetic of subjectivity, but the very condemning discourse of the powers that be, is evident in many places. Take the poem, "The Very Same," for example. In this poem "an idiot cousin / once-removed" tells Paul that it is "*time to turn / the page.*" After a brief put-down of this cousin's lifestyle, Monette protests "BUT THIS IS MY PAGE IT CANNOT BE TURNED" (Monette 20). Of course, the cousin did not say "time to turn *your* page, Paul," but Monette cannot get away from the fact that this book details himself, investigates precisely his *own* page, and not that upon which Rog inscribed himself. His romantic cry at the end cannot divert us from this self-love:

oh what a page Rog how can they not see

I am only still here to be with you

my best my only page scribbled on cirrus

the high air soaring in its every word

("The Very Same," Monette 21).

"Monette is not trying to resurrect Roger with this memoir," Murphy reminds us, and "neither does he mistake writing for taxidermy. It is not Roger's life that Monette is trying to hold on to here; it is his *goodness*" (313, original italics). Indeed, what Monette is doing—as I suggested earlier—is writing for himself. I do not mean by this to say that these are not elegies *for* Rog. What I am saying is that Miller is right to say "a kind of poetic therapy" (266) is going on. And this is arguably as strong a reason for elegy as is the memorial for the dead; this is why we invent alternative memorials such as the NAMES project, and this is why authors, for all their suppression, appear named in their texts and pictured in photographs.

From Monette's own testimony of the nature of Rog, we can be sure that Rog needed no such memoir. He gave his memories away ("Preface," Monette xi). He did not need them written in stone; this whole work is spawned of Monette's personal phobia of erasure, and his pathology of the transitory nature of discourse. It is such a pathology that allows us—*pace* Sontag, as Stevenson says (243)—to consider these poems in metaphoric terms without sacrificing the seriousness of AIDS. From filling up shelves with AIDS books to covering city centres with the elegiac Quilt, AIDS elegy faces up to reality and to those denying reality in ways that previous elegy does not (have to). "I don't pretend to have written the anthem of my people" ("Preface," Monette xi), says Monette, but AIDS elegy can never avoid speaking at large. Such consideration opens up doors in *Love Alone* to the history of elegy and allows us to forgive Monette his self-indulgent moments by reflecting on the fact that AIDS elegy always "becomes a vehicle for cultural criticism rather than self-validation" alone (Duncan 23).[17] Affect leads to action: we see the contribution to a real-world movement of politically active documentation when we feel grievously the physicality, the despair, and the ineluctable inscriptions of AIDS within modern literary and social discourses of the body.

1. For a detailed and rewarding examination of teaching gay literature to the "resisting reader" in the undergraduate classroom, see Barbara Frey Waxman and Eleanor Byington, "Teaching Paul Monette's Memoir/Manifesto to Resistant Readers," *College Literature* 24 (1997): 156–70.

2. My reading of the effects of Monette's powerful anger fundamentally disagrees with Susan E. Hill's reading of his memoir, *Borrowed Time*, of which she writes, "Monette uses textual strategies that appear to bridge the gap between himself and his reader in order to subvert them; exploiting the difference between himself and his readers, he simultaneously discloses and withholds spiritual meaning. Estranged from culture, the public expression of Monette's spiritual life is based not on common humanity, but on an individual's isolation" (157). I think this separates Monette from an implied "normative" spirituality and culture, nominated "common humanity," that is itself separationist.

3. I am thinking of the multiple voices in *Lycidas*, and the sharp breaks between voices; the self-reflection and pained question-asking in *In Memoriam*; and the claim of the poet to be at a loss for words and break off his quest to name Gregory in Yeats's elegy. I shall use *Lycidas* as a reference text for traditional elegy in this paper. However, as I am arguing, the very notion of an orthodox, traditional, stable elegy is suspect. See Stanley Fish, for instance, for a reading of *Lycidas* that foregrounds the poem's cynical awareness of its own conventionality and transgressions. For a recent brief revisiting of the issue of traditional versus "postmodern" elegy, see Roger Platizky, "Elegies in a Different Key: Tennyson's *In Memoriam* and Paul Monette's *Love Alone*," *Midwest Quarterly* 43 (2002): 346–54.

4. *Elégies manquées* is Abbie Findlay Potts's term. See *The Elegiac Mode: Poetic Form in Wordsworth and Other Elegists* (Ithaca: Cornell UP, 1967) 244.

5. Gregory Woods points out another specific reason to consider AIDS writing vital: "The notorious volatility and inaccuracy of written responses to AIDS—notably in the press and on toilet walls—have underscored, in the eyes of those whose communities have been affected, the need for a considered and considerate literature of the crisis" (158).

6. Roy Flannagan points out the possibility that changes in *Lycidas* between the Trinity Manuscript version and 1638 publication of *Justa Edouardo King Naufrago* on the one hand, and the 1645 edition of the poems on the other, were based on their dangerous, heterodox nature (*Riverside Milton* 98).

7. Peter Sacks has argued an alternative position that American elegists in particular have taken on the role of the child-like speaker, under pressure from a traditional elegiac figure of authority (314–15). He goes on to ask how Whitman, a poet of brotherhood and democracy, could write "When Lilacs Last in the Dooryard Bloomed" without reinstating such an overbearing figure (316). It may be the most successful aspect of Monette's elegies that they achieve this brotherhood and in the

process call in sympathy from many quarters, all the while vitriolically rejecting the legitimacy of authoritarian figures.

8. See Roy C. Strong, *Portraits of Queen Elizabeth* (Oxford: Clarendon P, 1963), for a descriptive, summarizing essay that draws on Sontag's book to discuss selected poems of loss.

9. Stevenson is citing Tom Young, "Crutches in the Sun," *The James White Review* 6.3 (1989): 8.

10. The NAMES Project memorial Quilt was first displayed in 1988 to provide a record of those who have died of AIDS and bring together a community of AIDS mourners. Mark Doty's "The Wings" emphasizes the directness of the woven "elegies"—the memorial panels—in the Quilt:

> In the Exhibition Hall each unfurled
> three-by-five field bears
> in awkward or accomplished embroidery
>
> a name, every banner stitched to another
> and another. They're reading
> the unthinkable catalog of the names,
>
> so many they blur, become
> a single music pronounced with difficulty
> over the microphone, become a pronoun,
>
> become You. (44)

Especially important, as Deborah Landau points out, is the second person employed in the tenth line (and again at the end of the poem, not quoted here) (212). "You" are drawn into the text at this point rather as one is when observing the Quilt. The experience of walking from section to section is extraordinarily evocative of textual elegy. Learned modes of mourning, such as written epitaphs and floral motifs, are sewn in with items of clothing and memorabilia. The latter trend is picked up on in many of the sections, giving an increased sense of community to the many individuals represented by the "Names." For an extended "reading" of the Quilt and quotations from its founder, Cleve Jones, see Judy Elsley, "The Rhetoric of the NAMES Project AIDS Quilt: Reading the Text(ile)," in Emmanuel S. Nelson, ed., *AIDS: The Literary Response* (New York: Twayne, 1992) 187–96.

11. Barthes writes, "Pop art thus features a philosophical quality of things, which we may call *facticity*: the *factitious* is the character of what exists as fact and appears stripped of any justification: not only are the objects represented by pop art factitious, but they incarnate the very concept of facticity—that by which, in spite of themselves, they begin to signify again: they signify that they signify nothing" (Barthes 202). The objects thus secrete importance regardless of the endeavour to

deny meaning. This may relate to the usefulness of Kleenex and brand names for Monette. Of course, these items are actually useful and serve a purpose; however, they are ineffective at the primary purpose of keeping Rog alive and thus stand as sterile objects. In their very iconic uselessness, however, they are imbued with meaning: they speak to the ineffectiveness of the world, of mass production, and by contrast highlight the necessity of humanity, love, and the non-sterile touch.

12. This kind of claim is open to objections of privileging white, affluent men in the "Western" world. It implies a superiority and primacy of experience that is not true in the worldwide historical picture of AIDS. It is justified, perhaps, since the context of the west is necessary for the prophecy, the west where developments in medicine and care imply the rescue of the masses, while doing nothing for ubiquitous grief.

13. "Ed Dying" is collected in Michael Klein, ed., *Poets for Life: Seventy-Six Poets Respond to AIDS* (New York: Crown, 1989) 172–74.

14. See Langdon Hammer for a discussion of artistic cultural production as substitute for political action.

15. Once more this radical truth is also conventional. Foucault reminds us, in "What is an Author?," that writing's connection to death is an extension of its role in survival, in deferring death, as exemplified in *The Arabian Nights* (Foucault "What" 1623–24).

16. Barbara Herrnstein Smith writes of the narcissism of the poetic speaker in *Lycidas*, "in focusing on the character of the speaker himself," the "coda" "emphasizes that quality of the poem that associates it more closely with dramatic monologue than formal elegy, and it allows the reader to relate the earlier resolution to particular personal motives and circumstances." Smith wisely adds, "By 'personal' I do not mean 'autobiographical.' The relation of the elegist to John Milton is another matter altogether. As always, I am speaking here of the fictional person whose utterance the poem represents. And Milton himself, by introducing a framing conclusion evidently written by someone other than 'the uncouth swain,' certainly emphasizes this fiction" (194 n.). We cannot claim so much distance between the poetic speaker and the author in Monette's poems; indeed, he is writing monologues and they are largely about himself—a fact he is not hiding.

17. See also Derek Duncan's engagement with Leo Bersani's objection to art as a culturally redemptive force, "'Solemn Geographies' AIDS and the Contours of Autobiography," *a/b: Auto/Biography Studies* 15 (2000): 22–36.

Bibliography

Abraham, Nicolas, and Maria Torok. "Mourning or Melancholia: Introjection *versus* Incorporation." *The Shell and the Kernel*. Vol. 1. Ed. and trans. Nicholas T. Rand. Chicago: U of Chicago P, 1994. 125–38.

———. "The Illness of Mourning and the Fantasy of the Exquisite Corpse." *The Shell and the Kernel*. Vol. 1. Ed. and trans. Nicholas T. Rand. Chicago: U of Chicago P, 1994. 107–24.

———. "'The Lost Object—Me': Notes on Endocryptic Identification." *The Shell and the Kernel*. Vol. 1. Ed. and trans. Nicholas T. Rand. Chicago: U of Chicago P, 1994. 139–56.

———. "The Topography of Reality: Sketching a Metapsychology of Secrets." *The Shell and the Kernel*. Vol. 1. Ed. and trans. Nicholas T. Rand. Chicago: U of Chicago P, 1994. 157–61.

———. *The Shell and the Kernel: Renewals of Psychoanalysis*. Vol. 1. Ed. and trans. Nicholas T. Rand. Chicago: U of Chicago P, 1994.

———. *The Wolf Man's Magic Word*. Trans. Nicholas Rand. Minneapolis: U of Minnesota P, 1986.

Adams, Kathleen. *George Eliot: A Brief Biography*. Hinckley: Warwickshire County Council, 1976.

Aiken, Lewis R. *Dying, Death and Bereavement*. Boston: Allyn and Bacon, 1985.

Alizet, Benoît. "Consolations de Vefves." *La calliope chrestienne, ou sommaire de la pure doctrine touchant la creation du monde, le peché de l'homme, la redemption & glorification des enfans de Dieu. Le tout descrit en vers françois, & compris en trois livres, remplis de consolations & meditations spirituelles*. N.p.: Antoine Blanc, 1596. 133.

Allen, Carolyn. "The Erotics of Nora's Narrative in Djuna Barnes's *Nightwood*." *Signs: Journal of Women in Culture and Society* 19.1 (1993): 177–200.

Ambrose, Saint. "On the Death of Satyrus." *St. Ambrose: Select Works and Letters*. Trans. H. de Romestin, E. de Romestin, and H. T. F. Duckworth. Vol. 10. A Select Library of Nicene and Post–Nicene Fathers of the Christian Church. Grand Rapids: Wm. B. Eerdmans Pub. Co., 1983. 159–97.

———. "On the Belief in the Resurrection." *St. Ambrose: Select Works and Letters*. Trans. H. de Romestin, E. de Romestin, and H. T. F. Duckworth. Vol. 10. A Select Library of

Nicene and Post–Nicene Fathers of the Christian Church. Grand Rapids: Wm. B. Eerdmans Pub. Co., 1983. 159–97.

An Old Seaman. *The Tears of the Ocean, an Elegy*. London: Anderson and Chace, 1818.

Angel, Rabbi Marc D. *The Orphaned Adult: Confronting the Death of A Parent*. New York: Human Sciences P, 1987.

Anon. *The Cypress Wreath: A Collection of all the Most Beautiful Fugitive Flowers of Poesy, strewn by the hand of Genius and Affection O'er the Corse of the lamented Princess Charlotte*. London: G. Smeeton, [1817?].

Anon. *Sincere Burst of Feeling! An Ode, to the Memory of her Late Lamented Royal Highness The Princess Charlotte of Wales*. London: J. Hatchard, 1817.

Arden, Heather. "Grief, Widowhood, and Woman's Sexuality in Medieval French Literature." *Upon My Husband's Death: Widows in the Literature and Histories of Medieval Europe*. Ed. Louise Mirrer. Ann Arbor: U of Michigan P, 1992. 305–19.

Ariès, Philippe. *The Hour of Our Death*. Trans. Helen Weaver. 1981. London: Penguin, 1987.

Ashcroft, Bill et al. *Key Concepts in Post-Colonial Studies*. London: Routledge, 1998.

Athanassoglou-Kallmyer, Nina. "Gericault's Severed Heads and Limbs: The Politics and Aesthetics of the Scaffold." *The Art Bulletin* 74.3 (1992): 599–618.

Attie, Alice. "Ineffable Mourning." *Pequod* 37 (1994): 105–12.

Attig, Thomas. *How We Grieve: Relearning the World*. New York: Oxford UP, 1996.

Augustine, Saint. *Sermons on the Liturgical Seasons*. Trans. Mary Sarah Muldowney. Vol. 38. The Fathers of the Church. New York: The Fathers of the Church, 1959.

Axelrod, Stephen Gould. "The Second Destruction of Sylvia Plath." *Sylvia Plath: The Critical Heritage*. Ed. Linda W. Wagner. London: Routledge, 1988. 313–19.

Baer, Marc. *Theatre and Disorder in Late Georgian London*. Oxford: Clarendon P, 1992.

Bakhtin, Mikhail. *Rabelais and his World*. Trans. Helen Iswolsky. Bloomington: Indiana UP, 1984.

Bargedé de Vezelay, Nicolle. (Alias Bergedé). "Accoustumance." *Les odes penitents du moins que rien*. Paris: Longis, 1550. Kiiij–a.

———. *Les odes penitentes du moins que rien*. Paris: Longis, 1550. Ciiij–b.

———. (Alias Bergedé). "Pleurer les mors." *Les odes penitentes du moins que rien*. Paris: Longis, 1550. Ma–b.

Barnes, Djuna. *Nightwood: The Original Version and Related Drafts*. Ed. Cheryl J. Plumb. Normal, IL: Dalkey Archive, 1995.

Barthes, Roland. *The Responsibility of Forms: Critical Essays on Music, Art, and Representation*. 1982. Berkeley and Los Angeles: U of California P, 1985.

Barton, John. "The Making of the Adaptation." *The Wars of the Roses: Adapted from William Shakespeare's Henry VI, Parts I, II, III, and Richard III*. London: BBC, 1967. xv–xxv.

Beadle, Richard, ed. *The York Plays*. London: Edward Arnold, 1982.

Beaulieu, Eustorg de. *Les divers rapportz*. Paris: Alain Lotrian, 1544.

———. "Rondeau lxj de resconforter ceulx qui se plaignent de la mort d'aultruy." *Les odes penitentes du moins que rien*. Bargedé de Vezelay, Nicolle (Alias Bergedé). Paris: Longis, 1550. Ciiij–b.

Behrendt, Stephen C. *Royal Mourning and Regency Culture: Elegies and Memorials of Princess Charlotte*. London: Macmillan, 1997.

Belsey, Catherine. "Tarquin Dispossessed: Expropriation and Consent in *The Rape of Lucrece*." *Shakespeare Quarterly* 52 (2001): 315–35.

Belshaw, John. "The Mourning After: Death and Mortuary in British Columbia Since the 19th Century." *Family Footsteps* (Kamloops Family History Society), 13.2 (November 1997): 3–8.

Berry, Edward. *Patterns of Decay: Shakespeare's Early Histories*. Charlottesville: U of Virginia P, 1975.

Berryman, John. *Collected Poems: 1937–1971*. Ed. Charles Thornbury. New York: Farrar, Straus, Giroux, 1989.

———. *The Dream Songs*. New York: Farrar, Straus, Giroux, 1969.

———. Dream Song 1. *The Dream Songs*. New York: Farrar, Straus, Giroux, 1969. 3.

———. Dream Song 34. *The Dream Songs*. New York: Farrar, Straus, Giroux, 1969. 38.

———. Dream song 42. *The Dream Songs*. New York: Farrar, Straus, Giroux, 1969. 46.

———. Dream Song 76. *The Dream Songs*. New York: Farrar, Straus, Giroux, 1969. 83.

———. Dream Song 145. *The Dream Songs*. New York: Farrar, Straus, Giroux, 1969. 162.

———. Dream Song 172. *The Dream Songs*. New York: Farrar, Straus, Giroux, 1969. 191.

———. Dream Song 235. *The Dream Songs*. New York: Farrar, Straus, Giroux, 1969. 254.

———. Dream Song 384. *The Dream Songs*. New York: Farrar, Straus, Giroux, 1969. 406.

———. "Henry's Understanding." *Collected Poems: 1937–1971*. Ed. Charles Thornbury. New York: Farrar, Straus, Giroux, 1989. 255.

———. *His Toy, His Dream, His Rest*. New York: Farrar, Straus, Giroux, 1968.

Billy, Jacques de. "De la misere de cette vie." *Sonnets spirituels recueillis pour la plus part des anciens theologiens tant grecs que latins*. Paris: Nicolas Chesneau & Jean Poupy, 1578. 189.

———. *Sonnets spirituals recueillis pour la plus part des anciens theologiens tant grecs que latins*. Paris: Nicolas Chesneau & Jean Poupy, 1578.

Blumberg, Baruch S. "Hepatitis B Virus and the Carrier Problem." In *Time of Plague: The History and Social Consequences of Epidemic Disease*. Ed. Arien Mack. New York and London: New York UP, 1991. 79–90.

Boffin, Tessa, and Sunil Gupta, eds. *Ecstatic Antibodies: Resisting the AIDS Mythology*. London: Rivers Oram P, 1990.

Bonaparte, Felicia. *Will and Destiny: Morality and Tragedy*. New York: New York UP, 1975.

The Book of Margery Kempe. Early English Text Series, original series 212. London: Oxford UP, 1940.

Bourbon, Catherine de. *Lettres et poesies de Catherine de Bourbon: 1570–1605*. Ed. Raymond Ritter. Paris: H. Champion, 1927.

———. "Stances de Madame, Seur du Roy." *Lettres et poésies de Catherine de Bourbon: 1570–1605*. Ed. Raymond Ritter. Paris: H. Champion, 1927. 209–10.

Bowlby, John. *Loss: Sadness and Depression*. London: Pimlico, 1980. Rpt. 1998.

———. *Separation: Anger and Anxiety*. London: Pimlico, 1973. Rpt. 1998.

Britzolakis, Christina. *Sylvia Plath and the Theatre of Mourning*. Oxford and New York: Oxford UP, 2000.

Broe, Mary Lynn. *Silence and Power: A Reevaluation of Djuna Barnes*. Carbondale: Southern Illinois UP, 1991.

Bronfen, Elisabeth. *Over Her Dead Body: Death, Femininity and the Aesthetic*. New York: Routledge, 1992.

Brooks, Peter. "Freud's Masterplot." *The Critical Tradition: Classic Texts and Contemporary Trends*. Ed. David H. Richter. New York: St. Martin's, 1989. 710–20.

Burton, Robert. *The Anatomy of Melancholy*. Eds. Thomas C. Faulkner, Nicolas Kiessling, Rhonda L. Blair. Oxford: Clarendon P, 1989.

Cady, Joseph. "Immersive and Counterimmersive Writing About AIDS: The Achievement of Paul Monette's *Love Alone*." *Writing AIDS: Gay Literature, Language, and Analysis*. Eds. Timothy F. Murphy, and Suzanne Poirier. New York: Columbia UP, 1993. 244–64.

Cardinal, Marie. *In Other Words*. Trans. Amy Cooper. Bloomington: Indiana UP, 1995.

Carroll, David. *Living with Dying: A Loving Guide for Family and Close Friends*. New York: McGraw-Hill, 1985.

Charpentier, Françoise. "Ecriture et travail du deuil dans les *Essais* de 1580 au troisième allongeail." *Revue d'histoir littéraire de la France* 88.5 (1988): 828–38.

Cixous, Hélène. "Le rire de la meduse." Trans. Keith Cohen and Paula Cohen. *Feminisms: An Anthology of Literary Theory and Criticism*. Ed. Robyn Warhol and Diane Herndl. New Brunswick: Rutgers UP, 1991. 334–49.

Cohen, Peter F. *Love and Anger: Essays on AIDS, Activism, and Politics*. New York and London: Haworth P, 1998.

Coignard, Gabrielle de. *Oeuvres chrétiennes*. 1594. Ed. Collete Winn. Geneva: Droz, 1995.

———. "Sonnet LXXIX" *Oeuvres chrétiennes*. Ed. Colette Winn. Geneva: Droz, 1995. 235–36.

———. "Sonnet LXXXIII." *Oeuvres chrétiennes*. Ed. Colette Winn. Geneva: Droz, 1995. 240–41.

———. "Sonnet XXIV." *Oeuvres chrétiennes*. Ed. Colette Winn. Geneva: Droz, 1995. 169.

Coles, Robert. *The Call of Stories: Teaching and the Moral Imagination*. Boston: Houghton Mifflin, 1989.

Colley, Linda. *Britons: Forging the Nation, 1707–1837*. New Haven: Yale UP, 1992.

Colonna, Vittoria. "Love Poem I." *Love poems*. In *The Renaissance Reader: Firsthand Encounters with the Renaissance Including Letters, Diaries, Orations, Autobiographies, Essays, Songs, Poetry, and Art*. Ed. Kenneth J. Atchity. New York: HarperCollins, 1996. 128–29.

Connor, Kimberly Rae. "'A Common Geography of the Mind': Creating Sacred Space in the Autobiographical Writings of Paul Monette and the NAMES Project." *Journal of the American Academy of Religion* 68 (2000): 47–68.

Cottrell, Robert. *The Grammar of Silence: A Reading of Marguerite de Navarre's Poetry*. Washington DC: Catholic U of American P, 1986.

Coulthard, Malcolm. *An Introduction to Discourse Analysis*. London: Longman, 1977.

Crenshaw, David A. *Bereavement: Counseling the Grieving Throughout the Life Cycle*. New York: Continuum, 1990.

Dalton, Anne B. "'This is obscene': Female Voyeurism, Sexual Abuse, and Maternal Power in *The Dove.*" *Review of Contemporary Fiction* 13.3 (1993): 117–39.

Dekker, Thomas. "The Wonderfull Yeare." *The Plague Pamphlets of Thomas Dekker.* Ed. F.P. Wilson. Oxford: Clarendon P, 1925. 1–61.

Derrida, Jacques. "By Force of Mourning." Trans. Pascale-Anne Brault and Michael Naas. *Critical Inquiry* 22 (Winter 1996): 171–92.

———. "Fors: The Anglish Words of Nicolas Abraham and Maria Torok." Trans. Barbara Johnson. *Wolf-Man's Magic Word.* Eds. Nicolas Abraham, and Maria Torok. Trans. Nicholas Rand. Chicago: U of Chicago P., 1986. xi–xlviii.

———. *Memoires for Paul de Man.* Trans. Cecile Lindsay, et al. Rev. ed. New York: Columbia UP, 1989.

———. *The Work of Mourning.* Ed. Pascale-Anne Brault and Michael Naas. Chicago and London: U of Chicago P, 2001.

——— and Maurice Blanchot. *Demeure: Fiction and Testimony. The Instant of My Death.* Trans. Elizabeth Rottenberg. Stanford: Stanford UP, 2000.

Des Roches, Madeleine. "Epitaphe de Feu Maistre François Eboissard, Seigneur de la Villée, son Mary."*Les oeuvres.* Ed. Anne Larsen. Geneva: Droz, 1993. 157–58.

———. *Les oeuvres.* Ed. Anne Larsen. Geneva: Droz, 1993.

———. "Ode IV." *Les oeuvres.* Ed. Anne Larsen. Geneva: Droz, 1993. 101–03.

———. "Sonnet I." *Les oeuvres.* Ed. Anne Larsen. Geneva: Droz, 1993. 174.

———. "Sonnet II." *Les oeuvres.* Ed. Anne Larsen. Geneva: Droz, 1993. 175.

———. "Sonnet VII."*Les oeuvres.* Ed. Anne Larsen. Geneva: Droz, 1993. 127–28.

———. "Sonnet VIII." *Les oeuvres.* Ed. Anne Larsen. Geneva: Droz, 1993. 127–28.

———. "Sonnet XXXVI." *Les oeuvres.* Ed. Anne Larsen. Geneva: Droz, 1993. 155–56.

Dickson, Lisa. "No Rainbow Without the Sun: Visibility and Embodiment in Shakespeare's 1 *Henry VI.*" *Modern Language Studies* 30.1 (2002): 137–56.

Doka, Kenneth J., ed. *Living with Sudden Loss: Suicide Accident Heart Attack Stroke.* Bristol, Pa.: Taylor & Francis, 1996.

Doty, Mark. *My Alexandria.* Urbana: U of Illinois P, 1993.

Dubrow, Heather. *Captive Victors: Shakespeare's Narrative Poems and Sonnets.* Ithaca: Cornell UP, 1987.

———. *Shakespeare and Domestic Loss: Forms of Deprivation, Mourning and Recuperation.* Cambridge: Cambridge UP, 1999.

Duncan, Derek, "Solemn Geographies: AIDS and the Contours of Autobiography." *a/b: Auto/Biography Studies* 15 (2000): 22–36.

Duplessis, Rachel Blau. *H.D.: The Career of that Struggle.* Brighton: Harvester, 1986.

Edelman, Lee. *Homographesis: Essays in Gay Literary and Cultural Theory.* New York and London: Routledge, 1994.

Eliade, Mircea. *The Sacred and the Profane: The Nature of Religion.* 1957. Trans. Willard R. Trask. New York: Harcourt, 1959.

Eliot, George. *Adam Bede.* 1859. London: J.M. Dent and Sons, 1960.

Elsley, Judy. "The Rhetoric of the NAMES Project AIDS Quilt: Reading the Text(ile)." *AIDS: The Literary Response.* Ed. Emmanual S. Nelson. New York: Twayne, 1992. 187–96.

"The Epistle of Paul to the Philippians." *New American Standard Bible: Old and New Testament*. Illinois: The World Home Bible League, 1971.

Ezorsky, Gertrude, ed. *Philosophical Perspectives on Punishment*. Albany: State U of New York P, 1972.

Felman, Shoshana. "Turning the Screw of Interpretation." *Literature and Psychoanalysis: The Question of Reading: Otherwise*. Ed. Shoshana Felman. Baltimore: Johns Hopkins UP, 1982. 94–207.

Feuerbach, Ludwig. *The Essence of Christianity*. Trans. George Eliot. New York: Prometheus Books, 1989.

Fineman, Joel. *The Subjectivity Effect in Western Literary Tradition: Essays Toward the Release of Shakespeare's Will*. Cambridge, Mass.: MIT Press, 1991.

Fish, Stanley. "Lycidas: A Poem Finally Anonymous." *Glyph* 8 (1981): 1–18.

Fleischer, Martha Hester. *The Iconography of the English History Play*. Elizabethan and Renaissance Stud. 10. Salzburg: Universität Salzburg, 1974.

Fleurs, Philiberte de. *Oeuvres. Les Bibliothèques françaises*. Ed. La Croix du Maine and Du Verdier. Paris: Sailliant et Nyons, 1772.

Foucault, Michel. "Different Spaces." *Aesthetics, Method, and Epistemology*. Ed. James D. Faubion. New York: The New Press, 1998. 175–85.

———. "What Is an Author?" *The Norton Anthology of Theory and Criticism*. Ed. Vincent B. Leitch. New York: W.W. Norton, 2001. 1622–36.

Frame, Janet. *An Autobiography*. New York: George Braziller, 1991.

Freud, Sigmund. "From the History of an Infantile Neurosis." *The Standard Edition of the Complete Psychological Works of Sigmund Freud*. Trans. James Strachey. Vol. 17. London: Hogarth, 1960. 7–122.

———. "Mourning and Melancholia." 1917. *A Metapsychology: The Theory of Psychoanalysis. The Standard Edition of the Complete Psychological Works of Sigmund Freud*. Vol. 11. Trans. James Strachey. London: Hogarth, 1960. 243–58.

———. "Mourning and Melancholia." 1917. *A General Selection From the Works of Sigmund Freud*. Ed. John Rickman. Garden City: Doubleday, 1957. 124–40.

Frye, Northrop. *Anatomy of Criticism: Four Essays*. Princeton, NJ: Princeton UP, 1957.

Girard, Rene. *Violence and the Sacred*. Trans. Patrick Gregory. Baltimore: Johns Hopkins UP, 1977.

Gittings, Clare. "Expressions of Loss in Early Seventeenth-Century England." *The Changing Face of Death: Historical Accounts of Death and Disposal*. Ed. Peter C. Jupp and Glennys Howarth. London: Macmillan, 1997. 19–33.

Green, Thomas. *Memoirs of Her late Royal Highness Charlotte-Augusta of Wales, and of Saxe-Coburg*. Liverpool: H. Fisher, [1818].

Greenblatt, Stephen. Introduction. *The First Part of the Contention of the Two Famous Houses of York and Lancaster (The Second Part of Henry VI). The Norton Shakespeare*. Ed. Stephen Greenblatt. New York: W.W. Norton, 1997. 203–10.

Grimm, Brothers. "Little Red-Cap." *Household Stories*. Trans. Lucy Crane. New York: Dover, 1963. 132–35.

Grisdale, D.M. Three Middle English Sermons from the Worcester Chapter Manuscript F. 10. No. 5. Leeds School of English Language Texts and Monographs. Kendale: Titus Wilson, 1939.

Gubar, Susan. "Prosopopoeia and Holocaust Poetry in English: The Case of Sylvia Plath." Yale Journal of Criticism 14.1 (2000): 191–215.

Gwilliam, John, ed. A Cypress Wreath for the Tomb of Her Late Royal Highness the Princess Charlotte of Wales. London: Sherwood, Neely, and Jones, 1817.

H.C. Elegy on the Death of the Princess Charlotte of Wales, Who Died November 6, 1817. London: W. Mantz, 1817.

H.D. Helen in Egypt. Intro. Horace Gregory. New York: New Directions, 1961.

Hall, Donald. Here at Eagle Pond Farm. New York: Ticknor and Fields, 1990.

———. Letter to Todd Davis. 20 July 1999.

———. The Museum of Clear Ideas. New York: Ticknor and Fields, 1993.

———. The Old Life. Boston: Houghton Mifflin, 1996.

———. The One Day. New York: Ticknor and Fields, 1988.

———. Principal Products of Portugal: Prose Pieces. Boston: Beacon, 1995.

———. String Too Short to Be Saved. Boston: Nonpareil, 1981.

———. Without. Boston: Houghton Mifflin, 1998.

Hall, Peter. Introduction. The Wars of the Roses: Adapted from William Shakespeare's Henry VI, Parts I, II, III, and Richard III. Adapted by Peter Hall and John Barton. London: BBC, 1967. vii–xiv.

Hammer, Langdon. "Art and AIDS; or, How Will Culture Cure You?" Raritan 14 (1995): 103–18.

Harpham, Geoffrey Galt. "The Business of Mourning." Southern Review 32.3 (1996): 537–55.

Harris, Andrea L. "The Third Sex: Figures of Inversion in Djuna Barnes's Nightwood." Eroticism and Containment: Notes from the Flood Plain. Ed. Carol Siegel and Ann Kibbey. New York: New York UP, 1984. 233–59.

Hastings, Adrian. The Construction of Nationhood: Ethnicity, Religion and Nationalism. Cambridge: Cambridge UP, 1997.

Hébert, Anne. Le Tombeau des rois/The Tomb of the Kings. Trans. Peter Miller. Toronto: Contact, 1967.

Hemans, Felicia. The Domestic Affections. London: T. Cadell and W. Davies, 1812.

Henry VI, Part Two. By William Shakespeare. Dir. Jean Howell. Perf. Julia Foster, Peter Benson. BBC Television, 1983.

Henry VI. By William Shakespeare. Adapted by Pam Brighton. Dir. Pam Brighton. Perf. Stephen Russell, Luce Guilbeault, Nicholas Pennell. Stratford Festival, Stratford, Ontario, 1980.

Henry VI. By William Shakespeare. Adapted by Peter Hall and John Barton. Dir. John Hirsch. Perf. Briain Petchey, Frances Hyland, Leo Ciceri. Stratford Festival, Stratford, Ontario, 1966.

Henry VI. Part One of The Plantagenets. Promptbook in the Shakespeare Centre Archives, Stratford-Upon-Avon. Based on Henry VI, Parts I, II, III. By William Shakespeare.

Adapted by Adrian Noble. Dir. Adrian Noble. Perf. Ralph Fiennes, Penny Downie, Oliver Cotton. Royal Shakespeare Company, Stratford-Upon-Avon, 1988.

Herring, Phillip. *Djuna: The Life and Work of Djuna Barnes.* New York: Viking, 1995.

Hibbert, Christopher. *George IV: Regent and King, 1811–1830.* Newton Abbot: Readers Union, 1975.

Hill, Susan E. "(Dis)Inheriting Augustine: Constructing the Alienated Self in the Autobiographical Works of Paul Monette and Mary Daly." *Literature & Theology* 13 (1999): 149–65.

Hirsch, John. "The Director's Notes About the Play." Programme. *Henry VI.* Based on *Henry VI, Parts I, II, III.* By William Shakespeare. Adapted by Peter Hall and John Barton. Dir. John Hirsch. Perf. Brian Petchey, Frances, Hyland, Leo Ciceri. Stratford Festival, Stratford, Ontario, 1966.

Hobsbawn, E.J. *Nations and Nationalisms Since 1780: Programme, Myth, Reality.* Cambridge: Cambridge UP, 1990.

Holme, Thea. *Prinny's Daughter.* London: Hamish Hamilton, 1976.

Hone, William. *Authentic Memoirs of the Life of the Late Lamented Princess Charlotte: with clear statements showing The Succession to the Crown, and the probability of the wife of Jerome Buonaparte becoming Queen, and her son, Jerome napoleon, being Prince of Wales, and afterwards King of these realms.* London: William Hone, 1817.

Horstmann, Carl, ed. *The Minor Poems of the Vernon MS.* Pt. 1. London: Kegan Paul, Trench, Trübner & Co., 1892. Early English Text Society, original series 98.

Houlbrooke, Ralph. *Death, Ritual and Bereavement.* London: Routledge, 1989.

House of Lancaster, The. Part Five of *The Wars of the Roses.* Based on *Henry VI, Parts I, II.* By William Shakespeare. Adapted by Michael Bogdanov and Michael Pennington. Dir. Michael Bogdanov. Perf. Michael Pennington, Paul Brennan, June Watson. English Shakespeare Company. Filmed at the Grand Theatre, Swansea, UK. ITEL, 1988.

Huish, Robert, ed. *A Scared Memorial of the Princess Charlotte Augusta of Saxe Coburg Saalfeld.* London: T. Kelly, 1818.

———. *Life and Memoirs of Her Royal Highness, Princess Charlotte of Saxe Coburg Saalfeld, etc.* London: T. Kinnersley, 1818.

Hungerford, Amy. *The Holocaust of Texts: Genocide, Literature, and Personification.* Chicago: U Chicago P, 2003.

Hutcheon, Linda. *A Poetics of Postmodernism.* London: Routledge, 1988.

"Hymn, sung at the Asylum for Female Orphans." *Select Poetry.* November, 1817. 445.

Irigary, Luce. "Ce sexe qui n'en est pas un." Trans. Claudia Reeder. *Feminisims: An Anthology of Literary Theory and Criticism.* Eds. Robyn Warhol and Diane Herndl. New Brunswick: Rutgers UP, 1991. 350–56.

Jarraway, David R. "From Spectacular to Speculative: The Shifting Rhetoric in Recent Gay AIDS Memoirs." *Mosaic* 33 (2000): 115–28.

Jeffords, Susan. *The Remasculinization of America: Gender and the Vietnam War.* Bloomington: Indiana UP, 1989.

Jerome, Saint. *Saint Jerome: Letters and Select Works*. Trans. W. H. Fremantle, G. Lewis, and
W. G. Martley. Vol. 6. A Select Library of Nicene and Post-Nicene Fathers of the
Christian Church. Grand Rapids: Wm. B. Erdmans Pub. Co., 1983.

Johnston, Alexandra. "*The Word Made Flesh*: Augustinian Elements in the York Cycle." *The
Centre and its Compass: Studies in Medieval Literature in Honor of Professor John Leyerle*. Ed.
Robert A. Taylor et al. Kalamazoo: Western Michigan University Medieval Institute
Publications, 1993. 225–46.

Johnstone, Peggy Fitzhugh. *The Transformation of Rage, Mourning and Creativity in George
Eliot's Fiction*. New York: New York UP, 1994.

Jones, Ann-Rosalind. "Writing the Body: Toward an Understanding of l'écriture féminine."
Feminisms: An Anthology of Literary Theory and Criticism. Eds. Robyn Warhol and Diane
Herndl. New Brunswick: Rutgers UP, 1991. 356–70.

Kahn, Coppélia. *Roman Shakespeare: Warriors, Wounds, and Women*. London: Routledge,
1997.

Kaivola, Karen. *All Contraries Confounded: The Lyrical Fiction of Virginia Woolf, Djuna Barnes,
and Marguerite Duras*. Iowa City: U of Iowa P, 1991.

Kannenstine, Louis F. *The Art of Djuna Barnes: Duality and Damnation*. New York: New York
UP, 1977.

Kantorowicz, Ernst H. *The King's Two Bodies: A Study in Mediaeval Political Theology*.
Princeton: Princeton UP, 1957.

Karl, Frederick R. *George Eliot: Voice of a Century: A Biography*. New York: W.W. Norton, 1995.

Kastenbaum, Robert. *Death, Society, and Human Experience*. 5th ed. Boston: Allyn and
Bacon, 1995.

Kaufman, Barbara A. "Training Tales in Family Therapy: Exploring *The Alexandria Quartet*."
Journal of Marital and Family Therapy 21.1 (1995): 67–75.

Kegan, Robert. *The Evolving Self: Problem and Process in Human Development*. Cambridge:
Harvard UP, 1982.

Kelso, Ruth. *Doctrine for the Lady of the Renaissance*. Urbana: U of Illinois P, 1978.

Kenyon, Jane. "Notes from the Other Side." *Constance*. Saint Paul: Graywolf, 1993. 59.

Kirk, Eugene. *Menippean Satire: An Annotated Catalogue of Texts and Criticism*. New York:
Garland, 1980.

Klein, Melanie. *Love, Guilt and Reparation & Other Works 1921–1945*. New York: Delacourte
Press, 1975.

Klein, Michael, ed. *Poets for Life: Seventy-Six Poets Respond to AIDS*. New York: Persea Books,
1989.

Kristeva, Julia. "La femme, ce n'est jamais ça." In *New French Feminisms*. Ed. Elaine Marks
and Isabelle de Courtivron. New York: Schocken Books, 1981. 134–38.

Kroll, Judith. *Chapters in a Mythology: The Poetry of Sylvia Plath*. New York: Harper and Row,
1976.

Kübler-Ross, Elisabeth. *Death: The Final Stage of Growth*. New Jersey: Prentice-Hall, 1975.

———. *On Death and Dying*. New York: Macmillan, 1969.

A Lady. *Lines Addressed to Prince Leopold of Saxe-Coburg, on the Death of his Consort, the Princess
Charlotte of Wales*. Colchester: Swinborne and Walter; and London: Hatchard;
Baldwin, Cradock, and Joy, 1817.

Landau, Deborah. "'How to Live, What to Do': The Poetics and Politics of AIDS." *American Literature* 68 (1996): 193–225.

Lazard, Madeleine. *Images littéraires de la femme à la Renaissance.* Paris: PUF, 1985.

Le Digne, Nicolas. "Sonnet pour les fefves." *Receuil des premieres oeuvres chrestiennes de N. Le Digne.* Ed. A. De la Forest. Paris: Jeremie Perier, 1600. 69b.

Maclean, Ian. *The Renaissance Notion of Women: A Study in the Fortunes of Scholasticism and Medical Science in Europen Intellectual Life.* Cambridge: Cambridge UP, 1980.

Malraux, André. *The Voices of Silence.* 1953. Trans. Stuart Gilbert. Princeton: Princeton UP, 1990.

Mankind. In *The Macro Plays.* Ed. Mark Eccles. London: Oxford UP, 1969. Early English Text Society, original series 262. 153–84.

Marcus, Jane. "Laughing at Leviticus: *Nightwood* as Woman's Circus Epic." *Silence and Power: A Reevaluation of Djuna Barnes.* Ed. Mary Lynn Broe. Carbondale: Southern Illinois UP, 1991. 221–50.

"Maria." *The Princess's Tomb: A Dialogue for the Nursery.* London: T. Gardiner; N. Hailes; T. Sizuer Juvenile Library, [1818?].

Marot, Clément. *Deploration sur le trespas de feu messier Florimond Robertet. L'édition originale.* 1534. Facsimilie. Paris: Chez l'auteur, 1938.

Marris, Peter. *Loss and Change.* New York: Pantheon Books, 1974.

Martin, Randall. "Elizabethan Civic Pageantry in *Henry VI.*" *University of Toronto Quarterly* 60.2 (Winter 1990/91): 245–64.

Martineau-Cenieys, Christian. *Le thème de la mort dans la poésie française: 1450–1550.* Paris: H. Champion, 1978.

Maus, Katherine. "Taking Tropes Seriously: Language and Violence in Shakespeare's *Rape of Lucrece.*" *Shakespeare Quarterly* 37 (1986): 66–82.

McGrath, Roberta. "Dangerous Liaisons: Health, Disease and Representation." *Ecstatic Antibodies: Resisting AIDS Mythology.* Eds. Teresa Boffin, and Sunil Gupta. London: River Oram P, 1991. 142–55.

Mellor, David. "Death in High Modernity: The Contemporary Presence and Absence of Death." *The Sociology of Death: Theory, Culture, Practice.* Ed., David Clark. Oxford: Blackwell/ *The Sociological Review,* 1993. 11–30.

Metcalfe, Peter and Richard Huntington. *Celebrations of Death: The Anthropology of Mortuary Ritual.* Rev. Ed. Cambridge: Cambridge UP, 1991.

Meyer, Kinereth. "The Mythology of Modern Death." *Genre* 19 (1986): 21–35.

Miller, James. "Dante on Fire Island: Reinventing Heaven in the AIDS Elegy." *Writing AIDS: Gay Literature, Language, and Analysis.* Eds. Timothy F. Murphy, and Suzanne Poirier. New York: Columbia UP, 1993. 265–305.

Mills-Courts, Karen. *Poetry as Epitaph: Representation and Poetic Language.* Baton Rouge and London: Louisiana State UP, 1990.

Milton, John. *The Riverside Milton.* Ed. Roy Flannagan. Boston: Houghton Mifflin, 1998.

Monette, Paul. *Love Alone: Eighteen Elegies for Rog.* New York: St. Martin's, 1988.

———. "Ed Dying." *Poets For Life: Seventy-Six Poets Respond to AIDS.* New York: Crown, 1989. 172–74.

Montaigne, Michel de. "De l'affection des peres aux enfans." *Les essais.* Livre II. Paris: GF-Flammarion, 1979. 56–74.

———. *Les essais.* Paris: GF-Flammarion, 1979.

———. "De l'amitié." *Les essais.* Livre I. Paris: GF-Flammarion, 1979. 231–42.

———. "De la tristesse." *Les essais.* Livre I. Paris: GF-Flammarion, 1979. 43–46.

———. "De trois bonnes femmes." *Les essais.* Livre II. Paris: GF-Flammarion, 1979. 406–13.

Moodie, Susanna. *Roughing It in the Bush.* New Canadian Library. Toronto: McClelland and Stewart, 1989.

Moyers, Bill. *Donald Hall and Jane Kenyon: A Life Together.* Princeton: Films for the Humanities, 1994.

Murphy, Timothy F. "Testimony." *Writing AIDS: Gay Literature, Language, and Analysis.* Eds. Timothy F. Murphy, and Suzanne Poirier. New York: Columbia UP, 1993. 306–20.

Murphy, Timothy F., and Suzanne Poirier, eds. *Writing AIDS: Gay Literature, Language, and Analysis.* New York: Columbia UP, 1993.

Myers, William. *The Teaching of George Eliot.* Leicester UP, 1984.

The N-Town Play: Cotton MS Vespasian D. 8. Ed. Stephen Spector. Vol. 1. Early English Text Society, Supplemental Series 11. Oxford: Oxford UP, 1991.

Navarre, Marguerite de. *Chansons spirituelles.* Ed. Georges Dottin. Geneva: Droz, 1971.

———. "Chanson I: Pensées de la royne de Navarre, estant dans sa litière durant la maladie du roy. "*Chansons spirituelles.* Ed. Georges Dottin. Geneva: Droz, 1971. 3–7.

———. "Chanson II: Autres pensées faites un mois après la mort du roy." *Chansons spirituelles.* Ed. Georges Dottin. Geneva: Droz, 1971. 8–10.

———. "Chanson XLII." *Chansons spirituelles.* Ed. Georges Dottin. Geneva: Droz, 1971. 117–23.

———. *La Navire.* In *Les dernières poesies de Marguerite de Navarre.* Ed. Abel Le Franc. Paris: A. Colin, 1896.

———. *Marguerite de la Marguerite des Princesses.* Ed. Ruth Thomas. Paris: Mouton, 1970.

Nehru, Jawaharlal. *The Vintage Book of Indian Writing, 1947–1997.* Eds. Salman Rushdie and Elizabeth West. London: Vintage, 1997.

Neill, Michael. *Issues of Death: Mortality and Identity in English Renaissance Tragedy.* Oxford: Clarendon P, 1997.

Nelson, Emmanuel S., ed. *AIDS: The Literary Response.* New York: Twayne, 1992.

Netter, Thomas. *Doctrinale Fidei Catholicae.* 3 vols. Venice: 1757; Farnborough, England: Gregg P, 1967.

Newtown, George. "From St. Augustine to Paul Monette: Sex and Salvation in the Age of AIDS." *True Relations: Essays on Autobiography and the Postmodern.* Eds. G. Thomas Couser and Joseph Fichtelberg. Westport, CT: Greenwood, 1998. 51–61.

Nussbaum, Martha C. *The Therapy of Desire: Theory and Practice in Hellenistic Ethics.* Princeton: Princeton UP, 1994.

Owens, Margaret E. "The Many-Headed Monster in *Henry VI, Part 2.*" *Criticism* 38.3 (1996): 367–82.

Parker, Patricia. *Literary Fat Ladies: Rhetoric, Gender, Property.* London: Methuen, 1987.

Parmet, Harriet L. *The Terror of Our Days: Four American Poets Respond to the Holocaust.* Bethlehem, PA: Lehigh UP, 2001.

Paterson, Arthur. *George Eliot's Family Life and Letters.* London: Selwyn and Blount, 1928.

Patmore, Coventry. *The Angel in the House.* London: 1854; republished 1863.

Patrologia Latina [PL]. Ed. J.P. Migne. 221 Vols. Paris: 1844–64.

Patterson, Annabel. *Reading Between the Lines.* Madison, WI: U of Wisconsin P, 1993.

Pearson, Michael Parker. "Mortuary Practices, Society and Ideology: an Ethnoarchaeological Study," *Symbolic and Structural Archaeology.* Ed. Ian Hodder. Cambridge: Cambridge UP, 1982. 99–113.

Peel, Robin. *Writing Back: Sylvia Plath and Cold War Politics.* Madison, NJ: Associated University Presses, 2002.

Perloff, Marjorie. "The Two Ariels: The (Re)Making of the Sylvia Plath Canon." *Poetic License: Essays on Modernist and Postmodernist Lyric.* Evanston: Northwestern UP, 1990. 175–97.

Perrault, Charles. "Little Red Riding-Hood." *The Fairy Tales of Charles Perrault.* Trans. Geoffrey Brereton. Harmondsworth: Penguin, 1957. 21–25.

Phillips, Heather. "John Wyclif and the Optics of the Eucharist." *From Ockham to Wyclif.* Eds. Anne Hudson and Michael Wilks. Oxford: Basil Blackwell, 1987. 245–58.

Pisan, Christine de. "Ballad I." *Cent Ballades.* In *Oeuvres poétiques de Christine de Pisan.* Ed. Maurice Roy. Paris: Librairie de Firmin Didot et Cie, 1886. 2–3.

———. "Ballad V." *Cent Ballades.* In *Oeuvres poétiques de Christine de Pisan.* Ed. Maurice Roy. Paris: Librairie de Firmin Didot et Cie, 1886. 5–6.

———. "Ballad VI." *Cent Ballades.* In *Oeuvres poétiques de Christine de Pisan.* Ed. Maurice Roy. Paris: Librairie de Firmin Didot et Cie, 1886. 7.

———. *Cent Ballades. Ouvres poétiques de Christine de Pisan.* Ed. Maurice Roy. Paris: Librarie de Firmin Didot et Cie, 1886.

Plath, Sylvia. "A Life." *The Collected Poems.* Ed. Ted Hughes. New York: Harper and Row, 1981. 149–50.

———. "All the Dead Dears." *The Collected Poems.* Ed. Ted Hughes. New York: Harper and Row, 1981. 70–1.

———. "The Beekeeper's Daughter." *The Collected Poems.* Ed. Ted Hughes. New York: Harper and Row, 1981. 104.

———. *The Collected Poems.* Ed. Ted Hughes. New York: Harper and Row, 1981.

———. "The Collosus." *The Collected Poems.* Ed. Ted Hughes. New York: Harper and Row, 1981. 129–30.

———. "Daddy." *The Collected Poems.* Ed. Ted Hughes. New York: Harper and Row, 1981. 222–24.

———. "Electra on Azalea Path." *The Collected Poems.* Ed. Ted Hughes. New York: Harper and Row, 1981. 116–17.

———. "Full Fathom Five." *The Collected Poems.* Ed. Ted Hughes. New York: Harper and Row, 1981. 92–93.

———. "On the Decline of Oracles." *The Collected Poems.* Ed. Ted Hughes. New York: Harper and Row, 1981. 78.

Platizky, Roger. "Elegies in a Different Key: Tennyson's In Memoriam and Paul Monette's Love Alone." Midwest Quarterly 43 (2002): 346–54.

Plowden, Alison. Caroline and Charlotte: The Regent's Wife and Daughter, 1795–1821. London: Sidgwick and Jackson, 1989.

Plumb, Cheryl. "Revising Nightwood: 'a kind of glee of despair.'" Review of Contemporary Fiction 13.3 (1993): 149–59.

———. Introduction. Nightwood: The Original Version and Related Drafts. Normal, IL: Dalkey Archive, 1995. vii–xxv.

Polkinghorne, Donald E. Narrative Knowing and the Human Sciences. Albany: State U of New York P, 1988.

Potts, Abbie Findlay. The Elegiac Mode: Poetic Form in Wordsworth and Other Elegists. Ithaca: Cornell UP, 1967.

Ramazani, Jahan. Poetry of Mourning: The Modern Elegy from Hardy to Heaney. Chicago: U of Chicago P, 1994.

Rando, Therese A. Grief, Dying, and Death: Clinical Interventions for Caregivers. Champaign, Ill.: Research P, 1984.

———. Grieving: How to Go on Living When Someone You Love Dies. Lexington, Mass.: Lexington Books, 1988.

Raphael, Beverly. The Anatomy of Bereavement. New York: Basic Books, 1983.

Rashkin, Esther. "Tools for a New Psychoanalytic Literary Criticism: The Work of Abraham and Torok." Diacritics (Winter 1998): 31–52.

Reinhard, Kenneth. "The Jamesian Thing: The Wings of the Dove and the Ethics of Mourning." Arizona Quarterly 53.4 (1997): 115–46.

Ricciardi, Alessia. The Ends of Mourning: Psychoanalysis, Literature, Film. Palo Alto: Stanford UP, 2003.

Richmond, H.M. Shakespeare's Political Plays. New York: Random House, 1967.

Riegel, Christian, ed. Challenging Territory: The Writing of Margaret Laurence. Edmonton: U of Alberta P, 1997.

———. Writing Grief: Margaret Laurence and the Work of Mourning. Winnipeg: U of Manitoba P, 2003.

Riggs, David. Shakespeare's Heroical Histories: "Henry VI" and Its Literary Tradition. Cambridge: Harvard UP, 1971.

Rise of Edward IV, The. Part Two of The Plantagenets. Promptbook in the Shakespeare Centre Archives, Stratford-Upon-Avon. Based on Henry VI, Parts II, III. By William Shakespeare. Dir. Adrian Noble. Perf. Ralph Fiennes, Penny Downie, Oliver Cotton. Royal Shakespeare Company, Stratford-Upon-Avon, 1988.

Roberts, Janine. Tales and Transformations: Stories in Families and Family Therapy. New York: W.W. Norton, 1994.

Rose, Jacqueline. The Haunting of Sylvia Plath. Cambridge: Harvard UP, 1991.

Rubin, Miri. Corpus Christi: The Eucharist in Late Medieval Culture. Cambridge: Cambridge UP, 1991.

Sacks, Peter M. The English Elegy: Studies in the Genre from Spenser to Yeats. Baltimore: Johns Hopkins UP, 1985.

Sanders, Catherine M. Grief: The Mourning After: Dealing With Adult Bereavement. New York: Wiley, 1989.

Schenck, Celeste M. "When the Moderns Write Elegy: Crane, Kinsella, Nemerov." *Classical and Modern Literature* 6 (1986): 97–108.

Schor, Esther. *Bearing the Dead: The British Culture of Mourning from the Enlightenment to Victoria.* Princeton: Princeton UP, 1994.

Seneca. *Seneca ad lucilium epistulae morales.* Trans. Richard M. Grummere. Vol. 1. Cambridge, Mass.: Harvard UP, 1917.

Shakespeare, William. *The Riverside Shakespeare.* Ed. G. Blakemore Evans. Boston: Houghton Mifflin, 1974.

———. *William Shakespeare: The Complete Works.* Ed. Alfred Harbage. Pelican Text Revised ed. New York: Penguin, 1969.

Shapiro, Ester R. *Grief as a Family Process: A Developmental Approach to Clinical Practice.* New York and London: The Guilford Press, 1994.

Shaw, W. David. *Elegy and Paradox: Testing the Conventions.* Baltimore: Johns Hopkins UP, 1994.

Shelley, Percy Bysshe. *An Address to the People on the Death of the Princess Charlotte. The Prose Works of Percy Bysshe Shelley.* Ed. E.B. Murray. 2 vols. Oxford: Clarendon P, 1993. I: 447–51.

A Shepherd. *Carmen Pastorale: or, a Pastoral Elegy, on the Death of Her Royal Highness the Princess Charlotte of Wales. An Humble Tribute to Her Memory.* Southampton: T. Baker for I. Fletcher; London: Longman, Hurst, Rees, Orme, & Co., 1817.

Smart, Elizabeth. *Writing in the Father's House.* Toronto: U of Toronto P, 1991.

Smith, Barbara Herrnstein. *Poetic Closure: A Study of How Poems End.* Chicago: U of Chicago P, 1968.

Smith, Ernest J. "John Berryman's Short Fiction: Elegy and Enlightenment." *Studies in Short Fiction* 30.3 (1993): 309–16.

———. "John Berryman's 'Programmatic' for *The Dream Songs* and an Instance of Revision." *Journal of Modern Literature* 23.3/4 (2000): 429–39.

Smith, Victoria L. "The Story beside(s) Itself: The Language of Loss in Djuna Barnes's *Nightwood.*" PMLA 114.2 (March 1999):194–206.

Smythe, Karen E. *Figuring Grief: Gallant, Munro, and the Poetics of Elegy.* Montreal and Kingston: McGill-Queen's UP, 1992.

Soble, Alan. *The Structure of Love.* New Haven: Yale UP, 1990.

Sontag, Susan. *AIDS and Its Metaphors.* New York: Farrar, Strauss, and Giroux, 1989.

Spurr, David. *The Rhetoric of Empire: Colonial Discourse in Journalism, Travel Writing, and Imperial Administration.* Durham: Duke UP, 1993.

Stamelman, Richard. *Lost Beyond Telling: Representations of Death and Absence in Modern French Poetry.* Ithaca and London: Cornell UP, 1990.

Sterne, Laurence. *The Life and Opinions of Tristram Shandy, Gentleman.* 1760. Ed. Ian Watt. Boston: Houghton Mifflin, 1965.

Stevenson, Sheryl. "'World War I all over': Writing and Fighting the War in AIDS Poetry." *College Literature* 24 (1997): 240–62.

Strong, Roy C. *Portraits of Queen Elizabeth.* Oxford: Clarendon P, 1963.

Sugnet, Charles. "'Nervous Conditions': Dangarembga's Feminist Reinvention of Fanon," *The Politics of (M)othering: Womanhood, Identity, and Resistance in African Literature*. Ed. Obioma Nnaemeka. New York: Routledge, 1997. 33–49.

Suleri, Sara. *Meatless Days*. Chicago: U of Chicago P, 1989.

Sykes, Egerton. *Everyman's Dictionary of Non-Classical Mythology*. 1952. London: Dent, 1968.

Szittya, Penn R. *The Antifraternal Tradition in Medieval Literature*. Princeton: Princeton UP, 1986.

Taylor, Robert A. et al. *The Centre and its Compass: Studies in Medieval Literature in Honor of Professor John Leyerle*. Kalamazoo: Western Michigan University Medieval Institute P, 1993. 225–46.

The Towneley Plays. Ed. Martin Stevens and A.C. Cawley. Vol. 1. Early English Text Society, Supplemental Series 13. Oxford: Oxford UP, 1994.

Tharoor, Shashi. *India: From Midnight to the Millennium*. New York: Harper Perennial, 1998.

The York Plays. Ed. Richard Beadle. London: Edward Arnold, 1982.

Tostevin, Lola Lemire. *Cartouches*. Vancouver: Talonbooks, 1995.

———. *Color of Her Speech*. Toronto: Coach House, 1982.

———. "Contamination: A Relation of Differences." *Tessera* 6 (1989): 13–15.

———. "Elizabeth Smart." Rev. of *Juvenilia*, by Elizabeth Smart, ed. Alice Van Wart; *In the Meantime*, by Elizabeth Smart, ed. Alice Van Wart; *Autobiographies*, by Elizabeth Smart, ed. William Hoffer. *Canadian Literature* 122–23 (1989): 169–72.

———. *Frog Moon*. Dunvegan, ON: Cormorant, 1994.

———. "An Interview with Christopher Dewdney." *Poetry Canada Review* 10.3 (1989): 1+.

———. "Paternal Body as Outlaw." *Open Letter* 6.5–6 (1986): 77–80.

———. "Reading after the (Writing) Fact." *Public* 3 (1990): 61–75.

———. "Remembered Conversation." *Brick* 38 (1990): 21–24.

———. Review of *the collected poems of Miriam Mandel*, Ed. Sheila Watson. *Contemporary Verse 2* 9.2 (1985): 51–53.

———. Telephone interview. 29 April 1999.

———. Untitled. *Sp/Elles: Poetry by Canadian Women*. Ed. Judith Fitzgerald. Windsor: Black Moss, 1986. 96–99.

———, and Smaro Kamboureli. "Women of Letters: Envois between Victoria and Toronto." *Tessera* 5 (1988): 13–26.

Tougaw, Jason. "Testimony and the Subjects of AIDS Memoirs." *a/b: Auto/Biography Studies* 13 (1998): 235–56.

Vendler, Helen. "Sylvia Plath." *The Music of What Happens: Poets, Poems, Critics*. Cambridge: Harvard UP, 1988. 272–83.

Vickers, Nancy. "'The blazon of sweet beauty's best': Shakespeare's *Lucrece*." *Shakespeare and the Question of Theory*. Eds. Patricia Parker and Geoffrey Hartman. New York: Methuen, 1985.

Walker, Michelle Boulous. *Philosophy and the Maternal Body: Reading Silence*. New York: Routledge, 1998.

Watterson, Barbara. *Introducing Egyptian Hieroglyphs*. Edinburgh: Scottish Academic P, 1981.

Waxman, Barbara Frey, and Eleanor Byington. "Teaching Paul Monette's Memoir/Manifesto to Resistant Readers." *College Literature* 24 (1997): 156–70.

Weeks, Jeffrey. "Post-Modern AIDS?" Boffin and Gupta. 133–41.

Weitz, Rose. "The Social Construction of Women's Bodies." *The Politics of Women's Bodies: Sexuality, Appearance and Behavior.* Ed. Rose Weitz. Oxford: Oxford UP, 1998. 1–2.

White, Michael, and David Epston. *Narrative Means to Therapeutic Ends.* New York: W.W. Norton, 1990.

Wilson, Deborah S. "Dora, Nora and Their Professor: The 'Talking Cure,' *Nightwood*, and Feminist Pedagogy." *Literature and Psychology* 42.3 (1996): 48–71.

Winn, Collette, ed. *Oeuvres chrétiennes.* By Gabrielle de Coignard. 1594. Geneva: Droz, 1995.

Wofford, Susanne L. "'To You I Give Myself, For I Am Yours': Erotic Performance and Theatrical Performatives in *As You Like It*." *Shakespeare Reread: The Texts in New Contexts.* Ed. Russ McDonald. Ithaca: Cornell UP, 1994.

Woods, Gregory. "AIDS to Remembrance: The Uses of Elegy." Nelson. 155–66.

Woodward, Kathleen. "Late Theory, Late Style: Loss and Renewal in Freud and Barthes." *Aging and Gender in Literature: Studies in Creativity.* Eds., Anne M. Wyatt Brown and Janice Rossen. Charlottesville: UP of Virginia, 1993. 82–101.

Worden, J. Wm. *Grief Counseling and Grief Therapy.* New York: Springer, 1982.

Wyile, Herb and Jeanette Lynes. "Regionalism and Ambivalence in Canadian Literature." *Open Letter* 9.4 (1995): 117–27.

Young, Tom. "Crutches in the Sun." *The James White Review* 6.3 (1989): 8.

Ziegler, Georgianna. "My Lady's Chamber: Female Space, Female Chastity in Shakespeare." *Textual Practice* 4 (1990): 73–90.

Zipes, Jack. *Fairy Tales and the Art of Subversion: The Classical Genre for Children and the Process of Civilization.* New York: Wildman, 1983.

About the Contributors

STEPHEN C. BEHRENDT is George Holmes Distinguished University Professor of English at the University of Nebraska. A scholar in British Romantic literature and culture as well as a widely published poet, he is also author of *Royal Mourning and Regency Culture: Elegies and Memorials of Princess Charlotte* (Macmillan, 1997).

TODD F. DAVIS teaches American literature and creative writing at Penn State Altoona. His scholarship has appeared in such journals as *Studies in Short Fiction, Style, College Literature, Interdisciplinary Literary Studies, Critique, Literature/Film Quarterly, Midwest Quarterly, and Western American Literature.* He is co author (with Kenneth Womack) of *Formalist Criticism and Reader-Response Theory* (Palgrave/St. Martin's) and co-editor (with Womack) of *Mapping the Ethical Turn: A Reader in Ethics, Culture and Literary Theory* (UP of Virginia). In addition Davis is the author of a book of poetry, *Ripe,* and his poems have appeared widely in such magazines and journals as *The North American Review, River Styx, Green Mountains Review, The Nebraska Review, Many Mountains Moving, The Worcester Review, The Red Cedar Review, The Midwest Quarterly, Yankee, Appalachia, and Image: A Journal of the Arts & Religion.*

LISA DICKSON is an Assistant Professor in the English Program at the University of Northern British Columbia. She has published articles in such journals as *Renaissance Drama, Camera Obscura, and Canadian Literature* and is currently working on a book-length study of the representation of violence and penal practice in modern productions of Shakespeare's dramas.

HEATHER DUBROW, Tighe-Evans Professor and John Bascom Professor at the University of Wisconsin-Madison, is the author of five scholarly books, most recently *Shakespeare and Domestic Loss: Forms of Deprivation, Mourning, and Recuperation* (Cambridge UP, 1999); her other publications include articles on pedagogy, two chapbooks of poetry, and a forthcoming edition of *As You Like It* for the New Riverside Shakespeare.

THOMAS M.F. GERRY is Professor and Chair of the Department of English at Laurentian University in Sudbury, Ontario. He teaches the program's first-year Introduction to Writing and English Studies, Canadian literature and culture, and various courses in Laurentian's interdisciplinary Humanities M.A. in Interpretation and Values. He is working on a book of text/image studies.

MELANIE E. GREGG is Assistant Professor of French at Wilson College. She has recently published a translation of Gabrielle Coignard's *Sonnets Spirituels* in the University of

Chicago Press series entitled *The Other Voice in Early Modern Europe*. Her current research interests include medical and pediatric literature of the Renaissance.

LEANNE GROENEVELD is an Assistant Professor in the English Department at Carleton University where she teaches medieval and modern drama.

BARBARA HUDSPITH holds an Honours B.A. in English and Religious Studies from McMaster University in Hamilton, Ontario, and a Masters in Religion from Wycliffe College at the University of Toronto. She has been involved with bereavement support since 1992 and works primarily with university students. Currently engaged in spiritual direction, she is nearing the completion of a Diploma in Spiritual Direction at Regis College, University of Toronto, where she continues to observe a close relationship between grief and spiritual growth.

LLOYD EDWARD KERMODE is an Associate Professor of English at California State University, Long Beach. He is the author of several essays on early modern literature and culture as well as co-editor of a volume of essays on Tudor drama (Palgrave, 2004) and co-editor for the *Broadview Anthology of Medieval and Early Modern Drama* (forthcoming).

CHRISTIAN RIEGEL is Assistant Professor of English at Campion College at the University of Regina where he teaches Canadian literature, Genre Studies, and a poetry course on the elegy and the long poem. He has published *Writing Grief: Margaret Laurence and the Work of Mourning* (U of Manitoba P, 2003), edited *Challenging Territory: The Writing of Margaret Laurence* (U of Alberta P, 1997), and co-edited with Herb Wyile *A Sense of Place: Re-evaluating Regionalism in Canadian and American Writing* (U of Alberta P/*Textual Studies in Canada* 8, 1998). He is currently completing work on *Twenty-First Century Canadian Writers* for the *Dictionary of Literary Biography* (Bruccoli, Clark, Layman/Gale Research, forthcoming 2005).

GARRY SHERBERT is an Assistant Professor of English at the University of Regina. He is author of *Menippean Satire and the Poetics of Wit* (P. Lang, 1996); he is currently co-editing a book entitled *Canadian Cultural Poesis: An Anthology* as well as co-editing *Shakespeare and the Renaissance* for the *Collected Works of Northrop Frye*.

ERNEST SMITH is Associate Professor of English at the University of Central Florida. He is the author of the book *The Imaged Word*, a study of poet Hart Crane. In addition, he has published on a range of U.S. poets including John Berryman, Michael S. Harper, Robert Lowell, Edna St. Vincent Millay, and Adrienne Rich.

KATHERINE G. SUTHERLAND is an Associate Professor at the University College of the Cariboo in her hometown of Kamloops, B.C.

KENNETH WOMACK is Associate Professor of English and Head of the Division of Arts and Humanities at Penn State Altoona. Womack has published widely on twentieth-century literature and popular culture. He serves as editor of *Interdisciplinary Literary Studies: A Journal of Criticism and Theory* and as co-editor of Oxford University Press's celebrated *Year's Work in English Studies*. He is the co-author (with Ruth Robbins and Julian Wolfreys) of *Key Concepts in Literary Theory* (Columbia, 2002) and the author of *Postwar Academic Fiction: Satire, Ethics, Community* (Palgrave/St. Martin's, 2001).

Index

U N